LEADERS

LEADERS

The Learning Curve of Achievement

Edited by
ANDREW FORREST
&
PATRICK TOLFREE

First published in 1992 by
The Industrial Society Press
Robert Hyde House
48 Bryanston Square
London W1H 7LN
Telephone 071-262 2401

ISBN 0-85290-906-3

British Library Cataloguing in Publication Data
Forrest, Andrew
Leaders – the learning curve of achievement.
I. Title II. Tolfree, Patrick
303.3092

Cover design by Milan Design
Typeset by The Setting Studio, Newcastle upon Tyne
Printed in Great Britain by
Billing & Sons Ltd, Worcester

Contents

Preface

In this book leaders from the private and public sectors talk about the influences and experiences that have been most formative in bringing them to their present positions. They also tell us something about their methods, styles and philosophies of management.

We hope it will be of inspiration, interest and value to all managers and professionals, but in producing it we have in particular had in mind:

- those who are looking critically at their own career progress and would like to learn from the experiences of others
- line managers and others responsible for management development.

We hope it will also be of interest to young people who have not yet begun their careers and may be wondering which particular direction to take. Many of the most important lessons described in this book were learnt in youth, at home or at school, or in the very early days of our interviewees' careers.

To make it as easy for the interviewees as possible we undertook to restrict the interviews, which were recorded, to one hour. This was a useful discipline: it helped us to concentrate on what at each stage in the individual's career had been most influential or beneficial in taking him or her forward. We were particularly interested to find out what particular mix of job and other experiences took the interviewee to his or her most recent position.

Interviewing people at this top level contains two time hazards: the period between the first and the nineteenth interview covers several months, and during the subsequent editing period some individuals' circumstances may have changed. Both of these hazards duly transpired. Where a significant change of role has taken place, it is mentioned in the appropriate chapter. But these time lapses do not in any way dilute the realism and value of the messages which emerge from the interviews.

The final chapter, The Learning Curve of Achievement, summarises the main themes and lessons that came out of the interviews. This review serves as a reminder of how much more there is to career development than merely attending formal training courses. In fact, if there is one lesson to emerge more than any other it is that, while formal training has its place, it is the influence of individuals which is possibly the most formative. Parents, teachers, bosses, inspirational managing directors, informal mentors, friends and colleagues . . . the career of each interviewee was at some point profoundly influenced by an individual. There are lessons there for all of us.

The title of this book is self-explanatory: we learn from the achievements of others. There is a slight and deliberate *double entendre* in the title, however; as they progress upwards, the most successful leaders learn from and build on their own achievements and, as many of them pointed out, from their setbacks and mistakes. The honesty and spontaneity with which they talked to us have resulted in a book which, we are sure, will encourage everyone with the ambition and the determination to lead full and interesting lives in their own, their organisation's and the community's interest.

We are extremely grateful to the leaders who both gave up their time to be interviewed and displayed such readiness to pass on to others the benefit of their experiences.

Andrew Forrest
Patrick Tolfree

Sir Richard Attenborough

Photo by Terry O'Neill

> **'***I work with a group, I always have.*
> *I enjoy playing the conductor,*
> *I enjoy holding the baton;*
> *I don't require*
> *dictatorship.***'**

Sir Richard Attenborough's career has moved through four phases – actor, producer, director, company chairman. But at each new phase he has maintained some activity from the previous stage, and has consciously transferred his skills. As an example, the concentration which he developed as an actor now enables him as chairman of several companies to 'operate within a box' and give his full attention to one organisation at a time.

His aversion to militarism has been well demonstrated in Oh! What a Lovely War and Gandhi, but he also shares with good generals the confidence to take large risks and to delegate, which stems from meticulous planning.

He has shown the notoriously prodigal film industry that commitment and financial discipline need not stifle entertainment value.

Sir Richard Attenborough is chairman, Channel Four Television, Capital Radio, RADA and the British Film Institute. In 1959 he formed Beaver Films with Bryan Forbes and Allied Film Makers in 1960. First stage appearance was in Ah Wilderness in 1941, his screen debut was in In Which We Serve in 1942. He produced and directed Oh! What a Lovely War in 1968 (16 international awards) and Gandhi in 1980–81 (19 international awards including 8 Oscars and 5 BAFTAs). Married with children. Educated: Wyggeston Grammar School, Leicester; RADA. Born 1923.

Chapter

1

How did you first decide that the stage was going to be your career? Was there any family influence in that?

No, my family are academics. My father was principal of the University College Leicester before it became a university. My mother was the daughter of a headmaster. All my uncles and aunts have been in education. But my father adored the theatre and there is, I suppose, inevitably a requirement in presenting yourself and to speak with conviction which is common to an actor, a teacher or a clergyman . . .

And so when I demonstrated my interest in the theatre at 10 or 11, I was not totally discouraged initially. I remember my father taking me to London to see Charlie Chaplin's *The Gold Rush* when I was 11. I thought that it was the most devastating occasion I could remember – there was somebody who could make you laugh and cry at the same moment, I suddenly felt, 'That's what I would love to do.' The mistake was that I allowed it to totally take over from my work at school and so by the age of 16 – shortly before war was declared – my father said, 'Look, this is hopeless. You're not going to do Higher Schools and you will not get to university. Your mother and I are at our wits' end. You spend all your time at the Amateur Dramatic Society. So we've applied to the Royal Academy of Dramatic Art. Because we can't afford to send you there you'll have to obtain a scholarship and there is only one with a subsistence grant. If you win it, somehow we'll find the money to send you there. If you don't you must promise that you will give it [the theatre] up for at least a couple of years.'

I entered for the scholarship and, partly I think because the war was on and the competition wasn't great, I was awarded it.

What did RADA teach you in particular? Presumably the craft of acting – but you were very raw no doubt when you started there, much more polished when you finished. What do you most remember?

It dealt with my accent, to start with, because I had a broad Leicester accent. With an accent comes a slightly different personality, and acting in large measure requires getting over the terrible self-consciousness and embarrassment that every actor experiences when he first faces an audience.

Was there anyone on the staff there that particularly influenced you?

Yes, there were two remarkable sisters, Dame Irene Vanbrugh and Miss Violet Vanbrugh; the principal Sir Kenneth Barnes, a marvellous old boy; and Ronnie Kerr who ran the Palmers Green Theatre; Robert Donat; and Billy Harcourt-Williams, one of the most eminent directors at the Old Vic.

You finished at RADA just as the war was getting into its stride, then you went into the RAF.

Yes, I volunteered and was called up for flying training in 1943. However, I was seconded to the RAF Film Unit to make a film called *Journey Together* where I met John Boulting, who influenced my life enormously. By the time the movie was over they didn't require any more pilots, which I was training to be. The commanding officer of the Film Unit suggested I take a cameraman and air gunner's course.

So I flew with the RAF Film Unit as an airgunner/cameraman. That's how I first became involved with cameras, really.

Then at the end of the war you were hooked on an acting career. You spent many years as an actor both on stage and in films. At what time did you feel impelled to start producing and directing?

They were different. I was cursed with a cherubic face. When I was 25 I was playing a 13-year-old schoolboy in *The Guinea Pig* with my wife playing my housemistress, which had its embarrassing moments! Nobody would allow me to move beyond these juvenile characters and I was convinced that ultimately my career was going to come to a grinding halt. So I decided to give up acting and go into production.

The first film I tried to set up and produce was *The Angry Silence* in 1958. The only way I could raise the money for that was to persuade everybody – the lawyers, the accountant, the designer, the composer – plus all the artists, to work for virtually nothing and to take a percentage in the film. But I could not persuade an actor to play the leading part, and three weeks before we were due to start shooting everybody said, 'Well there's no alternative, you're the only silly beggar who will do it for nothing, you'll have to do it yourself!'

So I actually played in the movie, not wanting to at all. That got me out of that terrible typecasting. I had a marvellous partner who is still my greatest chum, Bryan Forbes, and he used to write and direct and I would play in the movies and produce them – *League of Gentlemen, Seance on a Wet Afternoon* and so on. I was totally happy.

Then some madman sent me a biography of Gandhi and suddenly – it was like a blinding flash as I read this extraordinary story – I knew I wanted to direct. I wasn't satisfied any longer merely to produce. I didn't want to direct *per se*; I wanted to direct that story about Gandhi and for twenty years I tried to raise the money – from 1962 to 1982.

Once I had decided that I wanted to direct, to bring all those talents together, and mould them like a conductor does an orchestra, that's when it happened. Although I didn't make *Gandhi* for twenty years, people knew then that I wanted to direct and so I actually started by directing *Oh! What a Lovely War*.

If we stay with the theatre for a moment, it's arguable that being an actor gives you a fantastic opportunity of studying colleagues at unusually close quarters, including people of a different generation and people much more senior in the profession. Is that a particular advantage in trying to carve out your own style of acting?

> Yes, enormously so. Acting is a very strange profession. A number of distinguished actors have said that you act because you are dissatisfied with who you are and what you are. I don't know whether that is true or not. You either act by virtue of observation or by pure intuition or by a combination of those two plus often an enormous amount of research. For instance I made a film about a regimental sergeant-major. I worked with an RSM for a month, square-bashing, everything: it is often the only way to assimilate the characteristics and attitudes of other people. When you move into directing, experience such as that is of a value such that you can't put a price on it.

Coming on to your producing time, you have described how you had to grapple with this unusual situation when making *The Angry Silence*. It sounds as though you were willy-nilly having to become an entrepreneur as well, because you had to persuade people to do things, you had to arrange a lot of things, money was extremely tight. Had you been attracted at all to a business career?

> No, I don't think I had, but I do gain enormous satisfaction from impresarial activity. Although I can't add two plus two in terms of finance – seriously I can't, my strength is by no means finance as such – I run my own companies and I can operate a budget. I never go over budget, never, on any picture that I produce. I had an instinct of some kind. I remember the very first show I ever wanted to do. I was 11 and the hall I needed was the St Barnabas Hall in Leicester. I had to hire it for a Saturday in order to put on the show. There was a huge market in Leicester and I went into the marketplace and bought little notebooks and bits of coloured ribbon. I attached pencils and sold them for twopence halfpenny, having cost me a penny. That's how I raised the money to hire the hall. The cost was five shillings.

I suppose that indicates, in some measure, a passion, arriving at a point where you do something by virtue of a total commitment. The ultimate objective was the goal, but I enjoyed the grind of the business – raising the money – however frustrating it was. So to move into production and to have to control funds and plan the expenditure of those funds, I got and still get satisfaction from it.

I produce and direct my own movies now. Producing them is not merely a question of controlling the purse-strings and seeing that the production goes on and comes off the floor as it should. In addition there is the power that's vested in the producer. If you have raised your own money, if you have persuaded whoever it is to back you, then you're answerable to nobody else, and I love that. I enjoy my autonomy enormously, and that you cannot achieve unless you produce and direct, because you have somebody else who raised the money and who you're answerable to – why shouldn't you be?

Although you are very modest about your financial abilities, I would have thought most companies would give their right arm to have you as a finance director if you never go over budget on anything! How do you manage that?

Well I'm not sure about that – finance director – no I really couldn't do that. I don't understand the sophistication of finance – asset valuation, balance sheets, cash flow, reverse takeovers, etc. When I'm undertaking a production I plan it meticulously, usually with the same group of people. We've done many films together. The same executive producer, the same accountant and so on. We plan the schedule of the picture. We then plan all the pre-production, all the building, the costumes, the special effects, the casting budgets and so on.

I work a long time on the script because when we go on the floor we schedule very meticulously to that particular script. The script is the Bible to me – I don't ever move off it. When I know in my own mind how I'm going to shoot sequences and what sort of sets I require and what costumes and crowds and so on, I stick to it. All that I can control, and that I am meticulous about. So to that extent, yes I can manage funds in terms of achieving the particular end. But sophisticated financial perception is another matter. I don't think I could manage that.

Does your commitment, which comes through so strongly in some of the things you particularly want to do like *10 Rillington Place* and *Gandhi* – there's real energy and enthusiasm there. Does that make you find it difficult to delegate? Do you fuss and breathe down people's necks?

No, no, not at all. No, no, no, the antithesis. I delegate tremendously. I suppose that started really with *Oh! What a Lovely War* because I knew absolutely nothing. I didn't begin in the editing room where so many directors learn their skills. I didn't begin behind the camera. I was an actor and all I had done was to produce one or two movies – very different to directing. So I gathered together, by virtue of my experience in the business, the people whom I thought were the absolute tops of their profession – the best cameraman, the best recordist, the best designer, the best continuity girl, etc. And because at that time I really didn't know, I *had* to delegate. I had no alternative. I had to rely on them. They had to supply me with information which I was not able to supply myself. I relied on them enormously. I've continued to do that. Few of them still work with me, because they are producers or directors in their own right – but in broad terms, as I've gone along I've used the same crew in movie after movie, and because I have supreme faith in their capabilities I grant them absolute autonomy, in terms of what they bring to me.

May I use the analogy of the conductor: the conductor does not go and listen to his flautist practising his little phrase which is so vital in the second movement. You know that he or she will come up with it. Broaden that out and you have your production designer and your cameraman. What I have to do ultimately is to adjudge, when they present all their various elements, whether they work into the overall mosaic in the way I believe to be correct.

Like a conductor or a commander, there are occasions when you have to decide, 'No. That doesn't work.' At that time I'm cocky enough to say, 'I'm sorry, that's not the way I want it.' But up until that point I rely on them, and I don't know how else, in commercial cinema, you manage. If you are Charlie Chaplin and you go up to four hundred takes on one set-up, if you're Satyajit Ray and you take two years to make a movie, that's a different matter. But if you are in popular commercial cinema which I am, then I don't know how you can keep your hands on all those separate activities all going on at the same time.

And does the same apply to running Capital Radio and chairing Channel 4 or the British Film Institute and all the other things that you are in charge of?

Well, Capital Radio was interesting in that when we got the franchise, which we never expected to get I might say, we were in the particular circumstances under-capitalised. I decided when we started with John Whitney as the first managing director, that the only way in which we could get it off the ground would be if I became an executive chairman for six months. Unfortunately we went on the air at the time of the miners' strike and the three-day week, and we were very conscious within two or three weeks that we had insufficient funds, we had no listeners and we had no advertising. In fact we hadn't got any of the three ingredients which are absolutely vital in order to continue.

I had to go to the bank and say, 'Look, I have no money left. You've backed us so far. All I have is my art collection. May I put it in the vaults? Please, I need some money for Friday.' The Bank of Scotland were magnificent. They didn't take my pictures. They said, 'Your conviction is enough. You are sure it's going to work.' I said, 'I'm sure to the extent that if we continue I'm going to become executive chairman for a year rather than six months.' I had not intended to do anything other than set up the company. However for twelve months I worked in conjunction with John. I came in daily and did an executive's job. But once we were truly launched I got the hell out of it. I believe fervently that non-executive chairmen should. I employ exactly the same attitude in running Capital Radio now, or Channel 4, or the BFI, or RADA. I couldn't be involved in that number of activities if I didn't work by the same constraints or criteria, I again grant massive autonomy to the executives.

It seems to me, apart from anything else, to be eminently stupid to engage superb chief executives like Nigel Walmsley or Michael Grade or Wilf Stevenson and not to give them rein, real breathing space. To be sitting in the next office breathing down their necks is madness. You've got to be available and if they need you, you've certainly got to be there. I don't mean physically: it can be on the phone or by fax, or whatever. But you must be accessible. And equally you have got to do your homework. You can't – which I must say annoys me sometimes at board meetings – you cannot come to a board meeting unprepared. When the staff go to the trouble of preparing their papers, if you don't pay them the compliment of really working at those papers and knowing what they have said, you don't grant yourself the right to criticise them.

When you do feel that something has gone wrong, or there's something you're not clear about, you must bloody well say so. But you must say so prior to the meetings. I believe that absolutely. I do it on the film set – you must never humiliate the cameraman or the designer or first assistant – I would never question their commitment or their integrity or their skills in front of everybody. I believe that is exactly the same in the running of a company. I have a private meeting every time before the board, or on the previous evening, and I go through minutes and agendas. I've done my work on my papers and consequently I'm able to say, 'I'm not sure about this' or 'I can't support you on this' or 'Why can't you . . . ?' They will persuade me that I should support them, or the opposite and they give in to me.

What's the difference between the role of the chairman of a business and the role of the managing director or chief executive?

Well, I don't know whether you can generalise, so I can only speak from my own point of view. It seems to me that the chairman of a company has to bring the overseeing judgement to bear. Of course a good chief executive always keeps in his thoughts his product, his revenue, his shareholders, his public relations, etc. But inevitably the chief executive must, in some measure, have his nose very close to the grindstone and sometimes the balance between all those responsibilities needs an overview, and I would have thought that that was the function of a good chairman: to grant, as much as he may, autonomy and the loose rein – overridingly to the chief executive and perhaps the finance director – but to have fundamental knowledge of the operation and indeed to stand in loco, as it were, for the shareholders and not only for those who have invested in cash but those who by listening to Capital or watching Channel 4 have also invested in a way. He should speak from the outside in terms of an overall view. No company the size of Capital or Channel 4 can operate other than having three, four or five major executive directors. Obviously they are answerable to the chief executive, but the chairman has also got to watch the chief executive's judgements and possible errors in terms of those relationships. That I think is a vital part of his job. The job must be to hold the overview, to be available when he is required. The chief executive must, under all circumstances, keep the ball rolling.

Is it in fact a positive advantage to you that you have so many interests – you are involved with so many different activities, on the boards of different organisations – in that you can use a networking approach to your work. You can pick up ideas here and transplant them there. Do you do that positively?

Yes, I do, a lot – because many of them are interrelated. The BFI is related to the British Screen Advisory Council, which is involved with Channel 4 and so on. So yes, you do. And, of course, I am able in some areas actually to bring about marriages, not physical ones in terms of funding but of attitude, or concerns, of elements which are lacking in certain companies which you can draw on from some other company through your experience.

I think in some measure I spread myself too thinly. I do perhaps too much and I sometimes wonder whether I'm playing it correctly in that I chair too many boards. But I do continually say this to my colleagues and their reply is, 'Look, you are always available. I can always reach you; wherever you are, somehow within an hour you are available.' One of the things that actors have to learn is that – there's a terrible stage story, your favourite aunt has died. You learn that ten minutes before you go on stage either to play a very dramatic moment or indeed to play in a farce. There is no question whatsoever in terms of that performance, the grief for auntie has to wait till the performance is over. So you learn a mental discipline. Now that means that you have to operate within a box. I chaired a Channel 4 board meeting this morning. I chaired a Capital Radio board this afternoon. I don't find that anything lingers on. I am able to bring an actor's concentration in large measure to a particular function and responsibility.

You've described how you have tremendous confidence in the teams that you run, and you delegate to them and you let them blossom. If you are dealing with talent-spotting in a less experienced person than those reporting direct to you, have you any criteria in your mind when you are looking at younger people and saying, 'Will this person make the grade – have they got the makings of somebody good?' How do you look for talent? What are the key signs?

The terrible thing is that once an actor you're always an actor. Acting is born of two massive ingredients. One is a commitment which will not under any circumstances be moved. No matter how many times you are punched in the face you come on forward. This is what you are committed to come hell or high water – I don't mean by trampling over people, but in terms of your determination it's an absolute essential. The other is courage. You have got to be prepared to dare. You have got to be prepared to venture. Now if you marry those two things together, you've got a hell of a good start for a good actor or actress. I, in a way, apply that to people who come to see me. I see perhaps half a dozen young aspiring directors, writers, a week – every day I come up here I see one or more and they are spread now months ahead, but I see them always. I look for that absolutely passionate commitment. That doesn't mean they've got talent – you've got to discover whether they've got talent when you give them that break – but without that you might just as well not start. Now I think that applies in administration, in almost any area you can think of, not merely in the movie business but in business as such.

And if you've got somebody who has made their name as an actor or a performer where it's all about individual talent, how do you then help them to realise the need for teamwork in getting anything together?

Well you know the old impression that actors are totally egocentric individuals has gone in large measure. I don't mean that when they actually move on to the stage or in front of the camera that they are not there to present themselves. I don't mean it in that sense. But in terms of creating the overall piece of work, there is a massive commitment now to the ensemble. It started with Stanislavsky in Russia, in Germany with Brecht, with Olivier here at the National, and Trevor Nunn and Peter Hall at the RSC. There is a feeling of company. It's very interesting. I'm chairman of RADA, and we have a series of prizes which have been donated over the years: thirty or forty prizes. For five years now the students have begged the Council to abolish prizes, not because they don't wish to present themselves to the public to the best of their ability, but they say, 'I am not in competition with the other person on the stage. We are presenting a group – we don't wish to be compared, we don't wish to be rivals.'

I think in a way that's my feeling about cinema: that whereas there are the great *auteurs* and those who will pronounce that the cinema is a primary art form, I don't believe it is. I believe it's a co-operative art form and everything that I do – accepting that I am a dictator at times, although I trust a benevolent one – it's an ensemble operation which I enjoy. I don't enjoy being on my own, I don't enjoy being the top figure, above, isolated, away, no: I work with a group, I always have. I enjoy playing the conductor, I enjoy holding the baton: I don't require dictatorship.

You have an equally famous brother and I wonder whether you are able to spend any time together and to learn from each other and use each other's experience. Is that possible?

In some measure. We live very close to each other in Richmond. One of the sadnesses of our lives really is that we see as little of each other as we do. We try to have dinner together with our wives whenever we can. Dave is a different fish to me. My first film, *In*

Which We Serve, was shown in Leicester and if you coughed you missed me. In fact it was a part which was scarcely visible at all, but you wouldn't believe so if you saw the outside of the Leicester cinema. One of the boys at school said to Dave, 'Eh 'oop, Attie, is that Richard Attenborough a relation of yours?' Dave drew himself to his full height and answered very firmly, 'Only distant.' He had no desire at all to present himself in public. He's an intellectual, unlike me – I'm not at all – he's a highly erudite, highly educated, remarkable figure in many ways and he had no wish to 'cavort around in public' as he used to accuse me of doing. He only went in front of the cameras because of the cruel illness of a marvellous man called Jack Lester who was the keeper of reptiles at the London Zoo. He was dying and the series wasn't to go on the air because Jack was to be its presenter. At Jack's specific request Dave took his place and he just took off from that moment. He's quite shy but he's a marvellous raconteur. We both have a lower-fourth-form sense of humour, which I'm afraid makes us behave in the most outrageous way when we're together.

If you're not able to use him as a sort of sounding board because you are going off around the world in different directions all the time, who can you off-load to or can you think aloud about all the problems you're coping with?

My wife. We were students together, we worked together a great deal in the theatre up until the time our last daughter was born. We have shared everything always, so whatever I'm involved in, I debate the pros and cons with Sheila. On the other hand, Dave and I tend to talk to each other at crisis points. We always know where the other is. I'll give you an example. I got home one night and there was a message: 'Dear Dick, phone me for God's sake, doesn't matter how late.' And I rang him after 11 o'clock and he said, 'I'm on my way.' He came down the hill and said, 'The most terrible thing has happened, Dick.' I thought, 'Oh my God, this must be something quite dreadful.' He said, 'I've been asked to become the next director-general of the BBC – I can't do that can I?' There then followed, of course, a great debate as to whether he should be deskbound or continue doing what he did. Our mother was killed in a motor accident which was unbelievably dreadful for both of us. We worshipped our parents. My father never recovered from my mother's death so we tended to rely on each other much more than we might have done. Each became *in loco parentis* in some measure to the other.

How far ahead are you able to plan? If you take Capital Radio, looking back over the history of your first fifteen years, as an example, the purchase of the Duke of York's Theatre and the renovation of it. It sounds as though that came up as an unexpectedly early opportunity. How far can you plan those sorts of things, and how can you get the flexibility to respond when an opportunity presents itself like that?

The board at Capital has always had an executive element, more so now; I believe passionately in bringing management into the boardroom. I've done it here, I've done it at Channel 4, there are now six executive directors and there are four here. So I believe that's essential in order to be able to move quickly, in order to be *au fait*.

But at Capital, in particular, we had a number of delegatory directors: they represented the Evening Standard's shareholding, the Observer's shareholding, Rediffusion's shareholding, plus individual directors such as myself or Bryan Forbes, who have personal shares. Before we floated the company, the concerns and values were very different and it was hard to hold the company together and make decisions as quickly and as sensibly as one might have wished. I think it's fine now. We've refined the board, it's much smaller, neater, and it's a fully integrated board. So our flexibility of movement is very good

Channel 4 is a different matter. In Channel 4 you have to react immediately to certain developments. But because television broadly demands massive pre-planning, whether it be drama, light entertainment or documentary, you have to have a far-sighted view as to what's happening or is likely to happen.

In my own career, because I am my own master, I can in fact make my decisions immediately and I do plan a great deal, I do have a target, I do have an objective, and with I fear a frightening determination, I go for that target. But because I'm not answerable to outside shareholders, there's a very close-knit company. I have four or five directors, one of them is Sheila, one is my lawyer, one is my accountant, and others – the executive producer on most of my pictures, and my associate producer and marketing director who have been part of our companies for over twenty years. It's a very tight-knit little group and I can assemble them within half an hour, in actuality or on the phone in a matter of minutes. So I can move very fast and, of course, you need to move particularly fast when certain things suddenly come into the reckoning. In our profession people always want answers yesterday.

So you never wanted to run a business the size of ICI because of the sheer size of the thing?

No. I would hate that. I would absolutely hate it. I could never accept the impersonal element. I have an appalling memory for names, so people think that I'm simply a very flowery actor who calls everybody 'Darling'. The truth of the matter is I call everybody 'Darling' because I can't remember their goddam names! Man, woman, child or dog, they're all 'Darling' – but I do know them. I do have very real relationships with everybody from the dresser to the cleaner to the executives – in all the companies in which I'm involved. There are few people I don't know.

Baroness Tessa Blackstone

❝ ... I've had to combine my career with bringing up a family ... [this] required the development of organisational skills which many men don't have to develop in the same way. I think that, too, has helped me develop a real sense of how to use my time productively.❞

Tessa Blackstone's sheer intellectual ability could have provided her with a distinguished career in research and writing. But in her early thirties she exploited what she describes as 'an amazing opportunity' to join the Central Policy Review Staff, at the heart of the Whitehall machine.

What she learnt there about power and the formulation of social policy has proved invaluable in her subsequent posts. By the age of 36 she was a professor at London University, then as deputy education officer of ILEA she co-ordinated a wide range of services for hundreds of schools and colleges across the capital.

She was thus able confidently to take up the mastership of Birkbeck. She handled an immediate financial crisis with aplomb, and is sufficiently sure-footed in managing temperamental academics to find time also to be active in the House of Lords, the BBC and other organisations.

Master, Birkbeck College, since 1987. Tessa Blackstone is chairman General Advisory Council of the BBC and of the Institute of Public Policy Research. She is a director of the Royal Opera House and of Thames Television. Formerly she has worked with the Central Policy Review Staff, 1975–78; University of London, Institute of Education, 1978–83; ILEA, 1983–87. Two children. Educated: Ware Grammar School; London School of Economics. Born 1942.

Chapter

2

What determined your original choice of career as an academic?

I think I was on an escalator and I just kept going on up it. I had gone to the London School of Economics as an undergraduate, then become so fascinated by the subject that I was studying that I stayed on to do a Ph. D., at a time when the social sciences began a very rapid expansion. So before completing my Ph. D. I was offered a job at the LSE. That seemed to me a marvellous opportunity; to be given the chance to become an assistant lecturer in the place where I had been a student.

How did you enjoy the teaching part of the job – the student contact as distinct from the research, writing, bit of it?

I loved it. I tremendously enjoyed trying to encourage students. I enjoyed the contact with people slightly younger than myself, and I found teaching a wide range of people very interesting. For example, one of my students – whom I'm still in touch with – came from the British Cameroons. When he arrived he had some difficulty in being able to express himself in English, so even just teaching people how to write an essay I found an enjoyable challenge. Then, of course, it is always very rewarding when people you've taught make it in the world outside. I suppose towards the end of my career as a full-time academic with teaching responsibilities I found the teaching less exciting than I did when I started.

You had a period of about four years when you were writing prolifically. Was that a very creative, formative period – the last years before you moved on?

Yes, I suppose it could be described in that way. I was driven by a desire to get my ideas into print and disseminated. I suppose I was also ambitious and knew that if I was going to get promoted I would have to write. Writing is certainly the most difficult thing that I've ever done and continues to be so.

But you were writing an enormous amount, more than you needed to justify your position academically.

Yes, because I suppose in the end writing gives me more of a feeling of fulfilment and satisfaction than anything else that I do. Partly because it is more difficult than anything else – if I've spent a day writing something and it's been productive and I've achieved my ten pages I feel better at the end of that day than at the end of just any old day.

You were an academic for ten years. Looking back on it, what was the most formative aspect of it?

I worked in an interdisciplinary department with a mixture of various social scientists: economists, sociologists, historians, a lawyer – all sharing an interest in social policy.

What that experience gave me was an understanding of the way in which different social science disciplines can add to our understanding of how the world works, in particular in relation to social policy: how it's formulated, how it's implemented and its impact on different kinds of clients. That was enormously positive and valuable for me in relation to the things that I now do.

That was obviously paving the way to what happened next. How did that come about – the Central Policy Review Staff job?

Well, I started getting itchy feet and feeling a bit unsettled. In fact I had already felt that in 1971–72 and had had a year's leave from the LSE, which I spent partly at Harvard and partly at the Centre for Study of Social Policy. I then went back and found the year's leave had not been enough, really, and it made me realise that it was time for a complete change. I realised that if I was going to enhance my understanding of the system and how it worked, I probably had to get out of the universities and work in central government. Given my interest in social policy that seemed the right thing to do. We had moved from a Conservative government in February 1974 to a Labour government. I was obviously going to be more suitable as an adviser in a Labour administration. I talked to Claus Moser who is somebody who had been very influential over the years as far as my career is concerned. He, at that time, was director of the Central Statistical Office and he suggested seeing whether I could get into the Central Policy Review Staff. It happened that Ken Berrill had recently taken over as director and I knew him from his time as chairman of the University Grants Committee.

So then I got in touch with Ken Berrill, and it was extremely fortunate from a timing point of view that the CPRS had decided to do considerably more work on social policy and were looking for somebody with my kind of interests. I was offered a post.

Just coming back to you being ambitious, what was that born of?

I think two different things. My feminism and my determination to show that women could take on responsible jobs, influential jobs and make something of them. I felt that very strongly. Secondly, I think my own family background. I came from a very competitive family. I had brothers and sisters with whom I competed and I had parents who in different ways urged me on and regarded being successful as something that was important and believed that their daughters as well as their sons should achieve.

In a way your career took off with the job. What was it about it that came together?

> Well it's an amazing opportunity for somebody of 32 to be given, to get right into the centre of central government, to be able to see the Cabinet minutes when they come off the presses, to be able to establish a network all over Whitehall. So I was just lucky and privileged to be there at a time when the CPRS was fairly influential – perhaps more so than it was later. I also became involved in a particular study which had publicity – I suppose that established one as somebody who was working in the area of policy formulation. Although much of this publicity was quite hostile I gained a public profile as a result of it. Not everybody in the CPRS had such a profile.

Presumably it was in the nature of the job that you wouldn't stay forever?

> Yes, everyone who went into the CPRS went in on the expectation that they would be there for two years. I stayed for three.

Very much the sort of period that gives you time to make up your mind which way you jump next. You're at the heart of things, doing what you want and what you're good at. What kind of thoughts did you have about the direction to take after it?

> Well, unlike when I was starting off as a young Ph. D. student, I did give it some thought. I considered staying on in the civil service. Also I was approached by a couple of people in the private sector and discussed job possibilities there. In the end I suppose I took the same cautious route. I went back to where I had come from, the academic world, and took a chair at the Institute of Education in the University of London.
>
> I think I did that partly because I still felt a need to write a bit more and to consolidate on the nine years I had had at the London School of Economics. I also felt that I didn't have the qualifications really needed to go and become a businesswoman. I didn't have the

confidence to start in something totally new, and I don't know where I would have ended up had I done that. There's no point regretting what you have done in the past, because it happened and things have turned out quite well for me.

At 36 you were young to be a professor. Sometimes people move into top jobs a fraction too early and find they've missed out on some important chunk of experience. Did that in any way apply to you, or were you ready for it?

I don't think it applied at all in my job as professor of educational administration. I was perfectly able to take on the task of running what was not a very big department and I think that you don't need huge preparation for something like that if you've got the commitment and the energy. I think I would feel slightly differently if you asked me about becoming a chief officer in ILEA.

There was presumably some management and administration – how did you take to that?

I've always loved it, and always felt that it was quite easy to do in combination with research and teaching. Some academics make an enormous amount of heavy weather of it. Quite honestly the administration we had to do, compared with most jobs when you really are a manager in the public sector, is pretty simple.

In a sense doing the job of professor of educational administration took me away from administration because I then started research in a number of areas concerned with educational policy and how it's made, and in a way I was building on and deriving advantages from my inside experience of government. But, of course, I missed being at the centre of things. Everyone I knew who had been in the CPRS and then went out into something else and who said they didn't miss it, I found eccentric.

What was the most testing and challenging thing about the Institute of Education job?

> I think getting back to full-time research, writing and teaching was quite testing and particularly the more individualistic aspects of being an academic. I had got used to working in teams in the CPRS. I had done a lot of my academic work with others. Nevertheless it's a lonely job in many ways and I did find it lonely. I missed the team spirit of working in the civil service, and the special sort of solidarity that exists in organisations like the CPRS. So that was an adjustment that tested me personally.

In a sense as an academic with the LSE, you had been in charge of a team, working with people, but in the CPRS it was a team effort. You seem to have taken to the business of running something, even though it was a small department, without any difficulty.

> Yes, sometimes I think my lack of experience in dealing with personnel-type problems might have shown through. There are always some colleagues who are difficult for one reason or another, and I, of course, have had my share of them like everybody else. However, I think running a university department of that sort requires a fairly light touch because academics do work as individuals. You're not managing their time as you are in some other organisations. It's up to them to get on with it. I think what you have to do is set an example in terms of the standards that you set for yourself, and set targets and goals for people rather than organising them.

In a sense it was a preparation for what you are now doing?

> Yes, certainly, it would be more difficult to do my current job without having run a university department.

And you were there for just under five years. Do you feel now, looking back, that it fitted in with what had gone before and what was to come?

> Yes, it was part of a fairly consistent career pattern and made sense in that respect, whereas I think staying on in the civil service probably wouldn't have been right for me.

Having been responsible for the teaching of educational administration you then went on to practise it in ILEA. If you were ambitious when you left the LSE you must still have been pretty ambitious?

Yes, I think so.

And your first job with ILEA was as deputy education officer. What did that job involve?

I was one of three deputies. One was responsible for schools, a second for post-school education. My job was to take responsibility for a variety of services for schools and post-schools. They included research and statistics – the only activity for which I was well qualified – press and public relations, policy on development and buildings, industrial relations and personnel matters for ILEA's forty thousand non-teaching staff and the accounts branch. I also shared responsibility for the budget.

So it was a fairly hefty managerial/administrative task, not really in the kind of areas which were your prime interest.

It was a very hefty task and one for which in some ways I was ill-prepared. I wasn't able to keep up with all my interests in educational policy. However, if you sit in a job of that sort you are constantly drawn into discussions about where the Authority is going. If you're concerned with resource allocation you're going to be thinking about questions of priorities – nursery education as against improvements in the school-meals' service, for example.

Did you enjoy it?

Yes and no. It was a very demanding job which at times I felt that I wasn't doing adequately. I worked immensely hard. It was a job with a lot of frustrations because of the difficulties that the Authority was facing in various ways, including difficulties imposed from the external world, such as terribly complex and difficult relationships with central government. This was the period in which rate-capping came in. This was when the GLC was abolished and there were big questions about the future of ILEA: a totally new Authority had to be set up. There were also difficult relationships with elected members and between elected members. So I won't pretend that every day of the week was enjoyable. Even so I'm immensely glad I did the job, because although it was something of a baptism of fire it taught me a lot, I learnt certain management skills, it was tough, and I think it toughened me up for things subsequently which has made me much better able to deal with crises and difficult situations.

How many people overall were you responsible for?

In the eight branches that came under me there were six or seven hundred staff.

You comment very interestingly on how a professor leads an academic, how it was more by example rather than by coercion or by bringing somebody in front of you and telling them what to do. Was there more of that in the ILEA job, or did you take some of that style with you?

I think I took some of that style with me and I believe very strongly in the importance of delegation. There were large parts of my work that I had to delegate: first because I personally didn't have enough of a background in it to be able to do anything else, but secondly because it's highly desirable to give people their heads. After all, the people in the team working immediately under me had enormous responsibility themselves, and it was right to leave them to get on with those responsibilities. There were, however, times when, in providing a service to 2.5 million people living in inner London, you had to be sure that things did not go wrong and you had to make decisions and see that they were implemented. That occasionally requires a more directive style than is ever needed in a university context.

Do you want to comment briefly on the last few months when you were director of education?

My job changed then as a result of the abolition of the GLC. The Authority was restructured, I took over from the director-general of the GLC the job of being clerk to the Authority, which meant that I was responsible for the constitution, for committees and for their smooth running, and for supervising the legal adviser. By then I think I had decided that I wanted to do something different.

How did you come by your present job?

It is the only job that I've actually applied for as a result of seeing an advertisement in a newspaper. I had been thinking about the possibility of going back into the university world, possibly as the head of an institution. I was fairly clear that I wanted to stay in London.

By great good fortune the mastership at Birkbeck came up at exactly the time when I was beginning to think about a job of this sort. Birkbeck was an institution that was particularly attractive to me because of its long-standing commitment to part-time higher education and mature students. I had enormously enjoyed teaching them previously and I had come to believe in the importance and value of part-time higher education. The job at Birkbeck was one that, for me, had enormous advantages.

Do you think in any way that, subconsciously, you had been working towards that kind of job throughout your previous career?

I never had a target that one day I wanted to be vice-chancellor or principal of a college in a university. I have never planned my career in that sense as you can see. Things just happened.

But when that advertisement appeared, what was your reaction?

My reaction was absolute enthusiasm. This would be a wonderful job if I could get it.

And do you think you were equipped for it? You had had managerial responsibility in the educational field in ILEA, you had been professor of a department, you had been in the think-tank in the Cabinet Office – was that sufficient to prepare you for the job?

> I think it was really. What I hadn't done was to be a 'number two' in an academic institution. Quite often, when people take the kind of job I now have, they have been pro-vice chancellor, or pro-rector, or vice master, if I had done that it would have helped a bit. On the other hand, a lot of people who take on this sort of post had not had my outside experience of working in a big management job in local government, or an advisory job in central government, and I think those experiences have been very useful. They have meant that I haven't found it too difficult to take on the management side of the job, because by comparison with what I had done earlier it was relatively easy. Knowing how Whitehall works, how Westminster works is quite useful if you are running a university institution. In that sense I have had a bit of an edge over some others.

When you took the job, Birkbeck College was in some difficulties. What were those difficulties and how did you set about solving them?

> It looked as though the College might not survive because of a change in the formula for funding part-time higher education that the University Grants Committee had brought in, forgetting about Birkbeck and its very high proportion of part-time students. What it meant was that I had immediately to set about trying to find sources of funding that could keep us going. I came in at the tail end of a campaign that had been run in the College prior to my arrival but I became involved as soon as I was appointed.
>
> I can't claim any credit for the success of the campaign. It was the result of work by the chairman, Roderick Flood, professor of history, and various other people in the College. I'm very grateful for what they did because I believe they established in the minds of those members of the public, who have an interest in these things, a perception of Birkbeck's unique and valuable role, and in the minds of a number of politicians from right, left and centre that Birkbeck must be preserved. So I was fortunate in being able to build on that.
>
> What we then decided was that we should bring in an outside

management consultant to look at the College's financial situation and to make some recommendations. We were very lucky in getting support from the Corporation of the City of London who paid for Deloittes to do this. Deloittes gave the College an extremely clean bill of health in terms of its efficiency and in terms of the way it had been operating. They made it clear that the financial problems weren't going to be solved by slashing spending here, there and everywhere. Something else had to be done.

The management of the College came out well?

Yes, it did. The College had always been run with a very slim administration, there wasn't an awful lot of fat to cut in that respect. What we did was to come up with a proposal for increasing the number of planned student numbers without any additional staff which meant an increase in our recurrent budget from the UGC. After quite a battle that was eventually accepted by the UGC, and we have, over the last two years, recruited an additional five hundred students (equivalent to three hundred full-time students), and that has meant that our recurrent income has substantially increased. It has not meant that we have got out of all our difficulties, but it has meant we can survive.

The second thing I had to do, with the help of a new finance officer and the secretary of the College, was to be very tough about spending. It has been very hard for the academics here: they have had to accept a new regime where all kinds of things that they would like to do, they can't, because of the need to balance our budget. I hope that this year, after running in deficit for several years, we will be back to having a balanced budget but it will have been done at considerable cost and to the detriment of some activities we would like to have developed. As one example we had to close our refectory, which was a great pity and we have not been able to expand as much as we should have liked.

The problems and challenges again have been managerial and organisational rather than to do with the educational substance of the job?

> Well, yes and no. The College has been going through a period of very rapid development and change in terms of the content of courses, or put another way, the kind of higher education we are providing. We have also restructured our academic departments, grouping them into resource centres. We have been producing quite new courses at various levels – of course, much of this work is done by the academics with the registrar's help, but I must take the responsibility at the end of the day.

What is unique about being head of an academic institution – not necessarily Birkbeck, which is obviously unique in its own way? What does it have in common, say, with being a permanent secretary in the civil service or chairman of ICI?

> I think the permanent secretaryship or the chairmanship of ICI are both bigger jobs than running even the largest university, because, for example, ICI has far more employees and a far bigger budget than any university. If you are permanent secretary of a government department you are responsible for working out national policies for ministers in a whole variety of areas, putting the flesh on policies by working out the detail, thinking through their implementation.
>
> However, what is more difficult in a way about any university is that the command structure is much looser. You are a bit like a king or a queen with a whole lot of barons in a relatively decentralised state, and those barons must be allowed to develop their own areas in the way they think fit, but within a framework that you set, within guidelines about the policy goals of the institution as a whole. What vice chancellors or principals can't do is to operate in a strong hierarchy. Instead they have to persuade; they have to use committee structures; and they have to work with their colleagues.

In addition to being master of Birkbeck you are also chairman of the General Advisory Council of the BBC, you sit in the House of Lords and you are chairman of the Institute for Public Policy Research. Could you comment on how you keep all those things going, and what priorities you give them?

Birkbeck is my top priority without any question. I spend far more time at Birkbeck and on Birkbeck than on all the other things put together. I think that sometimes it is difficult to keep all those balls in the air but I've always enjoyed work and I've always worked long hours. I try on the whole to keep the mornings for Birkbeck and for that reason I don't sit on House of Lords' select committees or go to Westminster for any reason before lunch.

I suppose that after Birkbeck, in terms of time, the House of Lords comes next. I am a working peer and I do regard it as an obligation to my party to turn up. I am an opposition spokesman on education. I am also trying to develop my knowledge and interest in foreign policy further and to speak in debates on various subjects, and, of course, I have to be there for key votes. However, I am able to take my Birkbeck work with me and when I go to the Lords I often sit in the library and get on with that.

The Institute for Public Policy Research's success is very important to me. I am the chairman of the Board of Trustees. We have a full-time director and staff, and they do most of the work. But setting it up and getting it going took a certain amount of time. I believe it's extremely important that this first left-of-centre think-tank set up to fill the gap and counter the mushrooming right-wing think-tanks succeeds. It is very important that it uses the opportunity to provide new ideas and new thinking for the left. I think we're off to quite a good start.

The chairmanship of the General Advisory Council is an extremely interesting job. I've learnt a lot through doing it about how a big organisation of that kind operates. I've always been interested in broadcasting. I've done quite a lot of broadcasting myself – particularly during my period at the Institute and a certain amount since I have been at Birkbeck. However, the amount of time I give to the GAC is relatively small.

Looking back over the jobs you have done before this one, what would you say has been the most influential, the most testing, the most beneficial in taking you forward significantly?

I've loved every job that I've done, with the possible exception of some occasional bleak times in ILEA, but I got an enormous amount even out of that job, and most of the time I enjoyed it. I don't think it's very easy to pick out one job rather than another; they were all different. I suppose that getting into the CPRS gave me a special and unique kind of experience and my career took off after that; I think that's true. But I think each of the three jobs that I have done since then has given me different opportunities and experiences and those early years at the LSE were terribly important too. I owe a lot to the London School of Economics. It gave me my first chance, and I was appointed before I had finished my Ph. D.

One other thing, which I think is important, is that I've had to combine my career with bringing up a family. That in itself is testing and it has tested me all the way through. They're grown up now, and just about off my hands, but being a single mother, as I was during much of the time that they were growing up, as well as trying to do my various jobs reasonably well, and taking on various other things, required the development of organisational skills which many men don't have to develop in the same way. I think that, too, has helped me develop a real sense of how to use my time productively.

And have your children been part of your development?

Of course. My children are my toughest critics and they are immensely important to me. They are very close friends now, as well as my children, and I wouldn't have been without them for anything.

Sir James Blyth

6_I have fairly strong views about things…_
but I'm always prepared to listen
to the expert and I'm always
prepared to be persuaded
that I'm wrong.**9**

Sir James Blyth's energy and achievement of results have repeatedly caused him to be noticed by companies even in unrelated fields. By his mid-thirties he had acquired strong experience in three companies well known for their marketing: Mobil Oil, General Foods and Mars. His next move proved decisive – a complete change of industry and a major challenge as a general manager in Lucas.

After three periods in defence-related organisations he has now reverted to consumer goods, in a company (Boots) which provides plenty of scope for his favourite management activity: sales and marketing.

Running through his whole career is a thirst to keep learning. His style is to choose a challenging post, openly acknowledge gaps in his experience, gladly use help from experts and climb quickly up his learning curve.

Director and chief executive, The Boots Company plc, since 1987. Sir James Blyth is a non-executive director of Cadbury-Schweppes and of British Aerospace. He is a governor of the London Business School. Formerly he was head of defence sales, MoD, 1981–85; managing director, Plessey Electronic Systems, 1985–86 and then of The Plessey Co. plc, 1986–87. Married with children. Educated: Spiers School; Glasgow University. Born 1940.

Chapter

3

Can we go back over your career and find what have been the most important learning experiences? What comes to mind first in your early years?

I think I was lucky because among the many companies that I went to see in my last year at university, although there were several job offers, there was one that to me was enormously appealing – Mobil Oil offered me a graduate traineeship of which they only gave a couple every year. What I knew about business then you could have written on a small postage stamp, and what Mobil offered was a year of going round the whole organisation and seeing every department.

How did it go?

Fabulously. The other graduate trainee and I travelled all round the country. We visited the retail side of the business, the manufacturing side, research, head office, and we were given an enormous amount of time by some very senior people, in a way that very few organisations can probably afford to do now.

What do you remember best about it in terms of getting you motivated?

> I really do think the commitment of some very senior people, making sure that these two supposedly 'bright young things' that they had hired were properly used. We talked to the heads of all major departments. There was a fantastic commitment. The oil companies probably understood that requirement earlier than any of the other international businesses. They had been doing that for a very long time. So I have never for one second regretted (a) taking up that traineeship, and (b) the fact that it was an oil company that gave it to me.

What did you fetch up as in Mobil?

> I ended up as senior marketing planner for the UK, having spent some time in New York and having done a whole variety of things. I was assistant to the European purchasing agent and I sold on the road for a couple of years as a retail rep, which was tremendous experience. It was the absolute boom time of developing new filling stations in the UK and the reps did all the site acquisition work as well.

Do you still love selling – is that what you think you are best at?

> I could go into platitudes about the things I am best at – managing people and controlling organisations and thinking strategically, etc. All I can tell you is that I still love selling – no question at all. We've got a guy here who's the same – he runs Boots the Chemist – he can't walk into a Boots store without trying to sell something to somebody.

Was the love of selling there, or brought out by Mobil?

> I think it must have been there already. I think you can teach people to sell, but the people who absolutely enjoy it have a little bit born in them.

So you were there for about six years, then you moved on to General Foods.

I think that's probably the only genuinely deliberate career move that I've made. The oil business had started to sag worldwide in the late 1960s, before the real price crunch and just after the Seven-Day War. I had a marvellously exciting time during that period because I was in the purchasing area. We had to handle the banning of American oil companies while we were still drilling in Libya. But after all that settled down, it really did look like a business that was going to be pretty flat for some considerable time. I had just come back from the States, I had just got married and a big part of it was I absolutely hated commuting to central London. I frankly wasn't learning a great deal and I could see myself doing a planning job for another couple of years and then running one of the central retail departments or going back out as an area manager and marking time . . .

I decided I wanted to learn a lot more about marketing consumer goods, and it was the time when General Foods were planning a major European acquisition. The smart thing they did was to haul in a bunch of what the Americans would call 'benchwarmers' – guys who were slightly superfluous to the existing department but whom they could train in the way in which they did things. They paid us quite well – 30–40 per cent more than we were earning at that time. They were based in Banbury in Oxfordshire – a nice place to live and to bring up a family. They had a very good personnel director at the time, and made the whole package very attractive.

So what did you do?

They actually got several new businesses out of it. I helped to get them into catering products in a big way, then we launched the Maxpac System for British Rail. That was very much a marketing job. I was there for three years, ending up as a venture group manager, running a small series of new product ideas.

And what was the most important thing out of the General Foods experience?

I think really understanding how important being meticulous about the planning process is in marketing, and the value of good market research, which has always stayed with me. Also how very attractive it is to work with nice people, because that company had a talent for picking people who would get on well together. All that naked ambition didn't seem to breed too much hostility.

So what caused the move to your next company, Mars?

They were trying to fill a marketing manager's job in their catering division, which they were looking to merge with their whole human foods' business up in Kings Lynn – Yeoman mashed potatoes, Uncle Ben's rice, etc. Very soon after I went there, we merged those two together and I became sales and marketing director of that whole thing. It was relatively small beer as a Mars company, but highly profitable, and imbued with all of those extraordinary Mars management philosophies.

But it would have been very difficult for me to see myself spending the rest of my career in that company, especially because of the complete autocracy of John and Forrest Mars – the two sons who ran the business as a duopoly. They owned it to all intents and purposes, and they weren't wonderful at brooking opposition. But they still taught me the value of decentralisation, which they use to an extent that I don't think anybody else does. They still run the entire corporation with about twenty-five people at the centre, and they try to remove all of those trappings that are a barrier to communication and to effective methods.

So you're only paid for what you do, not for seniority?

Yes, and everyone is paid weekly, everybody clocks in, nobody has a parking space, everybody uses the same facilities, nobody has a separate office.

So what is your view on that meritocracy?

I think they carry it too far. One of the problems in Mars is that everybody is at everybody else's beck and call – vertically, sideways, every way. I just think that's tough to take for forty years – there aren't that many people who see their whole career through in that organisation. However, while they're there, because in the main they hire pretty bright people (says he modestly!) they do benefit. You certainly end up understanding what egalitarianism actually achieves, and although you might ameliorate it slightly yourself over time it still leaves you with a clear belief that in so far as you are able and, without rendering the entire atmosphere just too ascetic, you can still get a long way.

Nevertheless, you thrived in that kind of environment?

Yes, I enjoyed it. It was the heyday of American management style and a lot of us thought that if you wanted to learn how to run a business and to be successful, that was what you had to do.

So, just summing up on Mars, what was the most useful thing from that experience?

I think the genuine pursuit of excellence in every way: regarding the wrapper on the product as being as vital as building a huge manufacturing plant. They drummed that into people. And the pursuit of excellence in people probably is the most lasting one. They valued people and talent and they understood that reward in that context was very important.

So you went from there to Lucas – how did that come about?

Bernard Scott and Godfrey Messervy were looking for someone to run their battery companies. Bernard was chairman at the time and Godfrey had just become managing director and I had been using Pentagram as the design consultants on a tremendously unsuccessful attempt to get into the UK hamburger market. Lucas had also been using Pentagram and they took an extraordinary chance and gave this 34-year-old who had never run a damn thing in his life quite a big international battery business to run.

You went right in as a general manager?

> Absolutely. Straight from marketing director of a relatively small company in the Mars organisation to running quite a major undertaking.

Did they approach you?

> Pentagram were doing their corporate identity programme at the time and I think Bernard Scott said to Colin Forbes, 'We're looking for a guy to come in and change the way in which we run the battery business,' and Colin said, 'There's this guy in Mars – I would talk to him.' We had half a dozen conversations – and it came about.

What's your comment on the timing and experience that you need to move into your first senior post?

> They were very brave! When I look back on it they really did take a flier. There they were running this still quite conservative Midlands manufacturing company, and they genuinely wanted to effect change. They didn't think it could be done by the guy who had been doing it before, although he was actually a very sound technical operator. They really thought it wasn't that much of a risk.

You had something of a track record behind you?

> Quite a strong marketing track record. It's perhaps not as crazy as it seems: I had been involved with commodity-based businesses for a long time, and battery manufacture is very much a commodity-based business.

So there was method in their madness in a way?

> I don't think, to be blunt, they had fully assessed the risks! Much as I loved both of them! They desperately wanted to get some marketing talent into the company.

So you were swept in to what sort of turnover business?

It was about £55–60 million but it was only making about £350,000 profit.

So it was a sizable business. Do you think that going into general management you need more than that? Very often people get pushed into it, and although they are able enough to do it they're not quite ready for it. Were you ready for it? Was there anything missing in your armoury of experience and skills?

As it turned out, no – but there easily could have been. I've always been numerate, I've always enjoyed problem solving and I spent a long time in planning departments. Marketing planning in the oil business has very little to do with what you are promoting at the pump. It's where do you buy the product, and where should you be shipping it to, and, to the nearest four decimal points, what should you be paying for it. It's very much a distribution planning job rather than a promotion planning job.

The huge gap was industrial relations. I was dropped into quite a militant industrial relations environment having had no trade union experience whatsoever. I wouldn't have known a shop steward if I'd fallen over one. Mars don't have them, General Foods hardly have them and the oil industry is such a controlled business that you never encounter them. So that was the one thing I lacked.

Was that a stumbling-block or did you overcome that?

I loved it. I inherited a chap called John Mudd who was the personnel director, an ex-naval commander and very much a personnel director of the old school. He sat me down and gave me a 'Noddy's Guide to Industrial Relations' one morning a week. I was 34 at the time and he was 54. He was smashing, very very good, and well disposed to make changes. Actually we revolutionised the industrial relations.

We changed them quite dramatically, as a matter of determined policy. We removed a problem over pay differentials under circum-

> stances where people said it was absolutely impossible to do it. They
> would never agree to it, etc, etc. The sums weren't huge but they
> removed the disruptive influence that had been there since the
> war.

And you effectively turned the business round, because it was in trouble
when you took it over?

> Yes, it was in trouble.

Then you moved on to aerospace which was an even tougher nut to crack
than the batteries.

> The aerospace business was character building, yes.

What were the challenges there?

> First of all, we all of us forget how much of our time we used to spend
> on trade union affairs. Aerospace had a horrendous trade union
> problem. I don't know if you remember but they had a thing called
> the 'Shop Stewards' Combine' which produced strategic plans for
> the business and God knows what, and that was the time of planning
> agreements with the Labour government.

So were these trade union difficulties a barrier or a challenge?

> Oh, a huge barrier. They had to be got out of the way, they weren't
> just an intellectual challenge. They were absolutely preventing the
> change in the business that was necessary to make it successful. It
> was losing about £1 million a month in cash and profit on a turnover
> of only £119 million per year. It was in serious trouble. Again, what
> I knew about aerospace engineering you could have written on the
> back of an even smaller postage stamp.

How serious or significant was that – the fact that you didn't know the
technicalities of the business?

Very serious. It's a high-tech business and the customers talk the technology. People on the shop floor understand the technology – *really* understand it. So my learning curve was vertical. Fortunately I love listening to people talk about what they do, and I'm prepared to spend any amount of time on that, just listening and learning – as long as it takes. And I've always worked a very long day. So I just ploughed away at it and learnt about the business.

What was the most satisfying achievement of your Lucas experience?

I love getting the bottom line numbers right. To take a business that's turning over £120 million and losing £12 million, and in four years take it to a turnover at the thick end of £300 million and be making £26 million – that's my idea of what you're paid for. We shut factories, moved people, renegotiated prices and drove through productivity agreements . . .

Was the industrial relations side the hardest bit?

No. I think the toughest bit was getting the prices right on the contracts, but the industrial relations bit was the second toughest because the productivity gains depended on that, and if we hadn't made the productivity gains we would never have made any money. It's the toughest job I've ever done.

How did the move from Lucas to the Ministry of Defence come about?

There had been three heads of defence sales: they were all very good salesmen, very able. By then the MoD thought they needed somebody to reorganise that whole operation. One of the problems was that the organisation was trying to be all things to all men. They approached Godfrey Messervy, who was by then chairman. He was reluctant to let me go and I didn't particularly want to leave the aerospace business because it was doing reasonably well. After a fair amount of leaning from the system it was arranged that I would go and do it on secondment.

As head of defence sales what were the main challenges?

> Making sure the political will to do the job properly was completely there. Building an organisation that worked, because to be blunt a little of what had been put into the organisation in the past had been dross. Also, there was the matter of getting the facilities improved so that everyone could do their job properly. Their accommodation was horrendous and we had to change all of that, and that's not easy in the civil service. You go up to a civil servant, and say, 'Look, this is a sales office and it's got to look like that and not like the back end of some social security office in Soho.' It was difficult for them but we achieved all of that in time.

Did you find yourself moving fairly easily in Whitehall?

> Yes, I have to say that. It sounds blasé but it wasn't. I actually enjoyed the challenge of making that very complicated system work. To me that was one of the biggest thrills of that job. I got a tremendous amount of satisfaction from making the combination of the civil servants, the military, the politicians and industry and the customers work as an entity. That for me was the big attraction. That and setting some very clear objectives for what we were trying to do.

You were managing civil servants. How does that differ from managing people in industry and commerce?

> Not a lot really. You do have to thump them on the head and tell them that the first time they actually try to second-guess you on a 'Yes Minister' basis, you are going to get cross about it.

So how did it fit into your career as a whole?

> To some extent it was a hiatus. On the other hand, as an insight into how Government and governments work, and as a way of meeting people all over the world it was a great opportunity and I loved every moment of it.

So what were your options when that finished?

I was offered a lot of jobs, including a very attractive one back at Lucas. But by then my vaulting ambition had led me to believe that I really should be running a British public company.

Were you always ambitious?

I think so – greedy and ambitious!

Did you have some kind of long-term goal, or did you never think beyond the next job?

Very early on I wanted to run a company, but I didn't think what sort of company. I didn't want to live in the States. I had quite clearly decided that, very much aided and abetted and threatened by my wife. I wanted responsibility for running something substantial and Plessey seemed to hold that out.

I started with them as managing director of the electronic systems business – very enjoyable until along came Arnold Weinstock with a bid about two months after I got there, at which point I was catapulted into being managing director of the whole company. To be on the end of a major takeover bid is a very interesting experience. If you don't learn from it there's something wrong with you. To have fought off Arnold Weinstock is something.

Was that your major preoccupation?

I was at that in total for the thick end of a year. That was the first preoccupation. The second preoccupation was how the hell we got out of this mess on System X in the UK, which is what in the end led to putting the GEC and Plessey businesses together. The third was that the order book had been going to hell in a handcart for about five years, and sorting that out was something David Dey, who was running the telecoms business, and I set our minds to very hard. Those were the three big preoccupations.

Does fighting off a takeover bid divert management from running the business?

> Completely. The trick is to make sure you don't allow it to divert line managers. You need to have line managers in place – and you'd better get them if you haven't got them – who can run the business without supervision while something like that is going on, because you sure as hell aren't going to have time.

How would you describe your own management style?

> One of the problems is to see ourselves as others see us. I'm always prepared to change my mind. I'm always ready to be persuaded. I have fairly strong views about things, as most people who work with me will tell you, but I'm always prepared to listen to the expert and I'm always prepared to be persuaded that I'm wrong. And I often am persuaded that I'm wrong and I have no false pride about saying, 'You're absolutely right – let's think about it again.' I'm not long on patience, and I think that's generally agreed by people whom I work with. I think I'm fair – I think I spend a lot of my time considering – I don't think I'm fair by natural inclination. My impatience makes it difficult for me to be fair but I try to hold myself back and think what would be right and what some of the people that I have observed in the past would do under the circumstances.

You're obviously very confident and ebullient. What do you think that's born of?

> I'm like a lot of people with my sort of personality. We're like it in our public moments but not always like it in our private moments. I'm cheerful most of the time and I enjoy myself most of the time, but I have occasional moments of immense self-doubt – but not many of them.

How do you get over those moments of self-doubt?

> I wait for them to go away! I'm serious. I think a lot of those things are cyclical.

You are a governor of the London Business School. What importance do you attach to formal management training?

> In every company I have ever worked with there has been a strong commitment to formal management training, including Boots, and the only reason I took on the governorship was that I believe very strongly in it.

How many training courses have you yourself been on, other than updates or short courses?

> None! I've been trying to go to business school ever since I can remember and I don't think I'm going to make it! I've never had time. There has always been some new challenge. It doesn't stop me believing in it. It doesn't stop me thinking that I would have loved to have done it. I've never got myself ready for it.

Can you sum up your views on what goes into the making of an effective manager, based on your own experience and observations?

> I have to say that sheer intellectual horsepower is an enormous asset. Dogged perseverance can win through but it doesn't half make it more difficult. Having a good memory can be a huge asset.

And you have that?

> Yes, indeed. I think sheer physical stamina is an enormous requirement. Then you are into all those things like leadership and all those intangibles.

How do you keep fit, incidentally?

> I still play tennis at least once a week. Yes, I'll be on the court tomorrow morning at seven-thirty.

You have demonstrated that it's possible to move about at the top. To what extent do you think that top leadership skills are transferable?

I think they are transferable but I have to say that I think it's easier if you have been in the same industry. It's tougher if you haven't. That doesn't mean I haven't enjoyed moving about a lot – I have, enormously.

Ann Burdus

6Never, never hire anybody who is not as
competent as you. Hire people
who will challenge you –
it makes for an
easy life.9

Almost the whole of Ann Burdus' career has been spent in advertising and
public relations. She did not start off with a well-defined career plan, and some
of her moves have been due to being in the right place at the right time. But
equally, her self-reliance has enabled her to smash through the 'glass ceiling'
which inhibits many women's promotion to the highest management levels.

The mainspring of her working life has been an insatiable fascination with the
motivation of people. This began in her first job as a clinical psychologist and
continues in her present post with one of the most daring building projects in the
world.

Senior vice-president – Communications and Marketing, Olympia & York Canary
Wharf Limited, since 1989. Ann Burdus is a member of the Top Salaries Review
Board and joint deputy chairman of the Health Education Authority. Formerly she was
a chairman of McCann & Co, 1979–81 and a director of Interpublic, 1981–83 and
AGB Research, 1986–89. She was chairman of the Advertising Association, 1980–81
and of the EDC for Distributive Trades, 1983–87. Married. Educated: Durham
University. Born 1933.

Chapter

4

Starting at the beginning, what factor or factors determined your original career choice?

> Accident. When I came down from university, I got married and I went into clinical psychology because there was a big mental hospital quite near and I could get a job there. That was in County Durham. After about three years I realised I was not going to make a career in clinical psychology, my marriage broke up and, as I had been doing freelance depth interviewing for market research, I decided to find out more about a career in that field.
>
> I joined the research department of Mather and Crowther in London, which at that time was rather like a full research company within the advertising agency.

You say it was by accident – nevertheless, it was a reasonably natural progression from clinical psychology to market research.

> Yes, it wasn't all entirely whimsical. I began to question my career in clinical psychology when my superior left and the board of governors of the hospital offered his job to someone I considered less qualified

than I was. I didn't sweep out then and there, but I began to think, 'This isn't for me.'

Did that suggest to you that it was not just the career block which you thought was unjust?

It *was* a career block, but also I then began to re-evaluate what I was doing and decided I was going down the wrong road. So going into market research initially was an exploratory move. It happened at a time when the research companies and agencies were looking for psychologists, because attitude and motivation research had suddenly become very fashionable. When I joined Mather and Crowther, there was a psychologist there, a lovely man called Walter Gordon. He was a very good teacher and I learnt a lot from him.

So he was key, in developing and influencing you?

The whole department was. It was an extraordinary place to be. There was a very good feeling there. There was a very high intellectual calibre. People were very willing to help, teach and so on. It was formative in some curious ways: one of them was that it was my first real experience of the commercial environment and the people were so nice, which is not what you expect coming in from outside. It was intellectually challenging, it was fun.

Walter Gordon, quite straightforwardly, taught me my trade. I don't think he was an example in a management sense, but in the sense of teaching me the nuts and bolts of what I was supposed to be doing, he was very good indeed.

So it was a learning environment?

Very much so.

And what contributed to that? Was that part of the company's philosophy, or did it just happen because of the people who were running the place at the time?

It's a very serious company, it takes its people seriously. It understood them and does know that people are its resource. It has always taken the selection and training of people very seriously. It's also a company that gives you opportunities to do whatever you want to do.

What was your ambition at that point?

I didn't have any ambition. I wanted to enjoy myself. I had to earn a living and I found myself doing it in a very pleasant environment. Had I at that stage said, 'I want to be head of an advertising agency', I would not have followed the route I did. I followed it out of intellectual curiosity and genuinely took one challenge after another as they came along at that stage.

The 'intellectual curiosity' thing is part of it. The agency was growing very quickly at the time and we were shuffling round and sharing offices and so on, and for a time I had a desk in the information department – not the library. In the information department we kept a copy of every report that was written. The company at that time had a policy which said, 'We do market research in order to set the strategy for the advertising and we occasionally check on whether our work is effective, but we don't interfere with the creative process. We don't carry out any research on the creative work.' So I went to my boss one day and said, 'That's not true. At least once a week a report comes into the information department from a market researcher, which is research into the creative process and if we're going to do that, why don't we have a policy, an attitude, a position on research into the advertisements?'

At that time, the merger with Ogilvy in the States was beginning to take off, so they said, 'Why don't you go to the States and find out what you can about advertising research from our colleagues there.' So I went on secondment for several months to the US company and studied advertisement research – great fun! It had its ups and downs as a personal experience but as a learning experience . . .

When I came back, I said, rather grandly, 'They don't know anything we don't know.'

Why was it a good learning experience?

New country, different clients and intellectually stimulating people. I think I tried to make as much use as I could out of the time I was there. Then, when I came back, I said, 'The most important thing I have determined is that there is a negative relationship between creative people and research people. If we do do research, it's not getting applied because of this enormous hostility.' So eventually we set up a creative research department which was the first department of its kind and it broke new ground. I had enormous fun doing that. We built up our own techniques and we were very instrumental in the agency's new business development.

Then I took a long hard look. This has to be one of the times that I really began to take my career seriously. The head of the research department was roughly the same age as I was, and his deputy was also roughly the same age – two absolutely first-class men. I then looked round London and determined that there were only about five agencies who could afford a creative research department. It was an overhead. You didn't get paid for it. Times were becoming a little harder in the advertising business. So when I was offered a job at Garland Compton to run the entire research function, I took a step sideways out of the specialisation that was getting me into a box, into being head of research and information, which greatly broadened my base.

There does seem to be a pattern there – you stopped being a clinical psychologist because there was a career block and you did something about it. It looked as though there was a career block with Ogilvy's and you did something about it. So is there a lesson there that you shouldn't be put off by a career block?

You should act positively. You should assess the situation. As a young girl it was implicit in my upbringing that we are responsible for our own lives and indeed for other people's. So it would be completely alien for me, for example, to join a trade union, because that is abdicating your own responsibility for your life and job to somebody else. I'm not against trade unions – that's not my point – I'm saying that somehow it's implicit in my upbringing that I'm responsible for my life. If I'm unhappy it is not in my nature to say somebody is bullying me, or whatever. It's in my nature to say I'm unhappy, I had better do something about this and get on with it – which is probably why I walked out of my first marriage. A different person would have handled that situation differently. And it's the same thing in my career. It's up to me to do something about it.

So we've got to Garland Compton, head of a research department . . .

. . . in a company that was expanding. This is when I began to learn something about the business of business. They were in a takeover mode buying other agencies. And I was on the board and worked very closely with David Bernstein who was the creative director. He has been good enough in his books to say that I taught him everything he knows about research and I would say David taught me a great deal about creativity in advertising.

It's interesting that there were two people who were mentors in both of the jobs you have mentioned so far. They were obviously fairly influential in helping you forward and giving you the kind of experiences that you needed.

And there's another thread. There were some splendid people from whom I began to learn about management style, not necessarily the same people.

I think Jimmy Benson at Ogilvy was very important to me in that sense, but even more so at Garland Compton because I was now becoming more sensitive to management issues. Garland Compton was headed by a man called Dick Desborrow. I learnt some very practical things, like leading by example. Dick used to come into the office every morning, go up to his office on the top floor, do handwritten thank you notes for any hospitality he had received the day before and then he would walk down through the agency, stopping off at different departments saying hello, or whatever. That was something I put into practice when I was at McCann and it's interesting because there are clients who occasionally use it as a test. They come in and I say, 'Is there anything else I can tell you about the agency?' And they say, 'Walk me through it.' I used to have my own route and I walked them through it. I thought initially they were just interested. In fact it was a test to find out whether the chairman and chief executive really had their finger on the button as far as the company was concerned.

So there I was at Garland Compton and across the road was an agency of roughly the same size who headhunted me: McCann-Erickson. They had a very strong reputation for research with a very good head of research, a man called John Clements. What I discovered after was that John had been offered training in the States to become the managing director, but before he went he had to find his own replacement, so I was headhunted by McCann-Erickson to be his replacement as research director.

In straightforward career terms, it didn't really seem to make much sense. Garland Compton was a much more solid agency with a good local reputation and McCann-Erickson was exactly the same size. But I went to see them, and eventually joined them. The head of McCann London at that time – the man who now heads Interpublic – was such an enthusiast. He didn't bother to interview you in the normal sense. As you walked in the door, he would say, 'I think we're going to make £15 million this year and this is how we're going to do it,' – a wonderful enthusiast, but in the end, difficult to work for. But I think everybody would say inspirational, and totally dedicated to the business. There are stories about him as long as your arm – we would be having a 'new business' meeting on a Sunday morning and he would come in wearing his tennis clothes, because the only way his wife would allow him out of the house was if he said he was going to play tennis. Marvellous things like that. He has a great capacity for getting people to work for him which is very difficult to put your finger on, except for his dedication and enthusiasm.

So you'd got to McCann's. The things that you have mentioned so far are individuals and a good learning atmosphere, intellectual curiosity, determination not to be 'beat' if you come up against a block of some kind. What would you say were the most important learning experiences so far – up until the point that you joined McCann's?

I think watching people in senior management and watching how they work, seeing what works and what doesn't, confirming my own intuitive way of operating which is enormous respect for people – all sorts of people. I can't think of any other way to operate other than to assume the best of the people who are working with me and to respect what they are doing. Also learning little tricks, like hiring people better than yourself if you possibly can – that makes life much easier. Never, never hire anybody who is not as competent as you. Hire people who will challenge you – it makes for an easy life.

The thing that has come out in the interviews I have had so far with leaders from various walks of life is confidence. You obviously have to have confidence in order to take on someone who you know is very good. Where did you acquire this confidence?

I think it goes way back. Deep down I'm not necessarily all that confident. It's almost a self-assertiveness. Some of it is just common sense. I remember once at a client meeting in McCann I earnestly told a client how we were going to do this original research and what it was going to be like, and when we left the office, my assistant said, 'How are we going to do that?' I said, 'I don't know – you're the brains around here, now go and work out how to do it' – and he did. I had a wonderful stable of people because I just went out and hired the best. That meant I could conceptualise what we wanted to do and then ask them to go and do it, and they did.

Going forward, you fetched up as chairman of McCann's in this country. What took you there – it sounds like a signal achievement – what qualified you for it?

McCann was growing very fast. I was head of research and then head of research for Europe and eventually went on the executive committee. But I wanted to increase my US experience. By this time I was vice chairman. I was putting gentle pressure on the company and they transferred me to work on international business in New York. Then the head of the US company said to the international people, 'I'm desperately short of a strategic thinker.

Could we second Ann to work on US projects for me?' So I worked on a project for General Motors, and for Kodak and did some work for Sony and airlines. They liked it so much they asked if I would join the US company and run their research and thinking department. I think I had been on that job for three weeks when the head of the UK company resigned and after much heart-searching, the head of Interpublic said, 'Ann, you had better go back and run the UK company, because nobody else understands what Nigel was trying to do!'

At that time, McCann consisted of three agencies and I came in as group chairman. It was chaos, because Nigel had been a very brilliant, intuitive advertising man but he hadn't actually thought through what he was doing in management terms. I discovered that he had done something quite interesting. McCann-Erickson was the major company and he had spun off Universal McCann and Harrison McCann without really working through the relationships. One of the things that makes the Interpublic companies successful is their very good bonus scheme which relates to the profitability of the individual company. You can get up to half your salary again provided your unit produces sufficient growth and profit – it's a very good scheme.

I came back and found a situation where people in McCann-Erickson were saying those two companies (Universal and Harrison) were not profitable, were dragging down our profit and affecting our bonus. The people in Universal and Harrison were saying, 'We can't compete, carrying the overheads of McCann-Erickson, so we can't build our business and we can't be profitable.' So I created a new structure bringing all the services together and then the three agencies drew on these central services as they needed them. That caused trouble with head office in New York. I had one hundred and fourteen people classified as central services – everything from the financial men, chauffeurs, waitresses, office cleaners and so on. New York were horrified, because nobody else has ever added it up that way.

So I put in this new structure and things began to work a little better, but we kept having huge management upheavals. The entire board of Universal quit at one point and I had to put in a temporary manager.

So the job came suddenly. You were obviously well equipped to lead something at some point, but were you ready for it? Was there anything missing from your quiver that you might have had if you had remained a bit longer in the States? You were faced with massive organisational, structural and personnel issues.

> I learnt something which you had to live through. I don't think being longer in the States would have changed the situation. I didn't pay enough attention to boardroom politics. I got on with the job. With hindsight, I should have spent more time thinking about people and their ambition – including those who wanted my job!
>
> I did make several management mistakes. For example, I was on an absolute collision course with a director and I should have insisted that the company fire him, but I'm a very conciliatory person. I thought he had a lot to contribute and I worked very hard to keep him on board. I now know that I should have said, 'Fire him, or fire me – one of us has to go.' They eventually moved another of my key men, the managing director of McCann-Erickson, to Detroit. I knew it was a mistake for him and for the company. I didn't fight hard enough. I was a good corporate soldier and I let him go. It was wrong – it was a bad decision. So I was too conciliatory with senior management, my own management, and too conciliatory to the corporation, I assumed that they knew best. I didn't fight my corner hard enough.

Did you become less conciliatory as a result of that?

> Oh, much. And I'm much more of a political animal now. I try to work out what other people are trying to achieve rather than just throwing myself into it.

The job as chairman was more strategic and executive than creative?

> I'm into general management.

Was that your first major general management post?

Yes, I had run small teams before, I had been responsible for a media department at one stage with thirty odd people in it. I had had overall responsibility for the US research operation which was based in nine separate cities. But this was my first serious management job. The corporation did have problems, with which I can sympathise, in having a woman heading their major agency. The hard core of McCann business is in organisations like Exxon, General Motors and so on. I probably didn't pay enough attention to that. I knew that it is a problem for a woman to run a company – not so much now, we're going back twelve years – but it was then, particularly that sort of company. What I did was to surround myself with an executive team and delegate responsibility to them for these accounts. I was not sufficiently diligent in explaining to New York why I did this and they saw it as a slightly different structure from anything they were used to – why does Ann have so many senior people? They eventually decided that my thinking talents probably were better than my management talents and asked me to go and be director of strategic planning in New York.

What were the obstacles, as a woman, and how did you overcome them?

There's a belief in Interpublic that part of the role of very senior executives is to be a confidant to the chairman or CEO in the client company. They felt that at the most senior level they should be a boardroom presence in other people's boardrooms. They believe that there's a relationship between the head of the client company and the agency, and that the head of the client company will talk freely and frankly about things that he can't talk to his other managers about, or the rest of his board – and that this cements the relationship between the companies. When this works well, it's a very special relationship. They couldn't see how that could work between, let's say, the chairman of Esso and a woman manager of their office – and I think that in some senses they were right.

Even now?

I don't know. It might still be a problem, but then the whole business has become more professional and less dependent on personal relationships.

There are proportionately more women in the advertising/market research field than in others?

Oh yes. I'm delighted to say one of my protegées, Jennifer Laing, who I originally recruited as a trainee into Garland Compton, is now running her own agency, and there are now two other major agency heads who are women.

Is it surprising, given the nature of the industry, that more women haven't broken through?

It is and it isn't. I once held a meeting in Interpublic of the seventeen senior women in the company in the States and what was significant was that all of them were specialists. So they reached the position of being the head of a department, but the step from there to the main board is a very big one indeed.

What is the biggest step that you have taken so far? Was it going up to be chairman of McCann?

Yes.

Coming on now to the next job – strategic planning.

That was a staff role. It was extremely interesting. The first year was fine, because we were laying down the rules for a strategic plan for the group as a whole and for McCann-Erickson. I could see that once the thing was in flow it was going to be a record keeping, repetitive sort of job, not very exciting, and the probability of me moving up in Interpublic was zilch. So when AGB offered me a job, I said goodbye to Interpublic, goodbye to the States and came back here.

I have heard it said of you that you have the ability to inspire change without resentment. Was that said of you in regard to the AGB job?

> I think I probably caused more change in McCann than anywhere else. I think I do have this curious thing of just saying bluntly when I think things need to be done. I was joking about it last night with an old McCann colleague, and we were talking about the fact that while I was there I was very instrumental in setting in train something that became known as the 'Rye meeting' where, for the first time, the managers of the States company sat down at the same table as the managers of the agencies from around the world and, for the first time, the managers in the States learnt that they were less profitable and less successful than the international side of the business. And that was just from me saying, 'Having worked in both parts of the company this division is silly, we're one company, why don't we have a joint meeting?' This sort of trait of saying, 'This is silly' runs all the way through. When I came back from the States way back in the Ogilvy days I said, 'That isn't your problem; your problem is the relationship with the creative people.' This time I said, 'Our problem is that the US company is trailing behind the international company and doesn't know it – why don't we get together?'
>
> It was a question of seeing a weakness and digging it out. Rather like seeing and saying 'the emperor has no clothes'. At one point, the CEO of McCann US began to say, 'Ann, that's not your call.' He meant some things are none of your business. He began to say, 'You really ought to temper this trait of saying, "That's daft." ' But it was a strength – it did institute change. When I first went to McCann in 1971, I had a product development section that came under me but was totally separate from the rest of the agency, and I said, 'New product development is the most exciting thing people can work on. It should be an experience that everybody shares, has their crack at, and if you have a separate unit, they'll become sterile, they need stimulus – this is just daft.' There was that sort of 'the emperor has no clothes' which institutes change wherever you are.

So you rely on common sense and the courage of your convictions. But it needs something more than those to keep people with you.

Yes, you have to take people along with you and that you do by trying to understand where they're coming from. But interestingly I instituted change in AGB much more slowly than I originally thought was going to be possible. Some of the things that I tried to do when I first went there were only coming into effect by the time I left. I began to analyse the situation and ask why the context doesn't change and the reason was that Bernard Audley had very successfully gone round the world buying those successful companies but the people who had created those companies were still in situ. So people said, 'Yes, we're part of an international group, yes, conferences are great' – they hadn't changed one iota.

By the time I left – and nothing to do with me – most of those companies had professional managers instead of the founders who, instead of resisting coming together, were saying, 'For heaven's sake, what can the group do for me?'

You had no influence on that coming about?

I kept nagging away about what we wanted to do, went through the motions of communications and so on. The real change only took place as the people who built the companies began to go into retirement and truly professional managers came in behind them.

So were your six years with AGB – a new learning experience?

There were a lot of learning experiences, but most of them were quite small. One of them was recognising that professional/technical people must know that you understand what they are doing. I had an enormous breakthrough after I had been there a few months in that I was asked to help on a new product launch. At AGB a new product launch meant the investment of several million pounds, which for a relatively small company is a lot of money. So I took the documents home one night and read them with care. The head of this unit came to see me the next day and I said, 'John, before we start this conversation . . .' I asked him one or two technical points about the research and he said, 'You've read that, haven't you?' I said, 'Yes, and if what it says is right, this isn't going to work, is it?' A look of enormous relief came over his face because he knew I understood the technicalities of the project. I had also bothered to sit down and read all the small print. He and I got on well together all the time I was at AGB because he knew that I understood the technicalities.

Taking the trouble to understand your subordinates' problems?

Yes. That's right. Actually getting into what they are trying to do.

What brought about the move to your present job as senior vice-president, marketing and communications at Olympia and York Canary Wharf Limited.

AGB became part of the Maxwell empire. I was not put on the new board which was created for the joint company.

Were there any learning experiences in being at the receiving end of a takeover bid?

Some bits are just fun. It was very serious at the time, but you discover, for example, that the City advisers and so on actually like to work through the night. They don't go to bed. They come briskly in at 8 or 9 o'clock in the evening and settle down for yet another working session on the legal documents. Just seeing the whole technicality of working with the advisers fighting off a bid, or making sure that you end up with the right people, being exposed to a whole set of other experts you've never met before, the various bankers and so on – it's a very interesting learning experience.

Is that proving useful?

It's not proving useful at all in the job I now have. However, I anticipate being a non-executive director of companies when I retire from here, so it's all lodged in the back of my mind. I'm probably much more skilled than I used to be at understanding the structure of companies and what it's like to go through a situation like that.

What are the main tests in your present role?

> Learning about a whole new industry and knowing where you just have to rely on the experts. One of the rewarding aspects is to be associated with a great company which is doing something fantastic, to be within the small team of people here, and to work alongside architects and designers – people of enormous skill in their own professions. It's just a whole new learning experience, which is tremendous. I intend to retire in four years' time. To be able to spend the last five years of your career in a whole new area, but bringing to bear on that area everything you've learnt in the rest of your career (except the general management bits) is very exciting. Now, for the first time in my life I'm the client, and I'm buying advertising, public relations and research.

Can we talk just briefly about the Health Education Authority. What do you find most stimulating about that?

> Working in the public sector. This isn't the first time I've done it. I chaired the 'Little Neddy' for the distributive trades. That was an extremely interesting time for the distributive trades, and for me a most interesting process, because you are bringing together trade unions, the public and the private sectors – trying to move the industry forward. It was the first time I had worked closely with trade unionists and I gained enormous respect for the ones I met there.
>
> I had a very supportive team there who made things work. When I joined the Health Education Authority they were in a state of transition and we worked at enormous speed. We had to get a completely new team in. The Government had abandoned the Health Education Council in order to make a Health Education Authority. I had to begin to learn about the whole language and structure of the biggest industry in this country – the National Health Service. We had to appoint a new chief executive and a new chief medical officer. Then we had to develop a separate AIDS unit and to find a special advertising person. A lot of operational tasks to which I contributed quite heavily. I was bringing my administrative

experience to bear and a lot of other skills that I had picked up along the way.

I'm still not desperately used to the public sector. There are some aspects of the Health Education Authority which are difficult – one is that the Authority always meets in public and always has staff advisers at its meetings. I just find it extremely difficult to work with staff representatives at the board meetings.

I once caused havoc – I was at an Authority meeting and I was rather pressed; I had to go on to another meeting and we were discussing the budget. I said, 'I am sorry Chairman, I do have to leave before the end but I do want to say that I have never worked for an organisation with one hundred and twenty people that has six beancounters.' Once the staff representatives had worked out what a beancounter was, I nearly brought the whole Authority out on strike. They were were absolutely incensed. Later I realised that if you are interfacing with the Treasury you really do need five or six financial clerks or accountants – and I apologised.

Not only was I unguarded in using this slang expression with staff observers present, but I was wrong, in that in any public authority of that kind the whole budgetary procedure is such heavy weather when you are dealing with a government department that they really are necessary. So I was out of order on two counts!

So what about the substance of the job as vice chairman?

I think I contribute most now by giving support to professional teams.

Dr Neil Cossons

❛I am a passionate believer in the philosophy that if we serve our public well, then we don't have to worry so much about ourselves because as an institution we will be liked, respected and valued.❜

Neil Cossons' father, a history teacher, stimulated an interest in industrial archaeology, and Neil Cossons has spent his whole career in the management of museums. He finds this a dual challenge: to convey to visitors the function of an object clearly and dramatically, and to help his own staff find excitement in their work.

He is the antithesis of the cartoon stereotype of a museum director as a dry-as-dust lugubrious figure in starched collar. His restless urge to make his museums exciting has led to battles with his own staff who found the demands of the marketplace threatening. He is a perfectionist who sets high standards by up-front leadership. He sees himself as thinker, leader and manager, in that order.

Director, Science Museum, since 1986. Neil Cossons is commissioner, Historic Buildings and Monuments Commission for England; a member of the BBC General Advisory Council; NEDO Tourism and Leisure Industries Sector Group; and of the Council of the RCA and the Design Council. He is governor of Imperial College of Science and Technology and Medicine. Formerly he was director of Ironbridge Gorge Museum Trust; director, National Maritime Museum, 1983–86. Married with children. Educated: Henry Mellish School, Nottingham; University of Liverpool. Born 1939.

Chapter

5

Has there been any conscious pattern to the way you have learnt through your life, or have you used a variety of methods?

> I don't think there has been a clear pattern any more than there has been any conscious or predetermined career progression so, in one sense, I have been propelled by the vicissitudes of nearly thirty years in museums, responding to situations and opportunities as they have arisen, but of course learning all the time.

In childhood, what's your first memory of actually learning something?

> My father, who was a headmaster and secretary of the Nottinghamshire branch of the Historical Association, organised visits to places of historical and archaeological interest, and I used to go on those visits. I loved them and I still have vivid pictures of places I went to at the age of nine or ten. He also used to take me with him when he was doing his own research, much of which was on the history of turnpike roads and of canals. We would go off by Barton's bus to all sorts of places in the nether regions of

Nottinghamshire, Derbyshire and Leicestershire and bring pieces of loot back with us as well.

I remember rescuing a cast-iron tramway plate from the Ashby and Ticknall Tramway, standing at the bus stop with it, and walking down High Road, Beeston. Because we had to carry one end each, with me much smaller than him, it sloped down from front to back. I remember being very self-conscious and feeling an absolute fool . . . but it was worth it. I think that those memories go beyond learning, to a great extent shaping why I went into museums.

I think that was when I developed a sense of history and of landscape and of the meaning of objects, which I still feel. I have a passionate attachment to eighteenth and nineteenth century England, and in particular to its industrial history and archaeology.

The contrast to that is having been a medium performer at school, and no better than that, until I was 15 or 16. Through most of my early grammar school years I was very frightened, especially of bullying. From the first-form to the fourth I hated school because I was shy, terrified by the experience and inhibited, and achieved badly in those subjects where I was either frightened of the teacher or was worried. And I didn't do very well in the subjects I thought I was good at and that I liked because of the dread of the ones that I didn't. I eventually emerged out of that and found a self-confidence which I think, incidentally, is an important base for learning . . . In fact, I enjoyed the sixth-form enormously; I had my university place and I felt very confident about the future. I was a prefect and I feel I made a real contribution to the school in the second and third years of the sixth-form. I won the final year prize and became an expert rifle shot in the CCF; I was actually disappointed at my winning score in the North Midland competition of one hundred and twenty-three out of one hundred and twenty-five. All this would have been unimaginable four years earlier. I think, too, that I had my first sensation of wielding power and I enjoyed it. I learnt too that authority had to be underwritten by responsibility.

And all that was in spite of your father being a teacher himself. Did he give you any guidance about how to cope with the school situation?

I don't think he did actually, no. I don't know that I revealed it to him, I kept a lot of this fear to myself.

You bottled it up a lot?

I think so, yes.

But by the fifth or sixth-form, when you really were beginning to blossom, what feelings did you have then about your potential career?

I had no very clear idea of what I wanted to do. My father took me as a sixth-former to meet the then director of Leicester Museums, Trevor Walden, who was one of the great post-war museum directors in Britain. I remember Trevor said, 'It is only a part-graduate profession now, but within five years it will be a wholly graduate-entry profession, so my advice to you would be to go and get a good degree and come back when you have.' I don't know if he expected to see me again but I went off to university and after I'd graduated made my way back to Leicester and said, 'Well I've done that, now what do I do?' He said, 'You can start on 1 September as a student assistant', that is as a graduate trainee. There was no interview, no application form. That was in 1961.

What sort of guidance do you think people need when they're coming to the end of their full-time education, whether it's at secondary or tertiary level about careers? Is the system good? Are there gaps in it?

I find it difficult to understand what the situation is today but at the time I graduated it was almost non-existent. But one interesting thing of course is that when I left university it was at a time of full employment. It was in the early 1960s, and there was this bland assumption that anyone who was a graduate automatically got a job and sailed through the system. It's rather extraordinary, looking back on it, and was not particularly good for them or their employers. Certainly my own children have found things harder after they graduated. I think people of my generation often forget how tough it can be today.

There was also a belief that it didn't actually matter whether your degree was terribly relevant because you were the cream of society and you could pick things up as you went along. Now, I rather subscribe to George Bernard Shaw's view that 'all professions are conspiracies against the laity', but having said that I do admire *professionalism*. (There's a paradox isn't there; professions, as restrictive cartels, can't have much of a future but the need for professionalism has never been greater.) I also find generalists who believe they know what they're talking about – and especially when they are civil servants – somewhat irritating, just as I do captains of industry who believe that because they think they know how to do their job they can tell me how to do mine.

That sounds rather arrogant; I didn't mean it quite that way. In my summer holidays through the sixth-form and university I worked as a railway porter. I think I was pretty cocky until an old porter, who'd started his career on the Midland in 1919, took me aside and very carefully and gently showed me how to sweep a station platform. It made me realise that other people's jobs are not always what they seem. There is almost invariably more to it than one thinks.

So you place a high value on experience?

I place a rather high value on experience and I have no doubt that some of the tough times I have been through in my career, and the process of surviving them, have made me a much stronger and more capable person. I think that's why I find it rather difficult to take no for an answer – 'no' from somebody who is a practical, experienced and professional one can respect; 'no' based on administrative convenience or bureaucratic tidiness, or simply idleness or self-interest is like a red rag to a bull.

I think this is a real issue for the civil service. Dennis Trevelyan, who until recently was first civil service commissioner, wrote one of those lead articles in *The Times*' appointments section. The main thrust of what he had to say was that the civil service needed people who were real doers, can-do people, who had the experience of getting the job done and whose approach to life started from that point. I am passionately supportive of that view. As deputy director at Liverpool, where I worked with McKinseys, and even more so at Ironbridge, I became very much infected with that dynamic and it still provides a very strong impetus to the way in which I see my job.

You started your career in local authority museums. How would you describe your experience?

I went from Leicester as a graduate trainee to a brief period at the Great Western Railway Museum, Swindon, and then became curator of technology at Bristol City Museum where I stayed for five years. Bristol, which is a lovely city, was soft, easy-going and short-sighted and not in the least bit interested in its museums. In fact, the city was planning to build a rather grand new one but it lacked the get up and go and I think the site is empty to this day. That was a great pity and a lost opportunity because Alan Warhurst, who was director then, was totally devoted and committed and of course very good indeed. If I have any qualities of 'wiseness', if I can use that term, then I owe them to Alan.

Then, at the age of 29, I was appointed deputy director of the City of Liverpool Museums. Liverpool was quite different. It had a Conservative administration then, was very professionally run, particularly in terms of the quality of its senior officers, was very dynamic and was making real efforts to sort itself out in a post-blitz, post-war environment. It was really coming into its own and I spent much of my time working with Tom Hume commissioning the second phase of the post-war rebuilding of the museum.

But perhaps the most significant impact upon me came when the Corporation commissioned McKinseys to do a complete reorganisation of the city's management, based on a rigorous functional analysis. The deputy director of each department in the Corporation was seconded to form the team who worked with McKinseys. I spent an enormously exhilarating eighteen months working with this firm of management consultants who were then at the peak of their fame or notoriety, depending on how you look at it.

In 1969–70 McKinseys carried out a zero-based appraisal of the City Corporation and what it was there to do. The McKinsey experience had a profound influence on me. It was my first serious contact with management systems, which at that time was pretty unusual for a museum professional, certainly in Britain. The findings were implemented with very little modification and a major restructuring was well under way by the time I left Liverpool for Ironbridge. (Much of this of course went out of the window with local government reorganisation in 1974.)

So, almost exactly ten years after starting my museum career I left local authorities. I went from being deputy director of one of Britain's largest provincial museums, with a staff of between three and four hundred, to join a tiny charitable trust which had a staff of two – three including me.

What was the challenge of Ironbridge?

I think it was threefold. Firstly, I had been to Ironbridge in the 1950s and had kept going back at intervals because the place echoed to the voices of the past. It was one of those places where you could feel the life and vitality of the first industrial nation. It also had a rather romantic melancholy in its decay. The second attraction was that the newly formed Ironbridge Gorge Museum Trust wanted to appoint its first director in order to bring to life the archaeology and history of the area. Thirdly, I could be the boss.

One of the opportunities that had come my way in 1965, when I was in Bristol, was a travel bursary to visit the United States in order to attend the bicentenary celebrations of the Smithsonian Institution and then tour leading American museums. I came back with a new perspective on what museums could do and something of a frustration at the fact that British museums, at that date, were relatively drowsy and moribund. I was enormously excited by the new Smithsonian Museum of History and Technology (as it was then called) which had opened in 1964, and equally by places like Mystic Seaport – a reconstruction of a New England whaling port – which was also then quite new. The United States National Park Service was developing new standards of interpretation not only for the natural landscape but for sites of historical importance and this too was a revelation to me. So Ironbridge seemed to offer a huge opportunity to fashion a completely new form of museum which at that stage didn't exist anywhere. For at Ironbridge the objective was not to recreate history but to preserve what was there and to present it to the public.

You were director of Ironbridge for over twelve years. What were its main influences on you?

Lessons were learnt the hard way at Ironbridge. We were pioneering something entirely new and with a high rate of sustained and continuous growth. Without significant public funds to underwrite us we were also inordinately sensitive to short-term market fluctuations. (Jokes about eight rainy Sundays putting us out of business aren't funny when you've had seven of them.)

What Ironbridge taught me was the crucial importance of sound financial management and the need for good controls and reporting systems – nothing I've yet come across in the public sector can hold a candle to the quality of the monthly management accounts presented at Ironbridge. I also learnt that the organisational structure of a museum must equate with the nature and style of the job it has to do. If it doesn't then don't be afraid to change it and change it again as circumstances change. If the systems don't meet the needs of the day there probably won't be a tomorrow. The other very simple and rather obvious things were that visible leadership is essential to the morale and wellbeing of the organisation – it sets the style, tone and dynamic; that a small number of well-paid people achieve more than a larger number who earn less. I also learnt that getting about to see state-of-the-art practice is essential. Finally, of course, that museums can be both popular and set good scholarly standards: the two aren't mutually exclusive.

When you are going around places which clearly invigorate you tremendously, do you like wandering around on your own or do you like someone to guide you around, so you can ask lots of questions?

I like to go incognito, to devour it so to speak as an ordinary visitor would, and then to meet somebody to whom I can talk and find out how it's run, and see behind the scenes.

And when you've finished a tour of that sort, how would you marshal what you had learnt from it all?

> Well it's rather difficult. I think because so much of what one acquires by visits of that type is subliminal. It is also important, I think, not to assume that ideas transplant readily from one culture to another. You can be rather boring to colleagues telling them how wonderfully green the grass is elsewhere. So I don't feel, generally speaking, it's so much a question of marshalling one's findings as understanding the way in which one has changed personally, in terms of attitude, and applying that to one's management style and the definition of objectives. And if there is something really worth seeing, then send others to learn the same lessons.
>
> But you mentioned the marshalling of information, and that brings me to another important part of my development which started when I was in Bristol, and which has been a thread running through my career ever since, and that is communication. My curatorial and research interests in industrial history and archaeology meant that I was in demand for university extramural lecturing. I think I initially started doing it for the money; we had two small children then and Bristol Museum didn't pay very well. But very soon I became hooked and at the peak I was doing two or three lectures a week in places like Gloucester, Cheddar, Wells or Bath. I ran courses of twenty lectures and put an enormous amount of effort into marshalling data, preparing illustrations and doing visuals and that has been an enormous help to me ever since. I also began to like the theatre of public speaking.
>
> Later on, selling Ironbridge through lectures, radio and television broadcasts and overseas lecture tours was something I found hugely enjoyable. In fact I'll go even further because by the mid 1970s I was doing a series of big set piece lectures for the Open University combined arts and technology summer schools to audiences of four or five hundred and it really gave me a kick. Big audiences really do squirt the adrenalin round the system. In particular I remember the physics' lecture theatre at the University of Keele with its rather steeply raked auditorium, and standing on the bench so that I could get eye-to-eye with the majority of the audience and spending an

hour or so talking – without notes because I don't believe in them – about the development of industrial Britain, the take-off into self-sustained growth, and the extraordinary sequence of events that led this country to become the workshop of the world in the middle years of the nineteenth century. It was a very exciting story and I enormously enjoyed telling it. I regard it as a great challenge to hold an audience's attention and, on occasion, to make them chuckle a bit; and it's headily satisfying when one succeeds.

So is there a bit of entertainment that needs to come into education?

No question at all. I do think it's important, if you are going to speak to a group of people, to accord them sufficient respect not only to provide a lecture in which the content is good but to present it in a professional manner too. Sadly, most people who lecture are really awful and it's often because they have put no thought or consideration into how they present their information to their audience. I really hate going to a lecture where somebody of great distinction is presenting an important subject but where the presentation is unstructured, the illustrations are out of focus, or the lecture is being read in a monotone and occupies twice the length of time allotted in the programme. It really is a gross discourtesy to the audience, to other speakers, to the conference organiser; presentation is at least as important as content.

And the same goes through your approach to presentation here in the Science Museum as I understand it, where rather than acres of print on the walls explaining things, you like to use every possible method, pictures, videos and things you can touch and feel.

Yes, I think the Museum – any museum – is a peculiar and very specialised medium of communication which relies on original objects and the way in which those objects are presented and I find that quite challenging. There is also, of course, a great diversity of approach to presentation; what is right for an art gallery might be completely wrong for the Science Museum, and vice versa. Certainly, here we are conscious of the need to manage our presentation in a very careful way and to pay proper attention to design quality. I know I am something of a pain to my colleagues in the Museum for several reasons, but in particular because I cannot stand sloppy visuals and poor quality service to our audience. Felt-tip labels stuck with diagonal pieces of sellotape across a glass door saying 'Mind the Step', I find deeply offensive. I also feel that it is an insult to the people we are actually asking to come here, who it is our duty to serve, whether or not they pay at the door. We have a responsibility to provide something for them that is of real quality and is well run and has their wellbeing at heart. A museum is, after all, predominantly a visual experience, however interactive it is; people come here to look at things and the standard to which we present those things, in a visual sense, and the quality of the information we provide, is an important aspect of our ability to communicate about those objects and through those objects.

So are you saying that in education of any kind, whether it's visiting a museum or anywhere else, that the people putting the subject across need to, as it were, go halfway towards the customer and make it as easy as possible for people to absorb whatever it is?

Well that, of course, is a subject of intense debate in museums. It all depends, as Professor Joad would say, on what you mean by easy. I do believe museums should be challenging places. They are not there to spoon-feed. But in our case at the Science Museum – and this perhaps is where we differ radically from art museums – we recognise that we need to talk to our audience in terms that they will understand. That implies knowing a lot about the people we serve, having an insight into their levels of understanding of science and technology, and their educational background. We are in fact faced by three issues. One is that many of the people who visit the Science Museum have only the most superficial contact with or background in science and technology. (That is a problem for the nation as a whole.) Secondly, many of the contemporary objects and themes that we wish to explain in the Museum are not readily understood, even by people with quite a high level of pre-existing knowledge. And thirdly, the nature of our collections has changed.

If you go into the East Hall and see the great eighteenth and nineteenth century steam engines, some of which are operating, and look at them carefully and read the captions and perhaps talk to an engine driver, without an enormous amount of effort it is possible to get a pretty clear understanding of what you are looking at and what those engines did. Take the back off an Amstrad and you haven't a clue what it is you are looking at, let alone how it works. In visual terms, form is not an expression of function.

And so the process of explaining is itself an art or a science to such an extent that we have set in train a joint venture with Imperial College. We have appointed the first professor in the public understanding of science in order to push forward the boundaries of explaining. This isn't curatorship in the sense of doing research on the collections but is part of our wider 'Public Understanding of Science Initiative' designed to enable us to communicate about science and technology to a non-scientific public and to convey complex and abstruse theories and principles in a language which can be understood. That language doesn't just mean words, it might include complex interactive exhibits, cartoons, visual displays, demonstrators carrying out experiments in the galleries, explainers, actors and so on.

So you are trying to appeal, are you, to the fact that if one hundred people come into your Museum this morning they won't all have the same sort of natural learning style, some will like reading things, some will like doing things, some will like listening to things and some will like asking questions. Is it all of that?

Yes it is. This Museum is not only as diverse as its collections but also as diverse as its public. Museums are in a very curious position because they have to be all things to all people at all times and that's a pretty impossible brief. Some people like museums which are quiet and contemplative, in which they can have the opportunity to look at a museum object and gain some cerebral satisfaction from it. Now you can't provide that readily in a museum gallery which has four hundred hyperactive 8-year-olds busily interacting with manipulative technology exhibits. So we think that the answer may well be to segment the Museum into different qualities of experience – a series of museums within a museum, as it were – each related on the one hand to the nature of the stuff we have to present or the message we wish to convey and on the other to the types of people who we may be serving. Take for example the wonderful George III collection – one of the world's most outstanding collections of scientific instruments. It is not going to have an enormous amount of meaning or appeal to 8-year-olds, although they wouldn't of course be banned. But it will attract people who look at instruments as objects of beauty, or as examples of instrument making, or who have an interest in the history of science for which, of course, those instruments were the research and teaching tools of their day.

So the future development planned for the Science Museum sets out to create a multi-museum, each element dealing with a major theme or group of collections and designed to carefully manage our various audiences in order that they don't impact too heavily one upon another. That is why *Launch Pad* and the new *Flight Lab* gallery concentrate interactive exhibits together in enclosed spaces, because in the rest of the Museum the experience of looking at and learning from objects and collections is a rather different one requiring a different atmosphere and a different style and standard of presentation.

You are clearly a natural communicator, but perhaps some of the staff, that you have found yourself having to manage, whether here or at Ironbridge or the National Maritime Museum or elsewhere, may have got stale or sleepy or may not be such natural communicators as you are. What have you found to be the best ways of getting them up and running?

I think the nature of the relationship between a museum and its public is changing. Museums have moved from the twilight into the spotlight in the last twenty years. Not only are there many more of them but there are many museums which are now clearly doing a good job for their collections and their customers. The public can now discriminate between a good museum and a bad museum and is beginning to make choices. So we have, perhaps for the first time ever, a situation in which the public is making real and critical demands of museums and the services that they provide. The pace of this attitudinal change is faster than the rate of change of staff, particularly in large museums which have strong, well-established and traditionalist corporate cultures. One of the things that I have been very anxious to do has been to demonstrate that we have a clear obligation to deliver to our customers. For some of my staff that has been a novel and in some cases a quite distasteful rhetoric.

The last decade or so has been a quite extraordinary time for the national museums. We are all, of course, congenitally short of money and habitually blame government for all our financial woes. The present government has come in for even harsher criticism because of its policies of containing public expenditure but, in fact, when you look at the record of achievement by the national museums in the last decade or so, a lot has happened. There is a sparkle and a vitality, and a much greater sense of direction and purpose partly as a result of the government policies that have been thrust upon us. These include the transfer to Grant-in-Aid funding, the opportunity for us to retain all our earned income – itself a powerful incentive to self-help – the transfer of our buildings from the Property Services Agency to the museums themselves, and the insistence that we manage our affairs within the framework of a corporate plan coupled with our grants being allocated on a three-year as opposed to an annual cycle. The net result of that package of freedoms and opportunities, despite the shortage of funding has, I believe, been to challenge the national museums to demonstrate that they are worth having. Almost without exception they have risen to the occasion; today they represent one of the best cultural investments the nation could have.

I believe too that the way in which we run our national museums, with an arm's-length relationship with our sponsor department, the Office of Arts and Libraries, and through boards of trustees, is the best I have come across anywhere in the world. So, the money may not be all that we want but the freedoms and opportunities are there, we are substantially in control of our own destinies, and by the standards of most countries very free from direct political intervention or interference. That actually adds up to a lot and makes the job of running a major national museum like the Science

Museum challenging and enjoyable, with a good balance of stimulus and incentive.

It has also provided us with an opportunity to change the culture of the institution itself. The rhetoric of the nihilists has been to cast me in the role of being either a mouthpiece for government policies – which of course they oppose – or somebody who is trying to destroy traditional values and qualities, including qualities of service and scholarship, by a commercial and market-oriented approach. My counter-rhetoric has been that we need to fix our sights on some very clearly defined aims and objectives if we are going to move forward. We have outstanding collections and their welfare must come first; we can use those collections for the public good, and we must deliver them to a public in a manner and to a quality standard that the public itself is increasingly demanding. So, the strategy for restructuring the Science Museum has not been based on persuading groups of staff to do certain things but to focus the institution's attention on certain goals which have ranged from, for example, the development of proper collections' conservation facilities to opening on Sunday mornings and then pushing forward pretty forthrightly on those fronts. The net result has been that those staff with intelligence and foresight have embraced these ideas with enthusiasm, another group have been drawn along in the slipstream and are beginning to value and appreciate them too, leaving a small opposition, diminishing in number, who are still harking back to a mythical golden age of traditional values which, as far as I can see, means the situation in the 1960s when the Museum had – relatively speaking – plenty of money, no serious management and allowed a lot of its staff to pursue pretty self-indulgent and self-serving interests.

I think most of the staff here now recognise that the best future for them is to be part of a museum that is doing a good job and serving its customers with goodwill and to a high quality. I am a passionate believer in the philosophy that if we serve our public well, then we don't have to worry so much about ourselves because as an institution we will be liked, respected and valued. People will invest in us. The best thing that the staff of this place can have is lots of people going round saying the Science Museum is a wonderful place. It's already happening and I can see the enormous energising and motivating effect that it has upon people who, for much of their careers, have been largely overlooked.

It is also, of course, rather a 'chicken and egg' process. I remember talking to Sir Denis Rooke, who is one of the museum's trustees, before he retired as chairman of British Gas and suggesting to him that he might like to get some sort of corporate benefit out of the Museum, through holding parties, dinners and receptions here in return for an investment in the place. He said, 'I wouldn't give any money to that place, it's too scruffy.' I pointed out to him that we needed the cash in order to invest in the Museum to make it smarter but I went away and came back eighteen months later with the same message but a visibly improved Museum. The front-of-house facilities had been changed, the warders were in new uniforms, what had been one of London's dirtiest museums was now one of its cleanest, and there was a life and energy about the place which you could feel instantly when you came in through the door. Well, British Gas have invested in the Science Museum and they chose it for Denis Rooke's retirement dinner.

Clearly you can't make an omelette without breaking eggs. There must be times when you run into opposition to what you are trying to do, and times when you make mistakes about which, looking back, you could say, 'Why did I do that, or what can I learn from that?' When you feel you have made a mistake what do you do about it?

Well, like most people, I feel pretty sick but I don't keep a diary in order to record mistakes and I don't write notes to myself very much. But I think I do know when I've made mistakes and I think it's worth admitting to them and, where appropriate, apologising. It's something I try to encourage in my senior staff when they make mistakes too. Much better to say so, tell me and the rest of the team, and see what as an institution we can learn.

I think one of my biggest failings – that I know about – is my tendency to be impatient and occasionally sound off because we aren't making progress fast enough or achieving the sort of standards that I believe a great national museum should be setting. Whoever happens to be in the way tends to get the thick end of the stick, and it is not, of course, always their fault. It's taken me a little time to appreciate how seriously they view the director stamping about the place. Whereas I might feel better at the end of an outburst they might well feel a lot worse.

You mentioned opposition. That comes in two forms doesn't it. There are people who will present a counter-argument, offering an alternative course of action to the one proposed. They need to be heard and, if we have our consultative procedures properly established, their views should be picked up early on as part of the decision-making process. Then there are those who put their personal interests in front of those of the Museum and its public, or have an agenda of their own – perhaps politically based – and those again who simply do not like change. Some of the latter, of course, have criticised the status quo for years, but threaten to change it and their opposition will be vociferous.

I have to say that I have been shocked by some of the attitudes, attitudes that put self-interest before service, or the needs of the bureaucracy before the function it is there to perform. It's often little things, isn't it, that are symptomatic of a deeper malaise; preferring to see the information desk unstaffed for half an hour when somebody has been taken ill rather than have somebody else of the wrong grade stand in to keep the service running. I'd prefer to do the job myself. All that smacks of a system in which 'public service' actually meant the opposite; most of those views have now gone I'm glad to say. I think the direction in which we have moved the Museum forward has eliminated most of them; they are seen simply to be anachronistic and anomalous. With those who persist I am very tough and – at least as important – never give up; they either join the team or they go.

All of this has strengthened my belief in training, the setting of proper standards for staff development and systems to action them. After all if there are serious attitudinal problems, particularly among middle-range staff in a place like this, then it is a sign of management failure – poor leadership and direction or simply not having the skills at hand to do the job. As you know we've benefited considerably from what The Industrial Society has been able to offer, we now have a proper in-house training structure and we're aiming to devote about 5 per cent of all staff time to training and development.

How do you balance scholarship and its needs with the popular face of the Museum?

Well, as I've said, they aren't mutually exclusive. Indeed, you can't have the latter without the former. Again, it's partly a question of attitude. The foundations on which the Science Museum stands are its collections. Their cultural value is based on what we know about them and how they are delivered – interpreted – to our various publics. That demands people of scholarly inclinations and capabilities who understand material culture and believe in collections. Only by their scholarship will those collections grow and develop; only by their scholarship will those collections mean anything and have any lasting relevance. But, as the saying goes, scholarship is too important to be left solely to scholars. I believe it must be managed – in a broad strategic sense – to serve the needs of the Museum, support its policies and serve its public. You can't turn it on and off like a tap. It requires, first and foremost, good people, working to long-term objectives which have been agreed with the Museum. Without that the results are pretty hit and miss. Some will be doing worthwhile work, others will be doing good work but the wrong work, but worse, others will settle into cosy niches from which ultimately nothing emerges at all. And it is, of course, some of those people, who occupy the niches, who resent the Museum setting any sort of new direction and fight change. Quite often they're not very good scholars and exposure to the real world of scholarship is what they're trying to avoid.

If collections are the lifeblood of a museum then it is good curators – scholar-curators – who provide the heartbeat. But in the Science Museum we see scholarship going much further than that. Our Public Understanding of Science Initiative has, as one of its portfolio of objectives, the bridging of the gap between the object and the mind of the visitor. Science communication is of fundamental importance to us. Our objects often don't speak for themselves, and good curators are not always the best people to speak to the public.

Coming to my last question – you are obviously very busy, you are very energetic, you get things done. Do you get enough time to sit on a mountain top and think? Or sit somewhere else and think and reflect and take a long view? And how do you like doing that?

There are two issues. I don't get enough time – or I think I don't – and when I do have time I find other more immediate things to do. There is always some other pressure or priority. That is bad and at last I'm doing something about it – dedicating blocks of time, sometimes away from the Museum, in which to think or to keep my interest in industrial history and archaeology alive – even though the opportunity for serious scholarship is not really an option now.

I do think it's important to have stimulus that is outside the Museum and that helps to put what I do into some sort of perspective. For example, I'm an English Heritage commissioner, which I enjoy very much; it gives me a role – on the other side of the boardroom table so to speak – in the running of another quango and it enables me to apply directly some of my expertise – if I may use that term – in industrial history and archaeology. This has helped enormously in terms of my job at the Science Museum. And for recharging my batteries, I get away to the country most weekends.

But when it comes to thinking and reflecting, I need to do more. After all, I'm paid primarily to think, secondly to lead and direct, and lastly, perhaps, to manage. That means time should be consciously set aside for each of those activities. If I sum up my job it is – to serve the public and the interests of the nation's collections; to formulate policy; to recommend policy to the Trustees; to direct the National Museum of Science & Industry; to account for the proper expenditure of its funds; to promote the interests of the Museum; and to represent the Museum in Britain and overseas. The first three of those activities really require me to stand aside from the day-to-day tempo of the place and to think. I can do that thinking, however, in all sorts of situations. Walking around the Museum, getting away from the Museum, through travel – which I enjoy a lot

– and seeing what others are doing, or simply by sitting by the fire with a good single malt. But I probably could do with a sabbatical from time to time – even if it is only a sabbatical month – and I shall probably try to do that. Some people call it holidays. It's also important too, of course, for my senior managers to stand back and think, both individually and as a group. I go away with them for a couple of days each year to talk through ideas and that, I think, is enormously beneficial. It helps to release the tensions, renew the bonds, reinforce the mutual support which is an essential characteristic of a good management team, and lets me get to know them a little bit better.

The key thing is that we all do a good job, that we serve the needs of our collections and our publics, that we gain some real enjoyment from delivering, and every now and then get a pat on the back. We all serve the best interests of the Museum by maintaining and enhancing its great traditions, and by striving for excellence. If we achieve that then I believe we can realistically ask for more resources. And they will be forthcoming because our real value to society will be self-evident.

Sir Graham Day

❝There is nothing more important than on the one hand, having a business strategy, and on the other hand, developing your people, because developing the people will deliver the strategy.❞

Through his legal training, Graham Day honed his ability to get to the nub of issues and to define clear objectives. He has repeatedly displayed this ability, steering companies out of trouble and towards profitability.

He likes to analyse the situation facing a company in depth, both internally and externally. He will then make crisp decisions and communicate these starkly – 'I don't bluff, because I can't.'

Having himself benefited substantially from mentors during his earlier career, he balances his clinical decision making with a commitment to staff training and development.

Chairman: The Rover Group plc, since 1986; Cadbury-Schweppes plc, since 1989; PowerGen, since 1990. Sir Graham Day is a director of The Laird Group plc and DAF bv. In September 1991 he became acting chairman of BAe plc. He is also chairman of the review body on school teachers' pay. He began his career in a private law practice, 1956–64. He has since worked for: Canadian Pacific Ltd, 1964–71; Cammell Laird Shipbuilders Ltd, 1971–75; British Shipbuilders, 1975–76; Dalhousie University, 1977–81; Dome Petroleum Ltd, 1981–83; chairman and chief executive, British Shipbuilders, 1983–86. Married with children. Educated: Queen Elizabeth High School, Nova Scotia; Dalhousie University. Born 1933.

Chapter

6

What factor or factors determined your original career choice?

The negative factor was that when I was finishing my undergraduate course at university I had a significant weakness in science subjects. Also while I always recognised maths was important, for me it was a struggle. At school, I really hated it. That tended to lead me away from the quantitative subjects into the qualitative subjects, and hence to university law school. That was, for me, a very happy choice. I like things with a shape, and the law course has a structure. At the same time, it was flexible enough to give one room for personal development. For example, you could choose between property conveyancing and the Bar. I went into a law practice in a small community, taking on whatever walked in the front door, although over time my cases concentrated in the commercial area.

How real was the possibility at one point that you might have gone into showbusiness or on the stage?

It was very real in that I put a lot of time and effort into performing.

When I was in law school it provided part of my income, and in my early days in practice it was the only certain income I had. But I reached a crunch point in my second year at law school when I had an opportunity to go professional as a singer. It was the only time my father really leaned on me and said, 'No, you're wrong. It's an unstable way to earn a living.' He asked the critical question, 'How good do you really think you are?' And it was that key question, it wasn't the pressure. I went away and said to myself, 'How good?' and the answer was, 'Not good enough.'

In those years as a lawyer, what proved subsequently to be most beneficial to what you have done and become?

As a lawyer I had clients who came to me with a problem and I had to take the lead, to advise them and help them make up their minds. From that I learnt the necessity to be proactive rather than reactive. I have little patience with people who avoid taking decisions. I'm not suggesting one should rush, but there is a tendency to waste time. People say, 'No, no' when they know what the decision has to be, but they cannot actually take it because aspects will be difficult or there will be some unpleasantness, so they would rather harm everybody than perhaps harm a few.

How did you move out of the law into Canadian Pacific?

After about seven or eight years in the profession I was starting to realise that I had moved to a point when my work became repetitive, and at this point in time a senior member of the Bar, Gordon Cowan, (later Chief Justice) said to me, 'How happy are you, Graham, doing what you are doing?' And I said to him, 'Truthfully, I'm just going round and round and I'm not sure I'm progressing.' About a week later, he phoned me up and said, 'How would you like to work for Canadian Pacific?' What I didn't know when he put the initial question to me was that Canadian Pacific had approached him and said, 'Gordon, can you find us someone?'

Were you ambitious in your early years?

I think not, and I would say I'm not ambitious now, if ambition is movement towards a focused personal objective.

So what was the motivating factor in responding to Gordon Cowan?

A recognition that I was not being intellectually satisfied. I was doing well in what I was doing, but it wasn't testing me or pushing me any more. I believe I've always needed some intellectual stimulus.

It appears that individuals were important in determining your career path – first your father, then Gordon Cowan?

Yes. From school onwards I can point unerringly to the individuals who caused me to make all my career changes. I joined Canadian Pacific at a time when two people had moved out of the law department into other areas, so almost from day one I picked up a wide variety of activities. In my case, it tended to be the international business so I was the chap who, with monotonous regularity, went to Montreal airport on a Friday night and flew somewhere. So I was able to do a wide variety of work in Europe, in the Far East, as well as in Canada. I would say today that Canadian Pacific is the best school I ever attended.

What were the main things you got out of it?

I worked for people who gave one very high quality, comprehensive briefing. You might only be addressing one facet of a larger programme, but you were briefed on the totality of the programme and therefore you knew what your role was and how the whole would be impacted by your relative success or failure. I was with people who were good managers and who were prepared to place quite considerable trust and reliance in me – I was then 31. Undoubtedly that has coloured the way in which I try to deal with people. You always had the opportunity in those days in Canadian Pacific to say exactly what you thought. Ultimately, if a decision went against something you had recommended, that was all right because you had had your say. And you had your say regardless of rank.

Did this method of management rub off on you?

> Absolutely. And of course, as in any large organisation, you observe other people's styles of management, and you make the mental note to say, 'If that's ever me, I'll never do it that way' or 'That's how I'll do it.' In those days (from the mid-1960s to the early 1970s) Canadian Pacific was quite paternalistic and, probably, that was a good thing. Norris Crump, who was chairman, always said 'please' and 'thank you' – that was from a 60-year-old to a 30-year-old and it rubbed off too. He was always courteous. If he asked you to do something, you really wanted to do it.

How did the move to Cammell Laird come about?

> In any organisation you will find a mentoring system at work – working more effectively in some organisations than others. Norris Crump was retiring as chairman of Canadian Pacific. The man who had been my mentor, who would have become chairman, died. The man who ultimately replaced Crump had been a brilliant lawyer, but he operated very differently. He worked on the basis of, 'I'll tell you what you have to know, I'll tell you what you have to do, now get on and do it.' Against this background, and out of the blue, I had a phone call from John Gardiner, chairman of the Laird Group. He asked me if I would like to run a shipyard. He knew about me because I had spent four months in 1970 trying to sort out Cammell Laird's problems. Canadian Pacific was a customer of Cammell Laird. Cammell Laird, which was building us a number of ships, was heading for the receiver so, with the Industrial Reorganisation Corporation, we had worked out a scheme to keep the business afloat so that we could get our ships out. John Gardiner was speaking both on behalf of the Laird group, which owned one half of the company, and the British Government, which owned the other half.

So you went straight from being a very senior lawyer with a broad commercial experience to being a general manager. Did you feel that there was anything missing from your armoury of experience at that point?

Perhaps one of the strengths I had was that I didn't realise where I had significant shortcomings. First of all, there wasn't time. I had always been conscious of struggling on the maths side. During my time at Canadian Pacific I think I had put that as close as dammit to being right, because I worked very hard on business maths and on economics. I had had compulsory accounting training in law school in Canada. So I had enough handle on the numbers to feel fairly comfortable: I think it's absolutely fundamental to have an adequate degree of numeracy and a pretty good understanding of economics. And with Canadian Pacific, I had knocked around a wide range of engineering activities and had bought and sold more ships than Cammell Laird had built in ten years. I knew the blunt end from the sharp end in shipbuilding.

What was the most valuable lesson you learnt with Canadian Pacific?

That you did what you had to do; that you had to deliver. There were no excuses, you went out and you delivered and quite frankly it never occurred to Canadian Pacific that if you were trying to sell coal to the Japanese or do a joint venture on logs or whatever, you wouldn't actually achieve the objective.

What was the main challenge in Cammell Laird?

Cammell Laird had an engineering focus and an attitude problem. The challenge was to put commercial discipline into a business that had no commercial discipline whatsoever. To try to have the employees understand that ultimately they would live or die by how they performed in the marketplace, and that the marketplace is always totally unforgiving. Overall, I had to provide a strategy.

How did you set about putting your message over, down to the shop floor?

I talked till hell froze over. On Merseyside discussions are long, but nevertheless always interesting. With the history of that particular place, people did not so much query what you said as fundamentally doubt most of it. While you were talking you actually had to do things, because there was no bank credit. We couldn't borrow any money and our future was, quite literally, in our own hands – or there would be no future.

So we had to close the general engineering activity, we had to re-focus the business, try to find the money for capital investment, persuade the customers not to cancel orders, try to get new orders, put in an accounting system that one could believe and continue to change the management. After a while we started to make money and hold our own.

Then the Government changed – we were still half-owned by the government – and in December 1975 I made, in personal terms, a major mistake. I let myself be persuaded by the then Secretary of State for Industry that I should become the chief executive-designate of British Shipbuilders, which was going to be the nationalised operation.

What should you have done when that proposition was put to you?

I should have stayed with Cammell Laird until nationalisation occurred and then I should have left. I had a management structure there which could pick up the business and continue it. The worst year of my life as a manager was 1976. We were in the aftermath of the oil crisis. The Government of the day had a policy to nationalise but no strategy. The industry needed major restructuring. But I rapidly learnt that the Government was not in the least interested in a strategy for the industry, nor in restructuring. That, I believe, doomed the industry to more grief than was necessary. The only thing I got right was that I had a contract which died if the Nationalisation Bill failed to pass the House. It failed to get the third reading, so I had no contract, and myself and about five others on the board-elect declined to renew our contracts.

There I was, a professional manager, yet those who had appointed me did not want a professional manager. They wanted a do-as-you-are-told administrator. I don't take kindly to that sort of role. I was the wrong man in the wrong job at the wrong time. Even so, it was a learning experience. I learnt that if I was to be effective, I had to have a clear remit, and I had to be in a situation where I was actually able to manage.

Nevertheless, you temporarily stopped being a manager. How did that come about?

> At the time of declining to renew my contract with British Shipbuilders I was so pissed off that I decided not to take a fresh appointment for at least three months. I just wanted to think. In that period I had a call from Dalhousie, my old university, asking if I would run the new Marine Transportation Research Institute that was being set up, and also take on the post of professor in the Graduate Business School. I agreed to go there for two years, not seeing it as a career.
>
> It was a marvellous opportunity to marry practical experience with academic philosophies. I taught strategic planning (business policy) and transportation. The aim was to send the MBA graduates into the world armed with the full panoply of skills and the potential to exercise judgement as well. I also found myself sucked into doing consultancy, some for the Canadian Government, some for business. One of the firms I did advisory work for, Dome Petroleum, was having some serious problems. They asked me to come in and help them. Having learnt from my 1976 experience, I agreed very specifically what the task was and remained with that, to completion, for two years.
>
> After completing that task I was planning to return to Dalhousie. It was a comfortable life. I had control of my time. I very much enjoyed the students. I was doing enough outside work to challenge and stimulate me. I could actually see myself remaining there, though in the event I was pulled back into management in the UK.

Before we get on to that, can you elaborate on what you said earlier about mentoring systems. How would you describe a mentor?

> A mentor is where a senior selects one or more subordinates in whom the senior takes an interest on behalf of the employer and says, 'These junior people I'll try to cultivate and develop because they will be the bright lights of tomorrow's management structure.'

Is that a conscious thing?

> With me, it has become absolutely conscious. But I wonder, looking at the past. One of my professors at law school, Graham Murray, did it naturally out of genuine interest in a student, but possibly not consciously. In Canadian Pacific it seemed to be part of the culture that senior managers identified people and tried to bring them along, because there was no formalised scheme for fast-tracking. You were aware that you were within the ambit of a senior person. You saw by tasks assigned to you and how you worked that your loyalty might be to an individual, not necessarily your direct boss.
>
> When I went to Cammell Laird, I took with me from Canadian Pacific someone who had been my junior, on the theory that you had to have someone to watch your back, someone you could trust without any qualification whatsoever. Peter Mills worked for me ultimately for ten years. Within Cammell Laird I identified people – indeed hired people – whose careers I continue to watch. Mike Murden, who is now chief executive of Northumbrian Water Authority, was someone I brought into Cammell Laird in his late twenties. So I went from being mentored to becoming a mentor, and that's gone on throughout my career.

Can we now pick up again at the point where you were finishing your assignment with Dome Petroleum?

> For the second time I had a call out of the blue from John Gardiner. He rang me to say that the officials at the Department of Trade and Industry wanted me to think about returning to British Shipbuilders – they knew if they approached me direct I would decline. I said all the four-letter words you could think of. My impression was that British Shipbuilders had gone from bad to worse to God-awful. But John said, 'No Graham, life has changed.'
>
> The upshot was I had discussions first with Sir Peter Carey, permanent secretary at the DTI, and then with Norman Lamont, the minister responsible for shipbuilding. We talked it through, and this time, having learnt from my previous experience, I said, 'Minister, what do you want? What are your objectives?' Norman

Lamont was very explicit and said, 'Every day in every way we're losing more and more money: we have to stop that. The policy of the Government is to privatise. We want to identify those things which can stand on their own, get them back into the private sector, reduce the cash loss and, quite frankly, manage the government out of the shipbuilding business.' So we agreed a timetable we would work to and I went back to Canada and discussed it with my family.

For major decisions like that we had family conferences. My wife was neutral. My children then 23 and 21 said, 'Yes, you should go back.' My elder daughter said I had to exorcise something in my soul from the British Shipbuilders' past. So I did come back and delivered the agreement I had reached with Norman Lamont slightly earlier than we had settled for.

Then in December 1985 Peter Morrison, Norman Lamont's successor at the Department of Trade and Industry said, 'Graham, some of us think you should go into British Leyland.' And I thought, 'Oh God.' After Christmas, I started to look at all the British Leyland stuff that was in the public domain. Within the Department of Trade and Industry there were some officials opposed to my going into British Leyland but, in due course, it was clear that the Prime Minister was going to make changes, and that I was the change. In the aftermath of Westland the discussions about General Motors/ Ford were revealed and in the event I didn't start with British Leyland until May 1986.

In at least four of your jobs you have had the task of transforming the company's fortunes. Was there anything in common to each of those?

Common to them was a management at the very top which, at best, had lost its way through absence of strategy. Typically business problems end up being expressed in cash terms, and they start from having poor or no strategies. There were also overtones of difficulties with middle management, junior management and the trade unions, under-investment and so on, but you always had to start off by saying, 'Where should we be going, how do we get there?'

What I try to do when I move in is do all of the basic homework, identify what I think is a viable strategy, then try to deliver that strategy. British Leyland was no exception.

What is your method of getting management to come round to the changes that you know you have got to introduce?

First of all I try to identify how much time I've got to engage in a discussion. You never have enough time. In Cammell Laird I had no time, so it was authoritarian, autocratic, unilateral decision-making from the start, because there was no money and the company was in effect technically not entitled to trade. In British Leyland I 'guesstimated' that I might have four months if I was lucky. So then I put in some hard discussion with all of the senior people, basically saying to them truthfully, 'I have no background in this business.' I also had a little set speech, 'Please don't assume because I'm not an engineer that I am an engineering idiot. I've knocked around engineering operations for a very large number of years. I don't have to like what you tell me but if you try to deceive me I will hand you your head.' Sad to relate, despite those cautions up front, a number of people certainly tried to mislead me to the point of outright lies and I found some engineers trying to test how little or how much I knew. In both these instances my reaction was, first of all, not to reveal the fact that I knew I was being lied to, and then not to reveal that I actually knew I was not being told engineering truths.

Of course the then Prime Minister, Mrs Thatcher, has said – and I was able to give her book, chapter and verse – she believed that she was deceived and lied to. I was able to say to her, with some sadness, 'Prime Minister, you were right. You were deceived, you were lied to', and the only excuse I could give for these people is that they believed that that was essential to enable them to carry on the way they were carrying on, which they were sure was right.

I then put in hand two key exercises. One which I called the 'operational audit', which is an internal evaluation, and then an 'environmental scan', which is an external evaluation – 'What's going on out there in our marketplace?' You then have two packages of information and assessment from which you can analyse and from which you can develop a strategy. You then run like hell – because I had in effect borrowed the four months from the time when in theory we should have hit the floor running. From that point on I progressively changed out the top managers, of whom there were only a half-dozen, recruited only about two, and then promoted as rapidly as I could some people out of the second and third tiers. Then I started to address the financial problems like, 'Where are we going to get enough cash to invest in our forward model programme? Because if we don't have a solid model programme we're not going to be in business.'

To run to the end of the story, Rover today is profitable and has been for three years in a row – not as profitable as it might be. It is in a reasonable cash position. It is in the private sector; also, adding the belt to the braces, in a link-up in a formal sense with Honda. All of which places Rover, as it now is, with eighteen businesses gone, with its best hope for the 1990s and beyond.

You have now for the first time moved to running a successful company. How does that challenge look?

I was very fortunate, because I was approached by Cadbury-Schweppes to succeed Sir Adrian Cadbury as chairman. That was a surprise: I get all kinds of job offers (I'm very fortunate) but most have been somewhat poisoned chalices. So I thought, 'My God, can this be true?'

I had a series of discussions with the directors of Cadbury-Schweppes in which I was very frank with them and said, 'You do understand what my background is and what signals that may be likely to give?' They said, 'Yes, yes. The fact that the businesses you went into were in difficulty is not the important thing. What we are looking for is a managerial record, but we also believe it's important now to have someone come in from outside. We are increasingly a global business. It's multicultural – everything from Australia to the USA, from Japan to Africa.' In the event I said, 'Yes, I would like to do that, but why don't you get to know me a little better?' So I joined the board in January 1989 and we got to know each other during the course of the year.

It does seem that straight talking – forcing people to speak the truth and speaking the truth yourself – seems to be an important part of the way you work at all stages.

> I'm given to little homilies, I always say, 'I never lie and I never bluff.' I believe morally that lying may be the ultimate sin, but also if you do lie you are really on a slippery slope, because you are never sure what shade of meaning you are giving people. I learnt years ago that I bluff very badly, so I don't bluff because I can't. I'm not a poker player but the interesting thing is that, including in the early days at Rover, people assumed that I did bluff, and it's absolutely fascinating when you turn around and actually do what you said you were going to do and they say, 'I never thought you really meant that.'

Can you go back and pick out the most significant learning experience in your last few jobs?

> Two things. One is that one has to have a base of relevant skills. There really isn't any substitute for this. I think that education in a broad sense is desperately important, otherwise you get someone who typically has done one job twenty times rather than having twenty years' experience. Preferably you should get this skills' base early on: it gets harder and harder to pick it up as you go on, because the pace of the game is accelerating.
>
> The second thing is to identify the people who can contribute. You need to spot who the passengers are. They may be absolutely worth the salary or the wage which they are paid, but they are not going to contribute further, perhaps sometimes on the basis of ability or intellect, sometimes because they just don't want to contribute beyond the defined job which they do. The key is to identify those who can contribute beyond that which they are presently doing, get them to do it, then progressively to select from among them those who can move significantly up the structure and can move quickly. In other words who can be stretched, and stretched, and stretched again.

Do you see that as a line management role or something which in a large company you can leave to your management development manager?

> No, I don't think you ever do that. It's very important to have a good personnel director. In Rover, without Frank Saundry, I would not have achieved, because the time was such that Frank was a central player. But I don't think you delegate that job. I like to deal with it on a collegiate basis, in which the personnel or career development people are players. There is nothing more important than on the one hand, having a business strategy and, on the other hand, developing your people, because developing the people will deliver the strategy. You can have the best damn strategy, but without the people you're never going to get there.

Lord Donaldson

❝I'm not the judges' boss . . . We are a team. It's not a question of decisions but persuasion so that we all move in the same direction.❞

While still a young officer in the army, John Donaldson found himself in charge of a large staff of qualified barristers and solicitors. This proved to be the only time in his life when he was directly in charge of people.

Having practised as a barrister, he rose through the profession to the prestigious position of Master of the Rolls. He is careful to point out the nuances of this post. Because of its special structure the legal profession does not have leaders in the clear-cut sense in which they exist in companies. Lord Donaldson's 'choirmaster' role, as he describes it, is the classic example of leadership through influence rather than power.

Master of the Rolls, since 1982. Lord Donaldson was called to the Bar, Middle Temple, in 1946. He became a QC in 1961. Since then he has been: a judge of the High Court, Queen's Bench Division, 1966–79; president, National Industrial Relations Court, 1971–74; a Lord Justice of Appeal, 1979-82. Married with children. Educated: Charterhouse; Trinity College, Cambridge. Born 1920.

Chapter

7

What determined your original career choice?

> I was in two minds whether to do accountancy or law. I chose law, probably influenced by the fact that I enjoyed debating to some extent at school and, later, much more at Cambridge where I was secretary of debates.

When did you first think of becoming a lawyer?

> It must have been before I went to university, because in 1937 my father paid for me to become a student of the Middle Temple. But that was really a question of keeping my options open. The idea took root while I was at university.

I assume you read law at Cambridge?

> At my father's suggestion I read history for the first year, but I didn't like it. The second year I transferred to law, but I read very little law because it was 1939–40, the year of the 'phoney' war. Invasion was expected and much more of my time was spent delivering dispatches

on a motorcycle round the airfields of Cambridgeshire. I was actually in the army while at university. I enlisted in September 1939 and went on to what was called Class W Reserve, which meant they paid you one day's pay on enlistment – 1s 6d – and then told you to go back to university and stay there until you were sent for. In September 1940 I was told to go to Catterick for officer cadet training, so that was all the academic training I ever had.

You were commissioned into the Royal Signals in 1941 and went on to do four years' service in the army. Did that shape you in any way? Did it alter your ideas about things?

By VE day I was doing a signals staff job, and it was reasonably apparent that, owing to my relatively young age and seniority, I wasn't going to get out of the army as soon as I would like. There was a shortage of signals officers in Burma and it seemed likely that I would be sent there. I then conceived the bright idea that if I transferred to the legal division of the Control Commission, not only would I gain some professional experience but I would not have to go to Burma. I applied and was transferred. As I was being paid as a major in signals the authorities decided that I should do a major's job or the equivalent in the civilian administration. I was put in as deputy chief legal officer of Military Government of Schleswig-Holstein. The chief legal officer was a much older man, who promptly got out, and I took on his job as acting lieutenant-colonel. So you had the ridiculous situation that there I was, a Bar student, with quite a large staff of qualified barristers and solicitors working for me.

In the summer of 1946 I came out of the army and started at the Bar. At that time I really had no legal knowledge at all. In those days, rightly or wrongly, all you needed to do was to pass some very elementary Bar exams. You really learnt your trade after you were called, not before. In fact I took the Bar exams by correspondence course. There was a wonderful organisation which set out to teach you twelve questions and twelve answers for each paper. They guaranteed that you would be asked six of them. I enlisted with them while still in the army and learnt my twelve questions and answers by correspondence. So I was really totally unqualified when I was called to the Bar.

How would you say that a career in the law differs from other careers? What are the fundamental differences?

There are major differences, though you can't answer that question simply with regard to the law, because the solicitors' branch is so different to the barristers'. As far as the barristers' branch is concerned, it's a highly individualistic branch – an independent, one-man band operation. You don't have partners. You share expenses and work in a group, but you remain entirely responsible for your own work. In comparison with the medical profession where the structure is hierarchical – my father was a doctor and I have had some contact with it – the structure of the Bar is almost anarchical. The first thing you are taught at the Bar is that your opinion is as good as anybody else's and you've got to put it forward.

Does that mean that there's no sense of a team?

Well, there may be a team working on particular cases, where there are two counsel or even three. Nevertheless, you are all individually responsible, and while you try to work together, it's not unknown in Court of Appeal work, where two counsel have rights of audience, for the junior counsel to get up, when he's invited to add anything, and say things which perhaps are not wholly consistent with what his senior has said.

What particular aptitudes and gifts do you think are necessary for a successful barrister?

A barrister has to have an analytical mind in order to analyse the problem, strip it down to its bare essentials, and then be able to communicate those bare essentials.

Early on, as a young barrister, what are the most important learning experiences?

There's no one answer. It all depends on where you are. In my case, the particular work I was doing – highly specialised commercial work – was very poor in providing learning experience of court work. The cases were heavy and experienced people were employed to do them. So, beyond seeing them do it, there was not much you could do. I was very lucky because, owing to the shortage of barristers, somebody came to chambers and said, 'I want somebody to do County Court work.' So I got some County Court work to do on my own, and learnt by my mistakes.

Did anything particularly draw you to commercial cases, or was it just the way the cookie crumbled?

Entirely the way the cookie crumbled. Sir Henry Willink QC was asked if he would help me by my father – his wife had been a patient. I told him I wanted to do criminal work, but his chambers only did commercial work. He said he would introduce me to criminal chambers and then forgot all about it. So he got stuck with me, and I specialised in commercial and maritime cases.

What did you find most formative in your years as a barrister?

At every stage you learn by your own experience, and you go on from there.

Did you ever have any second thoughts about a career at the Bar?

At one time I did explore the possibility of leaving the Bar and taking up a job which would free me more for politics. The potential employer didn't see why he should employ a politician. I quite agreed and I came to the conclusion you couldn't have a family, run a full-time career at the Bar and be a politician. It was a three-legged stool, one leg of which would be likely to give way.

I suppose that, like a doctor, the expansion of a lawyer's practice very much depends on his reputation and the skill with which he builds it up?

I think there's a very large element of luck. You do need luck, and if you have the luck, you need to have the experience to be able to actually do the work. You're not going to succeed by luck alone, but you're not going to get very far without it.

Is taking silk – becoming a Queen's Counsel – a form of promotion in the profession?

Yes, and it's also a way of getting rid of a lot of work that's relatively ill paid and concentrating on heavier, better paid work. To some extent it's a change of functions and a way of moving forward as an advocate.

You went from being a barrister to being a Queen's Bench judge. To the layman, that seems a huge step. Is it?

Oh, yes. It's an enormous step, because you cut yourself off from ever returning to practise at the Bar. So you are taking on a job which, if you don't like it, will be an irreversible disaster.

Are you offered the appointment?

Yes, you don't apply as you do for County Court appointments, which deal with much smaller cases. The High Court deals with the big criminal and civil trials, and with particularly sensitive matters.

Does anyone ever turn down the offer of a High Court judge appointment, preferring to achieve eminence and success as a practising barrister?

In a sense you become a High Court judge *because* you have achieved eminence and success. Some do turn it down, but not many. It's quite a relief to be able to give it the grindstone of the Bar.

Would it be true to say of the law that in no other career or profession does the pure exercise of the intellect continue to be so important as you progress upwards? If you compare a judge with a vice chancellor, or with a permanent under-secretary in the civil service, or with a captain of industry, they couldn't do their jobs unless they were very clever, but they also have executive and operational roles. Lawyers and judges are lucky in the sense that they can go on using their brains, exercising their wits, for longer than others, as they go upwards. What's your comment on that?

> Apart from one or two jobs among the judges, including mine, there is practically no administrative work. Judges on the whole don't like administration, but I would have thought that somebody within industry, or say a permanent secretary, uses intellect to the same extent, but not so continuously because so much of his or her time is taken up with meetings, seeing to the execution of policy and so on. I certainly think it's true that to use your brain in court for two hours is a much more tiring operation than running a committee meeting for four – and I've done both.

In your progression upwards, where did the most significant changes occur?

> Certainly in transferring from the Bar to the Bench.

What were the essential differences?

> On the Bench you couldn't lose a case to start with! You may be reversed on appeal, but it does not follow that the appellate court is right. It just has the last word. You don't have clients, you don't have to worry about whether you are doing the best for them. It was much more relaxed, much pleasanter.

But you have a more onerous task in many ways, because so much hangs on the quality of your judgement.

> Yes, but you can only do your best, like a surgeon. He has his moments of anxiety, but he gets on and does the operation, and that's it. Becoming a judge is a change of job, but once you're into it it's merely a matter of exercising a different kind of judgement.

116

It seems that as a QC working with junior counsel, you were in no sense their boss and they your subordinates. They were collaborators, but you were all individuals. How did that change on becoming a High Court judge?

The judiciary is very much more hierarchical and everybody has an allotted seniority, but it's still incredibly individual.

You then went on to be an Appeal Court judge. What are the main differences there?

You don't see live witnesses anymore. You're working on paper to a much greater extent. That wasn't entirely welcome to me. I like my present job as Master of the Rolls because I've got a big administrative element too. I'm also concerned with the reform of the law. As an Appeal judge you go into court and decide endless cases on paper.

So far you've made it all sound remarkably easy. There must have been some hard bits, barriers to overcome, things which were hard. What were the challenges?

Obviously if you start at the Bar with very little money there are permanent anxieties about that. There's always the niggling worry – are you going to go bust? Are you going to lose your practice? (Practices do fluctuate quite wildly.) Every barrister is afflicted by worries, and I don't think I ever got to the point where I wasn't worried.

Like any businessman?

That's right, and in particular, like a small businessman, a one-man business with a cash flow problem.

To what extent and in what way in your capacity as Master of the Rolls do you in any sense exercise leadership over the judges?

Mainly I have an organisational role. I'm concerned with the throughput of cases. I'm concerned with delays. I'm concerned with providing a service to the public. The other judges of the Court of Appeal are concerned too, but it's my responsibility. So we have meetings regularly to discuss problems, everybody puts their oar in as to how we should overcome them, and we reach conclusions. I once said that the function of the Master of the Rolls is to act as choirmaster. You conduct, but you're conducting twenty-seven Privy Councillors, each of whom is perfectly capable of playing a solo part, and is entitled to do so.

Can you elaborate further on your responsibilities as Master of the Rolls?

I'm in administrative charge of all the Lords Justices in the sense of inviting them to undertake particular cases or particular jobs. The Lord Chief Justice runs the criminal side, but I have to give him Lords Justices to work with. I'm responsible for the work of the civil division as a machine, but not for any individual decisions, unless I happen to be hearing the appeal myself and even then I am only one judge among three. Apart from that, my major responsibility is for the solicitors' profession, because all their rules are subject to my concurrence. In practice this means the officers of the Law Society and I discuss problems and solutions. I put my two penny worth in, and eventually we reach a conclusion. I'm not the judges' boss, I have no right to hire or fire them. I have no right to instruct. I can advise – and will be asked for advice. We are a team. Ultimately it's not a question of decisions but persuasion so that we all move in the same direction. I have a major role in persuading them.

So you are *primus inter pares*?

Yes, I wouldn't ever interfere in a case. If other judges decide an appeal in a way with which I disagree, it's nothing to do with me. If it is wrong it's a matter for the House of Lords. On the other hand, if they asked me what I thought, I would tell them – though they might not agree. To give you an example, when I was a new and inexperienced judge, I knew I'd got a difficult bail application coming up. I went and asked Lord Parker, the Chief Justice, what his policy was, and he told me. I heard this bail application and came to the conclusion that it was so unusual that his policy didn't fit, and did the exact opposite of what he had advised. When I told the Chief Justice I had departed from his policy, he said, 'But, my dear John, that's what you're paid for.' And he was right.

How many people do you have accountable to you for the administrative work?

Strictly speaking, none. The job of the thirty or so members of the Civil Appeals office who undertake the administrative work is to work with me and in a sense for me. But as I am neither a civil servant nor a minister, they are not accountable to me. Of course I tell them what I want and lay down criteria, but they're not in my employment. Their 'pay and rations' and promotion are matters for the Lord Chancellor's department.

In the early 1970s, when you were a High Court judge, you were president of the National Industrial Relations Court. How did that fit into your learning experiences?

One of the joys of being a judge is that you only are responsible for one case at a time. In the National Industrial Relations Court we had, at any one time, sixty or seventy cases and as president I was watching the progress of each of them. It was like going back to practice, back to running a business. Apart from that what distinguished it was that it was a fairly exposed job, and was quite wrongly regarded as being political. I thoroughly enjoyed it. I had *carte blanche* to start something new. A lot of the subsequent courts, such as the county small claims procedures and the Employment Appeal Tribunal, are modelled on it.

Coming back to your role as a leader, let's ask how, if at all, you are comparable with, say, the chairman of ICI?

The only comparability is that he is a spokesman for his company

> and I believe that the heads of division have a job as spokesmen for the judges. We are, after all, public servants, and the public is entitled to know what we are doing. I think we ought to explain what we are doing and get a greater understanding of it. Ministers are not responsible to us, nor we to them, so we are a separate branch of the state. Like all judges I am responsible to the law and to no-one else. And no judge is responsible to me.

Who judges the judges?

> As every judge is independent of every other judge, in a sense the answer is no one. But their *decisions* are subject to appeal, so if they make mistakes, it can be put right. Every good judge judges himself continuously. Each has almost total security of tenure, and that's essential. So the important thing is to choose the right judges. If you choose the wrong ones, you have problems. High Court judges can be dismissed by the Queen upon a joint address of both Houses of Parliament, but this has not happened for over one hundred and fifty years. One or two have been persuaded by their fellow judges to retire if they became ill, but that is a different matter.

Is it a lonely job?

> Lonely in the sense that you are always personally deciding things. You're less isolated in the Court of Appeal, where you normally sit with others, but as a trial judge you're totally on your own. Socially it's not lonely at all. You have an individual private life, though it is subject to self-imposed restrictions like not becoming involved in public controversies.

Though as Master of the Rolls you are not a leader in a hierarchical, corporate sense, presumably there is a leadership role in what you do?

> Certainly. If I feel that particular types of cases should be tried in a particular way, and if it is generally thought to be a good idea, then other people will follow the lead. We all influence each other. If you

hold a senior position, as I do, your opportunity for influence is much greater.

How do you exercise that influence?

By talking to my fellow judges, by discussion, perhaps by example. Politically sensitive appeals will normally be heard by the Master of the Rolls. It's traditional. If there are other categories of cases causing problems, they would come to me to sort out. I accept that I am one of the senior members of the profession and in that sense a leader. Because of the peculiar structure of the profession I question whether there's room for leaders in the conventional sense of the word.

In most kinds of employment, as people go up the ladder they occasionally need a course – a management development course, for example, or a course in communication skills – is there anything comparable to that in the legal profession?

There used not to be, but recently a Judicial Studies Board has been created, which runs courses for newly appointed judges and for all judges in major developments in law such as the new Children Act. In the main we learn by experience, by discussion and by thinking the problems through ourselves.

Looking back, what has been the most beneficial experience in terms of equipping you to do the more difficult tasks as you have gone up the judiciary?

Everything is based on experiences. Experience in the army was obviously enormously valuable. At the age of 25, I had had experiences which very few 25-year-olds have had now. By good fortune I have subsequently had responsibilities which very few have had in quite different fields. The Bar is one of the great spectator professions: you're always looking at other people's problems, so you acquire a very wide range of knowledge. You get to know people in a way which you would never get to know in ordinary life.

I spent four years as a member of Croydon Council. That gave me a very considerable insight into political administration. That's all been very valuable now that I am dealing with the judicial work which affects government. I know quite a lot about how government works – how it really works, not how it theoretically works. Industrial relations taught me a lot about industry. I know how and why unions tick, which is timeless. Everything that you do probably better equips you to do something else. When young people at the start of their careers look at someone who's at the top of his or her profession, they may think, 'How could I do that job?' It's not a question they should be asking themselves. You've got to get on little by little, if only because there is not all that much room for people at the top. You may well not get there and you shouldn't be disappointed. There comes a point when you have done as much as you can and perhaps want to do, and you should be content with that.

How important was being ambitious? When you were a young man, were you ambitious to go onwards and upwards?

Ambitious, yes – but in a fairly generalised way. Like many others, I would like to have been Prime Minister, but not having followed that route that was not an option, so there it was. Initially I was ambitious to become a silk, but I wasn't too concerned about becoming a High Court judge. When I became a silk I thought I would like to become a High Court judge. When I became a High Court judge I wanted to go on to the Court of Appeal, and when I got there I found it was both enjoyable and challenging. Becoming Master of the Rolls was a bonus.

So you have a 'little by little' philosophy. At each stage you were ambitious to go on to the next one, but you didn't have vaulting ambition to be Master of the Rolls or whatever?

No. But it is also right to say I have a reasonably low boredom threshold. I like a change.

What advice would you give to anybody contemplating the law as a profession?

The only vital thing I would say to him or her is, 'Don't think that the law is a homogeneous occupation. Do have a good look at it and decide what kind of legal work you want to do and don't be over influenced by the money. Whatever you do you will need the ability to analyse and also not become emotionally involved. You've got to be detached, both in the interests of your client and of not self-destructing.'

Do you think you can get on without luck?

I think you can overcome bad luck. But I think you can get along a lot better if you have a bit of luck and the ability to use it.

What about confidence? Has the confidence to move on and act boldly counted much in your case?

I think in our profession confidence goes with independence, with being a one-man band. Without self-confidence you would go mad. It comes naturally with the job. You're professionally bred to it.

Brandon Gough

‘I see my role as setting the direction, the
creation and encouragement of
a vision for the firm, then
relying on other people
to execute it.’

Brandon Gough is very rare among leaders of major organisations in having
never worked for another company. The manifest risk of narrowness has been
overcome by the firm's culture which provides considerable variety and stretching
of individuals, and by Brandon Gough's own response to mentoring by two
senior partners.

He made his reputation by technical competence in the apparently
unglamorous sphere of auditing practice. But he was also developing broader
managerial skills, which led to his colleagues making the bold decision to appoint
him senior partner at only 44.

His assured leadership of an increasingly international business rests on three
skills: an acute sense of market trends, 'trailblazing' in the use of publicity and
a drive for all-round excellence.

Chairman, Coopers & Lybrand Deloitte (formerly Coopers & Lybrand), since 1983.
Brandon Gough is a member of the Council of: City University Business School; City
University; Business in the Community. He is a member of: Council for Industry and
Higher Education; the CBI Education and Training Committee. He joined Cooper
Brothers & Co in 1964 and became a partner in 1968; in 1989 he was Chairman,
Coopers & Lybrand Europe. Married with children. Educated: Douai School; Jesus
College, Cambridge. Born 1937.

Chapter

8

You are a leader in your role in Coopers. You are also a leader in the sense that you led the development of accountancy firms into becoming multidisciplinary organisations providing a range of management consultancy services. Can we go back over your career and try to identify what were the most important and valuable learning experiences in taking you forward. What comes to mind first?

> If I go back to the beginning, probably the most valuable experiences I have had have been disappointments rather than favourable experiences. What that means is an understanding that life doesn't go in a straight line; disappointments have to be expected. You have to seize your opportunities when they arise. I would summarise that by saying I think I have been able to develop in my earlier years a sense of objectivity which has benefited me in the last ten years.
>
> Having done National Service at the end of the National Service period meant that when I went to Cambridge, where I read sciences, I was thrown in with lots of people who had come straight out of school, so it was very hard work. My university period was very valuable in terms of developing a work ethic.

What was most beneficial in your time at Cambridge?

> I think literally the need to find one's own pace of work and, in particular, to be able to work very hard. The scientific method is very valuable in teaching anybody to order their thought processes to work systematically. It aligns very well with accountancy, which involves investigation, analysis, rationalisation and also a fair degree of judgement and luck. That is not dissimilar from scientific experimentation. I think I have a tendency towards idleness if I have the opportunity, and I'm sure an arts degree would not have done much for me in that sense – putting off the day when you have to write the essay.

What determined your career choice of accountancy?

> My father was a Bank of England official in Birmingham. He was very keen on accountancy and saw it as a good career, and a good entry point for business. The accountancy thing started when I was 16 or 17, had been put to one side, came back, and was an objective throughout my Cambridge period. I did very well in my final exams – I clearly had a bent for accountancy rather than management. I think I have a great aptitude for practising accountancy; I'm boastful enough to say that I don't know of many other accountants who are better at the job of public accountancy than I am myself.
>
> I was very well looked after in Coopers when I joined, was introduced to a wide range of fascinating assignments and hit the firm when it was growing very quickly and was very dynamic. I progressed rapidly: I was a partner after less than four years and had absolutely no reason to look anywhere else.
>
> Life was very rewarding and absolutely fascinating. The firm had the very attractive style of pushing people up to, and maybe beyond, their capabilities. It was very much a sink or swim environment but with a safety net. There was a great willingness to allow people to demonstrate their range of capabilities; it was a stretching environment. Obviously in those days there was much less emphasis on formal training or formal career counselling. At best, if you had some 'go' in you, the firm would give you a run.

What are the most testing experiences for a young accountant?

> As far as I was concerned it was simply being exposed to a whole
> series of new business situations. I worked mainly in the financial
> investigation area rather than the strict audit area. The two have
> always been very closely aligned in the firm, but I worked a lot with
> the man who was my predecessor as senior partner, David Hobson,
> who then had a very strong reputation with the merchant banks. He
> was invited to carry out quite a range of financial investigation
> advisory work and I was used quite a lot on that. So my experience
> was of being exposed almost every month to situations of which I
> had no prior professional experience. The particular experience that
> probably taught me more than any other was working with the Pye
> of Cambridge Group. That was a group that was highly
> entrepreneurial in the electronics fields. But it got into some
> difficulties and there was a massive range of work that we had to do,
> and I was heavily involved there.

By 'financial investigation' do you mean looking for potential problems
or advising on how to run their business better?

> It's a combination. In that particular case the emphasis was primarily
> on the financial health of the business, determining what was wrong
> with it and how it could be put right. There was also – this is not at
> all unusual in these circumstances – a boardroom row, and quite a
> lot of our time was spent in digging into the rights and wrongs of the
> relationships between the directors and the way the business had
> been run. The work that I did would these days be on the borderline
> of management consultancy.

And did management consultancy particularly interest you, excite you
and stimulate you?

> No. I don't know why. Probably because the financial element of
> our management consultancy at the time was very much geared to
> accounting systems and financial control systems, so it was
> procedure-oriented rather than advisory-oriented. The work that

> attracted me was working with boards of directors on takeover prospects, pre-acquisition – that kind of thing: policy and capital market-related rather than systems-related.

You seem to have been drawn to or become involved with City accountancy rather than other kinds. Is that a fair comment?

> Yes. From a relatively early stage, certainly from shortly after I became a partner, I had as much audit work in the City as outside. I always had the good fortune to have a mixed portfolio of clients. I like the City; if I were not working in an accounting firm I think I would still like to work in the City.

You became a partner at a very young age. That was obviously a landmark. What were the other landmarks in your twenties and thirties which made you feel that you were going up the ladder?

> The most visible sign of progress was a rapid rate of promotion, which may have irritated my peers in the firm! One has to live with the downs as well as the ups. Funnily enough promotions often came at a time when I thought I was perhaps not making as much progress as I would have liked. Maybe particular assignments were causing difficulty, or maybe there was some other problem.

Promotion means running a bigger team on a bigger investigation or a bigger audit?

> It means, first and foremost, recognition, particularly if your promotion rate is exceptionally quick and you are clearly marked out as somebody who is either better favoured or has greater ability. So the timing of promotion is something that people still monitor very carefully. There is a norm, so any deviation from the norm is marked out. It happened that in my case it did not of itself change the nature of my activity, but obviously as I got more senior I ran bigger jobs and managed more people. But, interestingly, up to the time I became a partner, I did not have a lot of experience of running very big teams. In the period before I became a partner, when I had

the responsibility for managing a team of thirty people, I relied a great deal on another manager to do the actual man-management side of the job.

In your late thirties and early forties, did you acquire significant management experience before becoming senior partner?

No. In fact it's really rather strange. Let me briefly outline the ten years before I became senior partner. There was a change in senior partner in the firm in 1975. Henry Benson, who had led the firm very effectively for years, retired. David Hobson, who had been my mentor, then took over. At that time the firm would have had a total of about two thousand staff, so it was a very substantial activity. It was decided at the time to make a stronger distinction between national, firm-wide activities and London office activities. Obviously, in the nature of a big accounting firm, the heart is in the City, so the City office has always been very influential. We put a London office organisation in place that had its own distinct partner in charge, then a series of subordinate partners responsible for segments of business: a very conventional organisation. I was given one division. That was my first real managerial challenge as a partner, but I was only in it for a year. There was an early rotation and I was given responsibility for what had previously been seen as a rather technical activity in the audit area – the development of our audit methods, the focus of our audit activity.

I have to say that at the time I wasn't very pleased to be asked to take on this job. It was highly political and rather risky. Basically I stayed with that almost until I became senior partner, because I moved progressively from running that segment in the UK to running it internationally, and then got sucked into the equivalent activity in the chartered accountancy bodies. In 1976 they joined together to form a single so-called 'Auditing Practices Committee' in response to government pressures. I was a member of that and subsequently its chairman.

So from 1976 to 1982 I was very much in the product development strategy area rather than the operating area. It was important in developing a sense of what the firm needed to be, and was relevant to subsequent leadership, but had no relevance to managerial experience. Certainly my experience is very different from your conventional industrial manager. I was required to think in a way that arguably was very beneficial in determining what the firm needed to do.

In 1981–2 David Hobson was within sight of standing down as senior partner and the process of determining what the succession should be got under way. We had no formal process for electing the senior partner, which was probably a good thing. So there was a lot of discussion: first of all about the candidates for the job and, but more important, about what the job should be. When it came to it – and there was obviously a fair amount of discussion in bars after partners' meetings – the choice was a fairly stark one. The partners could either have a senior partner who was about 55 or one who was 45 or under. The partners who were aged about 50 were not seen as candidates for the job. The partners were very brave when they chose someone who was under 45, and particularly as he had no managerial experience.

You used the word 'mentor'. How important was the mentoring that either or both Henry Benson and David Hobson gave you in what happened to you later?

Oh, fundamental. First of all, their willingness to give young people their heads, but more importantly the sheer experience gained by working with two people who were absolutely at the top of the accounting profession. They had different characteristics, but each of them in their way was outstanding. So working with them, drawing on their experience, seeing how they dealt with other people, was invaluable.

What was the most formative experience before you became chief executive?

I would have difficulty putting my finger on any single incident, because for many years I ran through a process of simply absorbing more experience about the environment in which we operate, and

130

so I was building up in my subconscious a sense of the way the demand for our services was developing, and therefore what would count for success within the individual firm. I guess the other characteristic that I was developing was a sense of the degree of importance that I would attach to success and position for the firm and the drive for excellence: not so much just where one stands in a league table of firms but a sense that a professional firm has to be different.

So the experience was cumulative?

Yes, very much so.

How does the role of senior partner compare with being the chairman of a public limited company?

Well, the way we have defined the role in the last three or four years is in essence to make the senior partner's job the job of a chief executive. So I am chairman and chief executive. I have responsibility for the management of the business, with very wide discretion as to how I discharge that responsibility.

You deal both with strategy and with overseeing the management and operational side of things?

Yes. We've had some debate about the desirability of having a kind of non-executive chairman, particularly at the time when we modified our working arrangements about two years ago. I said at the time that I had been elected senior partner – in other words head of the firm – and there wasn't going to be anybody over me!

Coming back to this question of management experience. Coopers & Lybrand is by any standards, a large organisation. You have commented on your relative lack of management experience. Very often when people get to the top slot they've got there because they are more than able to do it. But because of the need to get them there, the importance of getting the right man for the job, they have lacked some particular bit of experience which would have made it easier for them to start off. Did that apply in your case, or were you well enough equipped in all the necessary areas to take the top job?

> Looking back, there were two points in my favour. The first was that we were in a very favourable market; had the market been unfavourable things might have turned out very differently. In a sense it would have been difficult to run a big accounting firm badly from 1983 onwards. Secondly, the business is actually a relatively simple business compared with, say, making nuclear submarines or a whole lot of other things, and so it has been a much less demanding environment in which to operate as an inexperienced manager.

But is an accountancy firm – albeit one that has diversified as you have – one in which managerial skills are less important than in running, say, ICI or a large civil service department?

> No, I think the business is on such a scale that it does require expert management. A lot of our business is international in scope and therefore managing the international network requires a fair degree of subtlety, of guile. Nobody in the international firm is in a position to direct other national firms as to what they should do. Therefore, the range of managerial skills required is quite extensive – possibly a little different from those in a conventional corporation. From my own point of view I see my needs, my particular obligations, as less in the operational direction of the firm, than in other areas. I've been very happy to rely on other partners to make sure that the machine runs sweetly once it has been set up. I particularly place a lot of reliance on a managing partner.

So to some extent it's horses for courses?

> Yes. I've made something of a virtue out of seeking to devolve responsibility with authority into the firm.

It's interesting to see that you have terms like 'managing director' within the organisation. How does that fit in with the partnership structure?

There are two slightly different points which you may have picked up. The first is that internally we use titles that are manager-like – I'm referred to more often as the 'chairman' rather than the 'senior partner'. I have a managing partner. We have partners in charge. We have directors of human resource development. So we're simply drawing on other people's experience and using titles which are recognised. That's a little bit different from the constitutional quirk we have which is that the partnership is legally limited to chartered accountants and therefore the many non-accountants whom we have with partnership status are entitled 'director'. They are legally directors of a parallel company. We get a degree of confusion in terms because of the dual use. You would find a lot of our present audit clients came to us as a result of advisory/consulting work of one kind or another.

That way round?

Yes. The fortunate position I was in when I took over was that, whereas management consultancy in general had gone through a very bad patch in the late 1970s and early 1980s, and indeed our own consulting practice had declined in size, nevertheless we had stayed in the business. We had been able to undertake quite a lot of work outside the UK, which had kept up the skills and the staff resources. The market was picking up and, compared to some of our non-accountancy competitors, we were very well placed to exploit the demand. It's just sheer good fortune that when I took over as senior partner the consultancy market had suddenly reopened.

Our consultancy partners had positioned their segment of the practice very well to take advantage of the opportunity and it went like a bomb – and it was nothing to do with me! I was the happy beneficiary of the turn in the market and the fact that our own consultancy partners had seen what was going to happen and had reorganised to that effect. It went like a rocket for four or five years.

You modestly say that you had nothing to do with it. Obviously you presided over it and ensured that the opportunity was taken.

Yes. The prospectus on which I became senior partner was essentially one of 'be more aggressive', to adopt as best we could concepts of marketing which were very well understood in the business world at large but were relatively new to accounting firms, and generally to build a much higher profile for the firm. The reason for that was that there was a pent-up demand within the partnership ranks for a drive for leadership. It was a kind of morale-creating activity and my brief essentially was to energise the firm.

This drive for leadership; was it the drive to lead as an accountancy firm?

Yes. My sense was that the partners felt that we were not achieving our full potential. I believed that we had the potential, that we should be more aggressive in seeking to exploit it, and that in the process we should do things differently. That's not to say that the firm had been doing the wrong things. It was a time in our history when we were ready for a change in direction.

And where did that change in direction take you?

Well, it took us first of all very aggressively into areas of business opportunity where we had some advantage. I gave a lot of support to the development of the consulting practice, but the actual achievement was really to the credit of the consulting partners, not to me. I simply legitimised it. It took us, specifically, into a drive for a much higher profile in the market with a raising of awareness. For example, as the ethical restrictions on advertising and promotion fell away we were there at the forefront doing things differently. We had a classic 'cocking the snook' at our institute, which allowed accounting firms only a one quarter-page newspaper advertisement so we ran a full page recruitment ad! We were prepared to do things in a slightly irreverent way and I think that was quite motivating. But the more important issue was to adopt a somewhat different approach to the market, to try and understand what marketing really meant, and to adopt a strategically based market thrust for future business development.

You say that the firm had to be aggressive. You therefore had to be aggressive too?

Yes.

To be aggressive is difficult for lots of people and equally for lots of firms. How does one make a firm aggressive? How did you energise the whole organisation?

By example. By demonstrating that a somewhat different pattern of behaviour was still entirely appropriate for a professional firm. Take a very simple issue like access to the media – I showed the way. I made it clear to the partners that we had to be available to the Press and that if we wanted to get our point of view across, we had to have a point of view first of all and then be prepared to express it. I trail-blazed, and the rest were then able to follow. It's a legitimising process. At the same time we looked for other areas of development, other ways of achieving excellence, so, while we were trying to become more market-aware, at the same time we introduced processes like upgrading our recruitment and training facilities, took a more aggressive stance towards the introduction of information technology into the business – not always successfully – and a number of other initiatives that I triggered off, essentially designed to achieve excellence within the firm.

The theme of excellence is a term you have used once or twice. Was it something that you have consciously done?

Yes, very much so. We've always considered ourselves to be an excellent firm in terms of the service that we give our clients and, it sounds rather trite, but our history is one of seeking to do the job better than other people. A number of us thought that we were not given full marks for that. It's important in two respects. First, it does make a difference in the market, particularly a market which is much more willing to move from one adviser to another. The market in which we operate is very sophisticated and it recognises excellence. More important, the reason why most people stay in a professional firm like ours is because it gives them an opportunity for personal achievement. The vast majority of the people in the firm are professionals who look for their satisfaction in terms of their own personal professional achievement. The achievement of the firm is obviously important to them, but their own particular buzz is how well they think they are doing themselves. It is very important to create that kind of engine, of always driving to be better than anybody else. We don't always achieve it, but I'm very happy to have the partners competing internally against one another as to who is, say, the best tax advisory department, because that really is the heart of satisfaction.

Do you positively encourage that, or enable or stimulate it?

One tries to, in a rather inadequate way, but I can identify lots of inadequacies in the way we operate.

What would you describe as your style of leadership?

Rather than answer directly, let me give you some favourable and unfavourable characteristics that I see in the way I lead the business. On the plus side, I think my major strength has been in identifying trends and being able to articulate them and persuade people to go with them. It doesn't usually require much persuading if the points are the right points and if they are properly explained. I see my role more as identification and explanation rather than persuasion, and I think I've been quite good at that. I believe that through sheer force of necessity I've become pretty good at articulating messages to people in the firm. What I've been much less good at is the subject of management as a process. I can see all sorts of deficiencies in my management of individuals; good at the principle of delegating responsibility, not so good at requiring people to account. Therefore I've become very happy at the thought of moving up towards the role of executive chairman, and allowing much more of the operational activities to be in the hands of partners who are more comfortable with that. I see my role as setting the direction, the

136

creation and encouragement of a vision for the firm, then relying on other people to execute it.

You have connections with the City University Business School. What importance do you attach to management training?

I think it's essential for anybody who is going to stay in or near the business world, and obviously training can be given in a whole variety of ways. Probably the most encouraging development in management training in the last two or three years has been the opening up of a much wider range of training methods: distance learning, for example. We, as a firm, go to some lengths now to give our people training in the issues of management from a relatively early stage, for two reasons. One is so that they themselves can become good managers, whether they stay in the firm or leave. Secondly, and just as important, so they can talk to business managers, the people who are our clients. So there's a dual purpose: number one is understanding so you can do the job better, relate to our clients better; number two so we can actually manage our own affairs better.

Looking over your career as a whole, what do you now feel was the most beneficial or formative experience? What could you not have done without?

I think the two events that have made most impact have been, first, early recognition that success doesn't come automatically, and I would instance not being commissioned during National Service. That was a cold shower – learning that you don't automatically move from being a public schoolboy and captain of the rugger team to be a second lieutenant. So it gave me an awareness that other people had different views about one's capabilities and one has to recognise that and work to correct deficiencies. I think the other important landmark would be prizewinning in professional exams, particularly at the final stage. It acted as a corrective to some of my earlier set-backs.

It gave you confidence?

Yes, the confidence that I did have it within me to achieve excellence and, if I can be marginally vain about it, it wasn't just getting the first prize, it was getting it comprehensively with a number of subsidiary prizes. There was no doubt a lot of good fortune in it, but it was a very strong signal. One has to look behind that as well and see how it came about. It was obviously a lot to do with hard work, but the hard work was to a large extent based on being driven to do it by being married. I was married on coming down from Cambridge and by the time I had finished my exams we had two children. There was no possibility that I would have passed my exams in that way as a bachelor. So again it created in me a recognition that you need other people's support. I think from then on I have had a sense of detachment about personal success. I like being senior partner but it's not the be-all and end-all of my existence. I'm much more driven within the firm by my obligation to the other partners rather than by desire for personal recognition. In a sense it's a lonely job because of that, and I don't see myself moving out of Coopers & Lybrand to run another company, because that's not my particular personal buzz. So I think I do have an ability to stand to one side and take an objective look, particularly at my strengths and weaknesses.

Is there anything you would like to add before we finish?

Just about my own priorities as the head of the firm. I've introduced into the firm something it didn't previously have, a formalised planning and budgetary process. That's been a good discipline, requiring people to think year by year about the way forward and the areas where we're strong or weak, and how the market is changing. One of the first new appointments I made was to ask a senior partner to take on the role of director of planning and marketing.

On top of that I have evolved a process, almost unconsciously, of targeting one or two big developments each year, or at least sitting back and thinking whether there are any major changes in direction we should be allowing for. I think my own personal obligation is principally to do that and to look beyond the incremental developments to see if there is anything significant for the firm, to at least be sensitive to the big emerging issues.

Three examples of that. First, going right back to the beginning, my belief that we were going into a period when the rules for business development were bound to change very substantially. The move to take away the restrictions on advertising and aggressive business promotion I just knew would happen even before I took over as senior partner. It happened two years later. Secondly, and if anything we were rather late compared to many businesses, Europe. About three years ago I decided that we needed a very different approach in Europe so I embarked on a kind of political process with other partners, other firms in Europe too, to give the firm a rather different face and a different organisation – going from the federal to the rather more focused – and introducing the concept of a common strategy for the whole of Europe. Other competing firms had done the same thing, maybe done it more effectively. But my trigger was saying to the other Coopers firms in Europe, 'This is what we must now do.' Third, I said that 1989 was going to be the year of mergers. I was probably a bit later than some others, but within the firm it was for me to take that initiative, to say, 'I think that something is going to happen and we must take that into account.'

So I think I can justify my existence as the head of the firm simply by an ability, year by year, to see what the major developments are going to be.

A final question: you mentioned that, as senior partner, you were both chairman and chief executive rolled into one, although you had a managing partner and you were moving towards being executive chairman. How lonely is it? As one goes up the tree one is motivated by the people one works for and the work one does. You have nobody to work for. You have mentioned that you are very concerned about serving your partners and working with them – the team bit. How does one cope with the business of being at the top and having no one you can actually talk to and seek direction from?

I think the answer has to be in developing a team around yourself. That is a process that I've been working on rather more successfully over the last couple of years than hitherto. Peter Allen, my managing partner, and I work very closely together. I say to people, 'Whatever you say to me, Peter will know it.' I work on the basis that he and I have no secrets between us. There has been a desire, both on our part and on the part of the partners, to see that duo broadened out a bit and so we've been widening the team, partly in the mechanics of management, but also by creating an atmosphere where a group of people are more aware of what is happening.

The safest environment in which to work is one in which you create a sense of common values and a common commitment to what the firm should be seeking to achieve, and an awareness of the business as a group of people.

Sir Peter Imbert

❝... *if I hadn't had those few years on the beat ... I don't think I would have had the authority which I've got now, to run the whole of the police service here in London. One needs that apprenticeship.* **❞**

Peter Imbert's father was a small farmer on Romney Marsh. He went bankrupt in the 1930s, and the resulting insecurity was a major reason for Peter Imbert joining the police. He started as a PC on the beat, and later served in the CID and Special Branch. Until the final stages of his career he also studied at evening classes to make up for his inadequate education.

He negotiated the surrender of terrorists at the famous Balcombe Street siege in 1975 and was catapulted from superintendent to chief constable in only three years. He served in Surrey and in the Thames Valley before returning to the Metropolitan Police, and has been commissioner since 1987.

His style is calm and steady, belying the enormous pressures which afflict any commissioner. He regards the police as a service, not as a force, and devotes considerable energy to building confidence in it: on the part of its officers as much as of the public.

Commissioner, Metropolitan Police, since 1987. Sir Peter Imbert joined the Metropolitan Police in 1953. Following a variety of senior posts he became: chief constable, Thames Valley Police, 1979–85; deputy commissioner, Metropolitan Police, 1985–87. Married with children. Educated: Harvey Grammar School, Folkestone; Holborn College of Law, Languages and Commerce. Born 1933.

Chapter

9

What sort of environment did you grow up in?

I was one of seven children; my father had been a farmer but went bankrupt. During my schooldays he was variously a labourer, lorry driver, bus driver, taxi driver, garage worker. We were not an affluent family by any means; indeed we were middle to poor class.

My mother was a very Christian lady. We may not have been rich financially but probably we were so spiritually and morally. How did that influence my later development? I went to grammar school. Given the environment from which I came it was a surprise that two of the boys out of a family of seven should actually go off to grammar school; it didn't seem then to be within the reach of that class of family. I didn't go to university, it was never contemplated in our family. One expected that when you got to the age of 14, 15 or 16 you went out and earned your living. That's what happened to me. I grew up on Romney Marsh.

A very different environment from metropolitan London. The fact that your father had a business failure – did that affect the family very much?

Oh yes. I was born in 1933 and he went bankrupt about 1935. I can still recall at the age of almost 13 or 14 my mother insisting on repaying the debts that had been incurred at that time. My father was a small-time dairy farmer, selling his milk in and around Folkestone. When the Milk Marketing Board came into being a number of very small farmers fell by the wayside and he was one. That certainly affected the way we lived and our outlook on life. Who knows, that might be why I became a police officer, because of the family pressures and looking for something which had security.

Can you remember what view you had of the police as a boy, a teenager? You probably got into scrapes as much as anybody.

I recall getting caught three times in one afternoon by the same officer.

What were you doing?

Twice for riding two on a bike. There were about twelve of us with about five bikes between us and we were caught by the local policeman. He warned my father that if I did it again I would be up before the court. I don't suppose he meant it, but it was warning enough for me. It wasn't an urban environment like here – we weren't up on the eighteenth floor of a block of flats – he actually knew us without asking our names, and that makes a tremendous difference to the way one can deal informally with situations. Those instruments of informal social control are not there now – the bus conductor, the guard on the train, the local village bobby, the postmaster, the vicar and even the road sweeper.

So you left school when you were aged 16?

Yes. I was a clerk in the town clerk's office for two years, until I joined the RAF for National Service.

What sort of experience did you have in National Service?

I was an aircrew trainee, but that was only to last for one year. I had signed on for eight years, then realised it was not for me and so I reverted to National Service as you then could. I did my final ten months as a Royal Air Force policeman. It is an irregular life but leaves you some time to yourself. I think the companionship is what I enjoyed about the RAF, not necessarily the fact that one was in uniform. It was my first taste of police work.

So, coming to the end of your National Service, what were your plans?

There I had a problem. I began to realise that, in one sense, I wasn't qualified to do anything else. I also realised however, that there was a spark of intelligence somewhere and that I seemed to get on well with people. I wasn't really sure whether I was too late to do anything that needed training for about five or six years, whether it was architecture, agricultural, auctioneering or whatever else. What I had learnt was that I didn't particularly want to go back into local government. The cloistered life of a dusty town hall was not my burning ambition. I wanted something where there was a competitive spirit, plus the extended family atmosphere which I had found in the services, and where my contribution would be worthwhile and would be recognised immediately. That's what put me off going to do some full-time study. I felt that I wasn't giving anything.

Did you consciously decide that you wanted to move to London?

Much as I liked the country – I felt that there wasn't the exhilaration, the excitement, nor the opportunity in that area. I was a fairly active individual and saw a career in the police as challenging. I saw London as offering that degree of exhilaration and excitement. I wouldn't have been happy on the outskirts so I joined the Metropolitan Police and found myself patrolling the West End. I wanted to be part of the action, and so I went straight to Bow Street and to Gray's Inn Road, so I was right in the middle of where things were happening – good cosmopolitan areas.

Presumably now, as commissioner, looking back at yourself as a bobby on the beat, you don't at all regret having come through that experience, having learnt absolutely from the bottom and gone out and done all the things that a new constable has to do?

> Quite right. I think if I hadn't had those few years on the beat, if I hadn't known what it was like to have water dripping down my neck at three o'clock in the morning while trying to resolve a dispute, and if I hadn't had to deal with irate people, and nice people, and people in distress, and suicidal people, I don't think I would have had the authority which I've got now, to run the whole of the police service here in London. One needs that apprenticeship.

Would I be right in saying that as a junior police officer it is not so much the physical discomfort of standing on wet street corners, which obviously you have to do, but perhaps some of the aggro from the public that is the most difficult thing to cope with?

> They both have their difficult moments. But one of the difficult things for a country boy like me was actually developing the verbal repartee to cope with that sort of situation. When one has a crowd of a dozen youths on a street corner who, just by being there and being noisy, are worrying some other members of the public, as a police officer – although you have the authority of the uniform – you are still very much a human being. You experience all the fears and trepidations which anybody else would experience. You are just as vulnerable to pain and disaster. You learn by experience, you learn by watching others, listening to others . . .

How far did you learn by having a sergeant or an inspector above you with whom you could talk things through?

> We didn't only talk things through. What one did was patrol with a senior constable during your first few weeks and you would watch how they dealt with the public.
>
> I think in those days one also learnt, very occasionally, by the shortcomings of one's supervisors: I recall one occasion when there

were three drinkers who were causing something of an affray and an inspector told me to go and deal with it. I didn't come out of it terribly well – I lost my helmet and got a mild battering – but I managed to arrest one of them and another one later. I realised then the inspector had made an unwise decision in sending me by myself to deal with it. So one learns not only by good examples but also by bad examples.

Did you keep a diary, or make notes on how you were getting on, and look over it?

No I didn't. I do now. It isn't only that I find it helpful. I suppose it is one way of going over the day in a chronological fashion. It directs your thoughts back on to areas of doubt, for example, where perhaps you were chairing a meeting which you expected to be difficult and for whatever reason it has gone well. It helps to replay moments of drama which have affected the service or people within it. It also helps me to wind down at the end of the evening, to learn something about myself and the way I've handled things, and start again just a little better prepared the next day.

In the earlier part of your career in the Met you first came into the public eye at the time of the Balcombe Street siege – was that the time you first became a household name?

That's fair to say, yes. I don't think anybody knew me before those terrorists were holed up at Balcombe Street where they had taken hostages.

Did you find your training had equipped you to cope with that confidently?

I think it was my informal training throughout my career as a police officer that equipped me to do that. Firstly on the beat you are learning how to deal with people either by watching others or being told by others or through gaining experience yourself. Then, later on, in Special Branch and the CID, while questioning those who had something to tell you but were disinclined to do so, one learns certain techniques of building a rapport with people. I suppose it was then that every little bit of experience that I had built up and tucked away in little pigeonholes in the corner of my brain came to the fore at the right time.

So you found it came naturally to you to keep calm and to keep in control of the situation, and just take it as it came?

Yes. I think I had learnt that if you lose your temper you certainly lose the argument. If you lose your equilibrium, your sense of balance, then you are going to come off second best and there is one golden rule – to keep calm. But I don't think it came just from policing. Perhaps I didn't take full advantage of my schooling. I'm the first to admit that I didn't have a distinguished academic record, and I was very conscious almost immediately after I had left school how much opportunity I had wasted. So during my time as a police officer and throughout my career until about ten years ago I went off to night school to learn whatever I could, whether it was shorthand or Russian. I also took a commercial teaching qualification during which time I looked at the psychology of teaching and that, almost unwittingly, teaches you how to get on with people, how to capture people's attention, to keep them concentrating on what you are saying.

When you went to Surrey you went first of all as an assistant chief constable then rapidly became deputy chief constable, and you were 43 or so at the time? Is there a particular value in roles such as assistant and deputy, or is there an argument for saying that you ought to have one person in charge and get rid of a sort of intermediate clutter of deputies. There is one school of management which says deputies are all poison. Do you go along with that?

If as deputy you are only there so that you can act in the absence of the chief, then, yes, you could get rid of the deputy straight away. But that isn't the case in the police service. In Surrey as an assistant chief constable I had functional responsibilities for the CID, the traffic department, communications – as it's a small organisation I had 50 per cent of the operational side of the force. So it was not only giving you that very interesting and wide responsibility, it was also training you to become the chief at some time.

And you had set your sights on that when you went to Surrey – you were hoping to become a chief?

Strangely enough that wasn't a burning ambition. I had never said, 'I want to be commissioner' right from the start. As a much younger officer I had often passed the portraits of former commissioners on the fifth floor here at New Scotland Yard, and in my wildest dreams I saw myself actually wearing that rather fine uniform and being the subject of one of those portraits. But, frankly, never did I think that it would happen and I wasn't looking towards it. I was keen to do the job I was doing to the best of my ability and that has been so throughout my whole career; I have seldom looked more than one notch ahead, very seldom.

When I went to Surrey as an assistant chief constable I was quite frankly surprised to get the job and having got it, coming from the Metropolitan Police – an entirely different area to Surrey – I had to concentrate on what I was doing.

But nevertheless you moved and you were promoted again pretty rapidly to Thames Valley as chief.

Well of course, first of all, I became deputy in Surrey. I had only been there fifteen months and the general rule was that you stayed for at least a couple of years before you even looked anywhere else. But within fifteen months the man ahead of me retired and to my surprise the chief constable said, 'You might wish to apply for the job.' I did, but he didn't give me any promise about it. In fact I did get it.

You made this change to Surrey after a long period in London – you had to adjust to that. Then you had to adjust again to a large force, Thames Valley, with new problems. How did you find that double switch in a fairly short period?

I found it very demanding indeed – extremely demanding. I frankly hadn't had enough time as an assistant and deputy to know what being a chief constable was all about. I had had pretty rapid promotion. I was superintendent here in London, promoted to chief superintendent in the January and within a fortnight I had applied for the job in Surrey, so I had moved from superintendent to chief constable in three years. So although the Thames Valley Police Authority very kindly put their trust in me, I was very green in the provincial scene. I didn't have the right amount of experience to run a big police force like that. I knew that I had got to summon all my energies and political nous and use my personality, such as it is, to get the support of everybody around me.

Your style is to delegate – to let people make mistakes and learn from those mistakes. If I were very cynical I might be outraged by that. I might say, 'Well, it's all very well making mistakes but I'm the citizen who wants the best possible police service – what if I'm on the receiving end of one of your mistakes?'

I hope that I am at one with that member of the public. You can give a better service if you say to a commander of an area, 'Now it's your responsibility to give that service to the best of your ability to the people in that particular area. If you don't have the wherewithal to do it, that's my job to provide it.' It's also my job to ensure that the individual uses those resources to the best of his or her ability and it's also my responsibility to see that he or she is following the style of policing which has been laid down, because we only lay that down after consultation with the public.

Running the Met, you have something like forty-five thousand staff under your control, it must be one of the largest and best known police forces in the world. How far can the Met still learn anything from the police forces overseas, in New York or Chicago or Paris or Rome for instance – are there things that you can learn to your advantage?

Yes, it's not only learning from abroad but learning from colleagues in this country as well. Out there today in London alone there are probably going to be a million contacts between police and public. I take great pride in the fact that at the end of the year we only have about five or six thousand complaints or reservations about those contacts. Not all of our contacts will be good contacts and we will learn something from each of those. We've had rather difficult industrial disputes: Grunwick, the miners' strike, Wapping. We learn something every time, because every situation and every contact is very different, no two are alike.

To develop the answer about learning from police forces abroad, when the drug 'crack' began to appear on the streets we sent two officers to the States to study the problem. We sent them to New York, Washington and Boston. New York because it was the supermarket. Washington because it had suffered very badly with an increased number of murders related to drugs and it seemed to burst upon them so suddenly that they hadn't got the solutions. Boston because, on the other hand, it seemed to have dealt with it pretty well, and it hadn't got a hold there. So we wanted to learn not only what and how things went wrong but what went right. When the officers returned they made recommendations based on their experiences which were refined and put into operation in London – to do with intelligence-gathering, setting up units to deal with it – in that way we tried to be one step ahead of the problem.

One of the rather surprising things we notice in large organisations in this country is that often there doesn't seem to be a very well-developed system of sharing good practice: somebody perhaps running a sales force in the north west, is doing something which his colleagues in East Anglia or wherever could learn from.

In many organisations that doesn't seem to happen – there seems to be a very insular approach: 'My region, you keep out of it.' Do you have a system that you are encouraging of saying, 'Well, this part of the Met is doing something rather better than the rest. Can we share it around, or can we make it better known?' Do you do that?

Yes, we not only do it within the force but between forces in this country and abroad. I went on holiday to Denmark and while there, visited three police headquarters and a couple of prisons, and then spent six days in Hungary on an official visit, just talking to the Hungarian police. The object of that exercise was so that they could learn from us, but I learnt quite a lot from the way in which they are going. Wisdom doesn't just reside here in the Met or in Scotland Yard. It would be quite arrogant and wrong to think that it did. Within the forty-three separate and largely autonomous police forces in this country, in order to share our experiences, we have the Association of Police Officers. We meet every three months to discuss current issues.

In the Met every year we go through a planning cycle. Each one of the seventy chief superintendents – the local chief of police – must confer with his local authority, his consultative committee and the people in the area as to what ought to be the priorities for the police service in that area. They will then formulate their plans for dealing with those locally identified priorities.

So because that is such a thorough process you have a lot of confidence that what you end up with has got a lot of support, you have consulted widely?

My strategy, which I publish in January, will be a reflection of what the people of London want. It is put together after wide consultation both inside and outside the organisation. Each year all the senior managers, police and civil staff of the service, over a hundred of them, meet together to talk about the main issues which the service will face over the next five years. The issues raised by this conference and the priorities identified by local managers through the planning process are used to inform a meeting that I have with the seven most senior managers in the service. At that meeting we will decide the strategy for the service for the next five years. It will be a general strategy. It may be that there is an epidemic of burglaries in Barnet and of robberies in Brixton. What's good for Barnet isn't always good for Brixton.

As you said, you can't be everywhere throughout Greater London. How do you decide what priorities are top of your personal list?

First of all we have our strategy for the next five years and everything is aimed towards it. Within that there are issues arising daily or weekly. A crisis or drama may be dealt with by a police constable or the commissioner or one of the intermediate levels. It depends on whether an immediate remedy or a long-term approach or change in policy or strategy is required. Policing is a vibrant, exciting, demanding, and sometimes dangerous occupation. We must have long-term strategies, but my officers are also expected to provide instant solutions. Intelligent anticipation of problems, high quality officers, good training and adequate resources are an essential part of our constant endeavour to give a better service to our public.

Sir Alex Jarratt

*⁶I do not know of any business solution,
thought out at the centre and imposed
on part of the periphery, that worked.
At the end of the day if it's going
to work, people have
to own it.⁹*

As a young civil servant, Alex Jarratt learnt a great deal by working closely
under two different permanent secretaries. This experience has given him a
lifelong interest in the process of developing talent. He sees the relationship
between a senior and a junior manager as a contract, defining the limits within
which each party will work together. But he also likes to delegate as much
authority as the individual can accommodate.

In mid-career he made an apparently effortless move from the top level in the
civil service to managing director of a massive company. Since then, as chief
executive or chairman of several companies, he has been particularly keen to
define roles clearly – the respective roles of chairman and chief executive, of head
office and the operating businesses, of executive and non-executive directors.

---

*Chairman, Smiths Industries plc, since 1985. Sir Alex Jarratt is joint deputy chairman,
Prudential Corporation plc, since 1987 and chancellor of the University of Birmingham,
since 1983. He is a member of Council of the CBI. His career has encompassed: the
Ministry of Power, 1949–64; the National Board for Prices and Incomes, 1965–68;
Department of Employment and Productivity, 1968-70. He was managing director,
IPC, 1970–73 and chairman and chief executive, 1974; chairman, Reed International,
1974–85. Married with children. Educated: Royal Liberty Grammar School, Essex;
University of Birmingham. Born 1924.*

Chapter

10

What sort of family guidance did you get about careers – did you have any very clear ideas when you were young?

Not really. We got as far as which university I might go to, then I joined the navy during the war, and then my father died and I had no further family guidance whatsoever. I guided myself as the war ended, and at that stage I really wanted to improve my education which had been interrupted by the war. Not until well into my second year of university did I begin to feel I wanted to go into government, so I was about 24. I was the first Birmingham graduate to go into the civil service. I went through several interviews of the kind, 'Shall we take you as a management trainee?' But they concentrated far too much on, 'Come-and-make-biscuits' or '. . . ceramics' and no one said to me, 'Come and be a manager.' And then along came the civil service and said, 'Come and run the country' – not a bad selling point!

When I became chairman of Reed International we used to do an 'Introduction to Industry' course in the winter holiday. We had people from all the universities and we told them about being a practising manager, about being an account executive, not about making paper or books. It was very successful. To the person who stands outside it's far more interesting to learn about the activity rather than the output of that activity.

Going into the civil service in 1949 – a time of great stringency, the Stafford Cripps era – what was your first job?

I went into the Ministry of Fuel and Power, into the oil division. Then on to balance-of-payments work: we did most of our calculations on the backs of envelopes. Then I had my first tour as a private secretary to permanent secretaries, two of them, from whom I learnt a great deal. One was Sir Donald Fergusson, a pre-war permanent secretary, a Scot – quite outstanding. He would walk all round a room on the parquet flooring and on the edge of the carpet and dictate to me in longhand, and would explain to me why he was doing things, which was marvellous. A man with infinite understanding of government and the proper place for civil servants. He was succeeded by Sir John Maud (Lord Redcliffe-Maud), a man who said, 'With me you have to take the smooth with the smooth' – great personal style.

You learnt the different styles of those two leading civil servants. What did you learn about the way they got things done?

There were three main things. From Fergusson, hopefully, I learnt the intellectual rigour he brought to bear in reaching conclusions, and secondly, although he was an adviser, he always made a specific recommendation. He did not waffle. Nor did he care: he would put his reputation on the line at times. I saw it happen and it was very real, and as a young man watching it, that helped to stiffen my backbone. Then there were John Maud's great presentation skills. With a combination of those two, one had a quite formidable education combined with great knowledge, the use of context and an insight into how to work a system. Both did that in quite different ways.

An important thing which we don't always learn is the use of other people's time – something I've learnt as I've become more senior. People think you spend all day reading for seven days a week and are as passionately interested in every single subject as they are. Discriminating between what is important and what is not important is something that has to be learnt when you are serving ministers.

Are there ways of learning that?

To a certain extent it's trial and error. The civil service works heavily on paper so the ability to write clearly and simply and succinctly is important. Hugh Cudlipp at the *Daily Mirror* once told me that a leading article should have not more than ten words per sentence and no word should have more than two syllables, and you should be able to explain anything that needs explaining to anybody on that basis. There's a deep truth in that. You can partly be trained but it comes from usage.

So you had this privilege of serving at close quarters under two powerful and different leaders in the civil service. Who, if anybody, was pulling together your total training and development?

Nobody really. At that time they would appoint an assistant secretary – he was literally called a 'father confessor' – to a new entrant. That was really on the basis of 'Got any complaints lad?' – it wasn't much more than that. It would not be unfair to say that, with two exceptions, I was a 'guinea pig' and I had no formal training in the civil service at all. The exceptions were when I was on the first Treasury management course and the very first 'Node' mixed, service/industrial course. That was the sum total of my managerial training.

Did you feel the lack of a formal structure to your training?

I didn't at the time. I've felt it at times since – really the lack of other people helping me to keep up to date with the tools of my trade as I have progressed.

So in the absence of a formal programme, you must have relied very heavily on picking things up from studying people senior yourself.

| Yes.

So there is a theme coming through pretty strongly of learning by watching other experienced managers and picking up different strengths which each of them had. Each of those managers must have had a particularly strong suit. How did they compensate for any weaknesses that they had?

> They didn't always compensate. Not every one was a role model. They were all intelligent. Some of them not as well rounded as one would look for in the complete manager. Some were far more cautious than I thought government progressively required as the years rolled past. Some could be extremely pedantic.

You moved around within the civil service. The Ministry of Power was your base, but you were seconded twice, once to the Treasury and once to the Cabinet Office. Was that in any sense for your own development or was it to do a particular task?

> The Treasury secondment was for my development. I had two years there and came back to be a private secretary to three ministers.

What did you learn in the Treasury?

> When you talked to somebody on the telephone you could hear them standing up at the other end. It certainly was then and has remained the authoritative department. It has enormous power which, though it tends to be exercised extremely cautiously, does cause concerns. I suppose I learnt through seeing at first hand the command post of a very large administrative organisation.

Your stint at the Cabinet Office was about ten years after that?

> That's right, right at the end of the Alec Douglas-Home

administration and then the first eighteen months of the Wilson administration.

The transition could hardly have been more striking.

> The Conservative party had been in power for thirteen years and they had had enough by then. The Labour government came in with the famous 'white-hot technological revolution' and all that jazz. It was a very exciting period with relatively novel concepts of what a government's role should be. Then I got caught up in what became the only plank of their economic policy, the prices and incomes policy, and found myself saddled with it until I left the service in 1970.

To an outsider, looking at that sort of role in the civil service, on the one hand it seems that you are tremendously close to the centre of power, on the other that civil servants are grey faceless bureaucrats who don't actually *do* anything but just process a lot of things and prepare decisions to be made by other people. How much of a caricature is that?

> Oh, in the twenty years I was in the civil service it was increasingly a caricature. My senior colleague, Donald Fergusson, told the story of Baldwin receiving memoranda from his then permanent secretary of the Treasury which would say, 'You can do A or B.' He put up with this for so long and then sent one back saying, 'I agree.' So I suppose there were people who were like that caricature.
>
> But as time went on, and particularly in the latter days of Harold Macmillan's administration, with the beginnings of intervention by government, civil servants began to play an active role with ministers. Certainly I did that, as Donald Fergusson had taught me; when I put up proposals I recommended the course of action. With the prices and incomes policy, which got bigger and more all-embracing, one became involved with it. You couldn't step aside and say, 'Well it's all terribly boring stuff, but I'm doing it from Monday to Friday' – you couldn't be like that. You had to try to make it carry the economic weight that ministers wanted it to carry. Although I felt in my bones that the weight was too great I

became identified with it. I began to be known in the Press because of it.

So the impartiality of the civil servant doesn't preclude the commitment that you feel towards whatever policy it is?

No, I don't think it does. I remember going to see a very senior man in the civil service department about the promotion of one of my colleagues and he said, 'Oh, old so-and-so – his problem of course is that he gets so involved.' It wasn't unkind, it was just that he didn't measure up because of that. I have to say that one of the underlying reasons why I left was that I *was* involved, but increasingly I didn't agree with that with which I was having to become involved, and I couldn't divorce myself from it. From that point of view I wasn't a good civil servant.

When I was offered the opportunity to leave I spent two weeks debating it. I had undertaken to give Lord Ryder my answer on a Wednesday. My mother died the day before, which was important because she enjoyed her son being a civil servant – she could see his knighthood coming over the hill in a couple of years' time. I sat down that Wednesday with a sheet of paper, I drew a line down the middle and listed pros and cons. The things against leaving were getting longer and longer. I had a lunch date so I had to stop. As I walked down Pall Mall I said, 'I'm going.' It was a gut reaction.

Having taken that decision then I plunged into an entirely new life. There wasn't time to take stock. I suddenly, massively, changed my role. In reality, looking back now, the change was not as great as I thought it was going to be. I was acutely aware of a sense of insecurity where I had a sense of security before, of playing in an environment which I did not know instead of one which I knew well. But the basic elements of the task I had to do were very familiar. I was lucky to go into a publishing company; the collegiate atmosphere was still there in terms of people.

How many people had you been in charge of in the civil service?

In reality you weren't in charge of anybody. The complement is run by the establishment officer in the department and the Treasury. You commanded people in terms of policy making, and you did have your *say* on their promotion, but you did not promote and you couldn't kick them in the arse very often either; so it wasn't command in terms of the way you and I understand the word. The only time I got near that was in the prices and incomes board, where I was in charge of about two hundred and thirty people.

So presumably one of the enormous changes you were thrust into when you joined the International Publishing Corporation was being in charge of very large numbers of people?

Yes, about thirty thousand.

Was that frightening, or did you take that in your stride?

That was exciting. That really was the exciting bit plus the fact that publishing is a fascinating business. It was marvellous. It was difficult – the company was heavily into printing. I had all the print unions to cope with and also the National Union of Journalists. I had been accustomed to dealing with unions in my prices and incomes role, but when they directly affect what you are doing it gets rather different, sharper. But it was a very exciting time, you hardly had time to breathe or look round.

What sort of objectives did you set for the organisation when you got your bearings in it?

Restoring its credibility as a profitable organisation. It had lost its way and it was certainly an asset-rich and profit-poor organisation. It was under-managed but it wasn't under-managed. The managers were there but they had not been led properly. Once they realised I was on their side and could see the potential this enormous company had got – indeed now certainly has – I got a very quick reaction from them, and that helped enormously.

When you say 'under-managed' do you mean that the unions had taken the thing over?

> There was that element to it, but more important was that the place was anarchically inclined. There were very strong personalities sprinkled throughout the organisation. The organisation itself was formed of famous household-name publishing companies, each one of which, only a few years before, had been proud, independent and very often a family firm. Those people were still there and had to be brought together, not to worship the parent company, but to operate effectively in the environment of a new company, and do so in a co-ordinated way – which they did.

You went in as managing director of IPC and you were there for four years. Then you became chairman of Reed. What is the essential difference between the role of managing director and that of chairman?

> The difference between those two roles is what two people make of them. As a generalisation, the managing director's task is to run a business on a day-by-day basis. The chief executive's task is to run the business on a day-by-day but increasingly a future basis. The chairman's task is to supervise that activity and to represent the company externally. This is where the US titles are very useful – COO, CEO, president, CEL and chairman.

Going back to the start at IPC, your main objective was to restore credibility. Was that primarily in the City?

> Within the company, first of all: to give the people back the dignity they had lost. Then secondly in the marketplace. But the vital thing is to start within. Get that right and virtually everything else falls into place.

What were some of the early things you did to make that clear?

> I revised and reintroduced the basis of budgeting. I had quarterly reporting bringing the central staff and the operating group staff

together so we could debate it out – good, bad or indifferent. It had been a confrontational situation before. I increasingly defined the objectives of the organisation. We began to improve the personnel relationships within the organisation. Then we faced up to some of the very tough decisions that had to be taken if the company were to weather the future, which involved quite a bit of rationalisation and some very severe trade union battles.

How do you like to define objectives?

You sit down and work out what are the strengths and weaknesses, where your potential is, what the marketplaces you're in are like, are they going to develop, what the competition is like, how you can win out on both of those and what the resources are that you need to do it. Only part of these are objectives, the rest are strategies. Sometimes you have to proceed crabwise. You can't always just sit down with a blank sheet of paper and do it.

Do you like having that done by a small central staff who prepare a lot of papers for you, and a lot of alternative scenarios?

As time went on I did have that facility. I had a very small corporate planning staff and a finance staff which also did the business planning, but it was essentially done by a process of debate: internally with my staff, but critically with the operators. The staff were there to generate and excite thought, and make sure the issues were thrashed out. I do not know of any business solution, thought out at the centre and imposed on part of the periphery, that worked. At the end of the day if it's going to work, people have to *own* it.

Is there a problem there? If you've got a large organisation and you want to delegate a lot of authority to the operating business you want them to feel the strategy has been formed by them, at least to some extent. The sheer timescale of going right the way down the line and asking everyone's views and getting it all back up again means time has marched on. Can you afford to do that?

Not necessarily. Of course it can be done, but there has to be a limit to how far strategic thinking goes down in each operating group. When it comes to really long-term thinking you're talking of a relatively small number of people being involved at the critical operating points of the company. That process must be iterative and it does take time.

But you must try to avoid it becoming a set piece so that every year you pull up the roots and look at them again. I used to try to avoid that. I guess you take the time when you first set out doing it to get people into the habit of thinking beyond next week. There are some businesses that force you into long-term thinking. In aerospace and defence there is no way you could operate on an annual basis let alone a weekly basis. Likewise in papermaking. In publishing, the horizons are much shorter, you don't start fussing about whether women's magazines will still be there in five or ten years' time. The key is, 'How am I doing for the autumn issues?' You get people into the habit of thinking as far forward as their natural business horizons require them to look.

Does that usually stretch people's thinking a bit longer in timescale?

Yes, and many people don't like doing it. It's uncomfortable. So many things could happen, couldn't they? Maybe I'll be dead! Equally, if people's sights are always way ahead and they are not looking at what's happening immediately in front of them, then that's just as dangerous. It's finding the right balance between those two. Your point about time is important there. You somehow learn to ration the time that you devote to each of those forward looks.

So were you feeling at IPC that you were able, within a reasonably short period of time, to get some momentum going again?

I think we did. We got back into profit, which was something.

There must have been some very difficult decisions for you when you went to Reed. To divest the wallpaper business, for instance, because at that stage it was the largest in the world and people might have said,

'What on earth are they getting rid of that for? It's the jewel in the crown!'
Did you have to explain that very carefully to the people affected by that
decision?

> Yes, we did. We did a lot of divestment in sorting the organisation
> out. We took our decisions to divest as privately as we could. Once
> we had taken them, we tried to play them as openly and honestly as
> we could with those primarily concerned. Very often people did not
> welcome them because the security of a large devil you know is
> better than one you don't.

In an organisation as large as Reed you must have had a problem. People
come up through one part of the business, but you would no doubt have
been looking for generalists and spotting the helicopter ability. Did you
develop any particularly good ways of spotting that skill?

> Nothing clever, I must admit. You've put your finger on a very real
> problem. At the end, as with any conglomerate without a large
> central office – and we had a pretty flat organisation – that leap from
> running a subsidiary to running a division is quite a big one. The
> leap from there to running the whole thing, or being number two, is
> a hell of a leap.
>
> It's very hard. You can undertake the obvious training. We
> did that increasingly, but you are looking for the more exceptional
> person – not necessarily exceptional intellectually, but in a
> collection of personal resources they've got and can bring to bear.
> Succession in a conglomerate is a very difficult task. A conglomerate
> these days does not necessarily mean a group of businesses doing
> quite separate things. Any big company made up of a large number
> of units has that problem. There aren't many pencil-sharp shaped
> companies nowadays.

Do you look back on your own earlier experience where clearly you learnt
so much from studying the management style of some key people, and do
you use that consciously as a way of developing your people?

> Yes. We've had things we call 'springboard jobs' which we identify

in the company. They were sometimes concerned with the nature of the job, but usually meant they are under the command of a lively person who could help the person to develop. We did achieve some switching around between different types of operation. I had a PA system which helped to bring a more diversified group of people forward. I'm never quite sure how successful that is. It's nice to have a PA, and I enjoy them greatly, but it can be a difficulty. I guess the bulk of the management development which we progressively and successfully introduced was more divisionally based than corporately based. When it got to a corporate development you were chancing your luck with individuals.

We notice in some of the work that we do that organisations at the very highest levels are now saying that they want at least two members of the main board to get to know the people two levels down instead of just one, as often happens. People sitting round the boardroom table often rely on the comments of just one person on whether X is a good person or not. But the balance to that is provided by somebody else getting to know that person. That seems to be becoming more common.

Yes, I've had different experiences of that. Reed is quite different to the ICIs of this world, because it had come together in quite different ways and was formed from different businesses. In ICI, where people tend to stay with the company, the knowledge shared by the executive directors of the people who are coming up is huge. They can have a genuine debate on the worth of Mr Smith or Mr Jones. Likewise Smiths Industries, although it is composed of different parts, has a great past in instrumentation, automobiles, aerospace and the executive directors can have a pretty extensive knowledge of people who have come through the company. I watch and envy that, because I didn't have that when I was running Reed. I agree with you: it's important to have more than one perception.

The other point is the importance of international experience. So many top people now say that one of the most developmental things they ever did was to go abroad for two years to run the US business, or whatever.

I think that is true too. The opportunities are not always there in the right forms. For example, if you are working on defence in the USA, as we are, you cannot readily play a part in the line of command because of their security arrangements. If you are operating in Europe in the medical business you're not the same size as the UK business or the US business, so you can't get the same European input for a senior man. So unless you are a genuinely international company your opportunities can be rather spasmodic and can't be structured that well. But that's no excuse for not looking for them.

How do you go about managing your time, because you are not only chairman of Smiths Industries, but you are deputy chairman of the Prudential and a director of ICI, and you wear so many hats. How do you cope with that?

I suppose I have to now. I had open-heart surgery in 1989 and was instructed that I should not go to London more than three days a week. It concentrates your mind on how you run your life. You do get accustomed to picking up what is important and what isn't. There's a lot you get to know and you carry that knowledge with you like a private briefcase. And you need a certain amount of application! I suppose to carry that sort of portfolio you have to have been a very busy person for a number of years so that you have become accustomed to apportioning your time.

Have you ever found it difficult to delegate?

No, not at all. When I was in a subordinate position I always wanted to be given as much authority as the bloke above would let me have, and I have remembered that. The only way you can let people develop is to give them as much authority as they can possibly carry. Don't overdo it – don't crush people – but give them as much as they can carry.

Inevitably they are going to make some mistakes and you can't bankrupt the business in the process. How do you decide how far to go?

I think it is something in the nature of a contract you have between yourself and your next executive. It takes the form of a business plan, a development plan, or a strategic plan – particularly a business plan. You set up authorities on capital spending, salaries – all the paraphernalia of a management regime. You define the limits within which you and he or she are going to work together. You reinforce that with good reporting – that's vital. It should then be surprise free in the sense that whatever *you* do, you don't cause surprises: some rotten swine outside will cause them. With those two things combined, with luck the company won't be bankrupted by an act within the company. People will know the borders beyond which they can't go, but also know the frontiers they are expected to get to.

And they will give you some early warning – they won't try to cover up?

Absolutely. No rewards for trying to spare one's feelings. They need to keep you informed. Equally, they shouldn't be running around every time something goes slightly wrong. A lot of this is subjective but, when possible, there should be remits laid down, normal procedures for reporting and the ability to check those out. In this company it's done by the controller mechanism. You are part and parcel of the management's team – the chief executive of that division with his controller. The relationship between the centre and the operating groups is tight and clear. By and large they don't get caught out. But the people who run the businesses are given an incentive – they're expected to perform, it's their marketplace. That is the key to all this. Sitting at the top of Reed or being the chief executive of Smiths Industries, you don't make anything, you don't sell anything, you haven't got a marketplace except your own people and the banks. The one thing the people out there have got to know more than anything else is the marketplace. That's the bit they feed back to you and within which you make your contract with them. If they don't know about that bit and push their frontiers too far, they shouldn't be there in the first place.

What's the most difficult thing about being a senior manager?

Firing people. The sort of relationships I have been talking about are co-operative ones, not confrontational. I don't think you get the best out of people by shouting at them all the time. But occasionally it goes wrong and you have to 'let them go' as the Americans say. Magnificent euphemism that is. Although there have been occasions when I have had to fire people with whose performance I had been very displeased, I have never been able to do it without pain.

Is it lonely, being a chairman? Who can you talk to about problems?

It's lonely if you carry both jobs, if you are chairman and chief executive. There are very few people you can talk to, either because they could be heirs apparent, or because they're not of a kind who could help you, or because you don't want them to know that you are worried – you're supposed to be cool, calm and collected sitting in the middle like a great big fat spider. It is lonely. It's one of the most marked characteristics of the job. Less so when the chairman and chief executive are separate. That is the key argument for separating them, but you will find that roughly half the companies have got the job combined and half have got the job separated, and in ten years' time you'll find the half and half are different companies!

You obviously take a great interest in the development of people, and you are heavily involved with Henley and Ashridge and with the CBI. Do you have any feeling about the relative place of formal training in management, of mentoring, counselling or reading – all the various techniques there are of developing people?

My own lack of training, particularly concerning the tools of the trade – things I've had to pick up for myself as I've gone along – must have reduced my efficiency from time to time. Having been closely connected with business schools for so long and as a university chancellor I am very much in favour of formal training – anything from a distance learning course to two days, two months or a year, depending on what you are trying to achieve. The role of training within a development programme is far more important than it appeared to be during my own career.

But training is not development, it's part of it, and I believe that the areas into which you appoint people are very important in themselves: you give them the chance to blossom. The point of delegating is to give them an environment in which they can flourish, to encourage them as much as possible, and, at the senior level, to get outside perceptions. I'm very much in favour of executive directors having outside directorships. I've always had them. I do believe I've been made a better executive by having outside directorships; hopefully I have brought something to them, they have certainly brought something to me.

To read about your environment, your subject – yes. I do find a lot of the literature on management a load of rubbish and jargon-ridden, and you have to be very discriminating about that. That's where, if you go to the right training schools, they will help you discriminate. It's a variety of things. The key is to have development programmes and make them happen.

At the end of the day life's all about human beings, not organisations. Help people develop and, if you do it well, you will develop the company too.

Professor Anne Jones

‘It's a blend of trying to keep a long-term
vision, combined with feet on the
ground, taking little attainable
steps towards a goal.’

Anne Jones resisted the prospect of a television career and made a positive
decision to be a teacher. Her career in education has now taken many different
forms. Starting as a French teacher, she became a pioneer school counsellor
while her three children were young. Later, as a head teacher, she involved staff,
children and parents in agreeing the school's aims and objectives. She encouraged
her staff to develop their students by giving them more responsibility for the
management of their learning.

Her style as head of two schools in turn was to have high expectations of
people and to reward them for achievement. Her success as a head, notably in
her involvement of her schools in the community and in education/industry
links, led to her being appointed director of education for the Department of
Employment, where she was in a position to influence education policy and
practice at national level.

Consultant, author and professor of continuing Education, Brunel University since
1991. Anne Jones is member of council: Royal Society of Arts; CRAC; Grubb
Institute; Queen Mary and Westfield College. Formerly she was head teacher: Vauxhall
Manor School; Cranford Community School. Director, Education, Department of
Employment, 1987–91. Three children. Educated: Harrow Weald County School;
Westfield, King's and the Extra-mural department, London University. Born 1935.

Chapter

11

Did you always want to go into teaching?

> It was an early ambition, when I was under the age of 10. However I went off the idea at university. The reason I read modern languages rather than English was not in order to become a teacher, but to be a diplomat or an international EC/OECD/Unesco type of person. In the event I became a teacher after all, though ironically I am doing some work for the EC and OECD.

How much did your family influence your career?

> There was no tradition of going to university in my family. I am the first person I know of in my family to go on to higher education. There was some argument in my family, particularly from my father, about whether this was a worthwhile investment for a woman. For me this proved to be an incentive: I decided I *had* to get a state scholarship to justify the decision. And I did. But originally I was advised to become an executive officer in the civil service: I suppose if that had happened I might still have ended up as a senior civil servant but by a more orthodox route! Very ironic.

Did you grow up at home with a lot of books and learning materials to hand?

> My parents both came from relatively modest backgrounds, but where learning was very much esteemed. My parents were passionately keen on books and reading. We used to have family play readings and poetry readings on Sundays, that kind of thing. My mother herself went on learning during my lifetime: she went from being a 'real full-time housewife' into educational welfare and youth club work, took an extramural diploma in sociology and continued to learn and develop. I remember her writing essays late at night to get her homework done and my father took up the cello at the age of 40 and oil painting at the age of 60. And so they provided a model for me, which said something about people's capacity to go on learning all their lives.

And at what stage did you make your final career decision?

> Well, it certainly wasn't a *final* decision, and I made it initially for expedient reasons. I was president of the students' union at Westfield College, London. Somehow or other I managed to get an upper second as well as being president. I was then asked to become vice president of the University of London Students' Union, which of course is a vast union, and I took that on combined with my postgraduate certificate of education.

And that's where you met a number of people who have since moved on to all sorts of influential posts?

> A lot of the people I met as student leader have done very well. It's absolutely fascinating to find one's erstwhile debating colleagues popping up in the Cabinet and so forth.
>
> However, during the course of that year I also nearly became a television star. I was auditioned for *What's My Line* to take over from Barbara Kelly as a permanent member of the panel. I got a contract for just a few weeks. It was absolutely fabulous because it paid my grant for the whole year. But, although it was wonderful to

take part in those television programmes, I then made a conscious decision to turn my back on the lights, the fame and the glory, and to do something really solid. So I then went into teaching thinking that this was what I really wanted to do. I also happened to get engaged during that year, I wanted to have a lot of children and I wanted, therefore, to be able to combine the two. Education both served my genuine motivation to be useful and serve people and my desire to be a 'good mother'. I have not had too much conflict about that.

One of the fascinations of going into teaching must be that you are faced with a group of students who are all individuals and all different. How do you set about getting the best out of each individual?

I think it has got more difficult since the days when I began teaching. I began teaching first in a girls' public school – Malvern Girls College – and then at the Godolphin and Latymer School – a famous London school – both of which were selective. I think I was considered to be a very successful languages teacher and I certainly managed to get the whole class to participate. But it was much easier in a relatively streamed situation. Now I haven't actually taught French for twenty-seven years, in fact I only ever taught for five years in the first place. After that I hardly ever taught at all. I diversified with the education profession.

Did you find that the training that you had at teacher training college was adequate?

It was very good for its day, but then there was a much more limited concept of what education was all about. Later, I went from teaching academic French into counselling. In the first place this was mainly individualised support and guidance to adolescent girls growing up.

What was your reason for making that switch?

I think it was a frustration about teaching French. You actually couldn't engage in very much meaningful dialogue with your pupils because, if they were only up to Whitmarsh Book Three, or something boring like that, they couldn't actually converse with you very fluently. Yet I was always exceedingly interested in my pupils as individuals. I had a natural bent for pastoral care and counselling, but I found that I had to do that on the side, as it were, I couldn't really do it through my own subject. So, when I was at Godolphin and Latymer, I was made head of the sixth-form at the age of 26 and the head teacher, Dame Joyce Bishop, asked me to run a discussion group in the lunch hour about personal relationships and sex. There was a lot of concern about pregnancy among young people at the time. I had been inspired by Rose Hacker, of the Marriage Guidance Council, who had come into the school and done some preventative work with senior pupils.

I continued her work by setting up a club which met regularly. I used to run group discussions where the girls would come to me with their problems and talk them through. So I was already into a counselling role. I then retired to have my first child at the age of 27. When I was at home with my first two children I undertook marriage guidance counselling training, part-time, and did group work in schools on personal relationships on a voluntary basis. At this stage I was very fortunate in meeting Dame Margaret Miles, the head of Mayfield School. She invited me to join her staff as a part-time counsellor in 1964. I believe I was the first school counsellor in the UK. I set up the counselling and guidance system at Mayfield School *ab initio* in a very part-time and flexible way. I actually became pregnant at that point and had my third child, and then went back to the part-time counselling until all the children were at school; only then did I think of going back into teaching full-time.

Did the mixture of being a mother and being a teacher or a counsellor work out all right? Did the one help the other?

Oh, infinitely, yes. I think having children combined well with the lateral development of doing the counselling training which was a very enriching experience. Like my mother I also did a diploma in sociology at that time, so I studied and read enormously. I loved the years at home with the children. They were very full and rewarding.

All of that gave me a broader perspective: I could not have done what I have done afterwards if I hadn't spent those years with the children, who themselves are an enormous learning experience – extremely good for me. So I had a great deal more to offer at the end of my time at home. I also wrote a book on counselling and did a certain amount of lecturing and broadcasting during this phase. In a way, I was already testing out the 'freelance consultant working at home' mode which is so popular now.

Is there a general message there about people getting additional qualifications? Sometimes they feel it's a terrible sort of chore to go through, a tremendous slog. Is there any way in which people could be helped to realise that these additional experiences enrich the rest of their work?

There's rather a vogue at the moment for collecting qualifications for the sake of getting a better job. I've never done anything that way. I've done them because they are intrinsically interesting and I wanted to do them. It is the learning rather than the qualification which has made a difference. So it's something to do with one's own genuine desire to learn. In me this is very deep and will never stop.

How does one help somebody who hasn't got such a burning motivation to learn as you clearly have?

Well, how do you sell the message that learning throughout life is a very important part of being alive rather than dead? It's a bit like education itself. People either get the message or they don't. People have observed people like me – not only me of course – progressing because they've gone on learning, and so people have jumped on the bandwagon. If they are collecting qualifications mechanistically I don't think it necessarily gets them a better job. I do think that's a serious point. I see a lot of people grubbing for qualifications for the sake of getting an MA so that they then will get their deputy headship. But this does not necessarily make them better than people who haven't got the MA, even though it does indicate a willingness and a capability to go on learning. When I was a head teacher I looked not so much at the qualifications *per se* as for evidence that this was a person who was clearly going to go on learning and, therefore, would create a learning environment around them.

Does that seem rather heretical, that people were perhaps taken on who hadn't got the paper qualifications that would be the norm?

Oh they usually did have them, but that wasn't why they got the job, I didn't sift out the ones with MAs in education, I went by the person. If they happened to have a qualification, so much the better. But if they had evidence of having gone on learning, but it was not born out in practice by the way they behaved, spoke, looked and their attitude, then I wouldn't appoint them. And I would never appoint anyone to a senior post in my school, who hadn't got the capacity to go to the very top. So we had a very high quality of staff. The members of the senior management team have now all been promoted to headships or deputy headships.

You said in your book that the experience of counselling was enormously helpful when you became a head teacher. Thinking back to when you were first a deputy head, or a head, what were your feelings about that? Were you exhilarated, were you frightened?

I was amazed, because when I applied for the deputy headship – my first application – I hadn't actually taught for six years. Previously I'd only ever taught in the grammar school/public school sector. I'd been working as a counsellor one day a week only and I was a 'temporary terminal' on the lowest pay scale with no security of tenure. I had done an awful lot of community work, writing and broadcasting in the gap, but I hadn't actually worked as a professional teacher. The appointments panel took note of the things I had done that were not to do with my teaching career and seemed to value them, which was marvellous – 'accreditation of prior learning' ahead of its time.

But when I got the job I was absolutely flabbergasted, and I went back and said, 'Well I wasn't expecting to get this job, and I'm not

sure if I am prepared to take it on unless you understand that I shall
stay at home if my children are ill. I shall only stay late after school
for specific meetings. I shan't hang around after school, but I will do
a good job. Do you want me on these terms?' And they said, 'Yes
please.'

When I began I was terrified. I had never taught in a multicultural
school before. Thomas Calton school in Peckham had a
multicultural intake which was mainly Afro-Caribbean. In my first
term I was quite overwhelmed, and didn't do very well. After that, I
was fine. I learnt quickly.

In a multicultural situation, where you have people from all sorts of
backgrounds, some of whom probably feel as if they are treated like
second-class citizens at the start, what's the secret of getting learning
going without being patronising?

It's quite simple, it's high expectations really. I had a positive policy
of high expectations: praise and recognition of achievement at
whatever level. So, if you weren't doing very well, but you did a bit
better, then you got a lot of strokes, but if you were doing well but
being lazy, then you got encouraged to do a bit more. So there were
high expectations and encouragement rather than low expectations
and punishment.

And is the recognition best done in a very public way in a school assembly
or is it best done privately?

Well, both really. I used to make a point of interviewing the children
in one academic year. Not all the children in the year, but I would
ask the heads of school or year to send me people. First they sent me
everyone I could praise, and then all the rogues. I remember in my
last school being told there were about twenty-five so-called rogues
in the fourth year who were all real problems. So I had them all in
for a chat. Their first reaction was, 'What have I done?' and I said,
'You haven't done anything, I just want to get to know you.' That
was exceedingly useful because, when they did turn up on my
doorstep with some problem, dragged in by the ear, we had

established a relationship. I knew a lot about them because my counselling skills had come in useful again. I found that as I went round the building, or did dinner duty, I could often defuse a tricky situation. There were one or two children, for example, who used to get very angry and sometimes they would swear at the staff. I made it quite clear I did not accept swearing at the staff: if they felt very worked up about something they should come and see me. So, occasionally, one or two would burst in and let off steam, then go back and be perfectly well behaved in the classroom.

So it was possible to do a lot of unobtrusive work like that, to help the ones with the real problems. But, at Cranford, we also had a merit system where if a pupil achieved so many 'merits' they came to see me. I wrote a letter to their parents and to their junior school: in other words, success was given a lot of recognition. The children loved that and clamoured to do better. I had found previously that if you concentrated on the pupils with problems, and you only saw people with problems, you'd get a lot of people with problems at your door. It's important to have positive expectations, and reward the good things people do. Everyone can contribute something good, so in fact you can actually recognise most people.

And did you find any particular pattern among the so-called troublemakers, those ones about whom other teachers would say, 'We must throw this person out because they are so disruptive. I have tried everything I can and they are still no good.' Did you find any pattern when you did your individual discussions with them?

Oh no. A little word with me wouldn't save a child with real problems. What we had to do then was to work with parents and the staff in a team effort. In my last school we had an excellent student support department which would give very subtle and sophisticated help to young people with behavioural difficulties to help them stay in the mainstream and not be hived off into a sink group. But it wouldn't work at all unless you had a whole network of support which you pulled together so that everything was integrated. You had a strategy for helping each pupil, but you had to weigh up each individual pupil according to his or her actual situation.

Do you see the role of the head as being the leader of a team and mobilising a lot of resources?

> Yes. The head who tries to do everything him or herself is hopeless. That's not the right model, it demotivates everybody else and it doesn't use their ability. One of the tasks of the head is to mobilise everyone's ability including the pupils'. You can get the children to take a great deal of responsibility for the management of their own learning. They will grow as a result of that, they do not need spoon-feeding all the time. The more the pupils took responsibility the more they behaved like extremely sensible young adults rather than children. The extreme example of that was during the teacher action when there wasn't too much help around in the dinner hour. The children were very sensible on the whole, they were marvellous. I think they responded to my saying to them, 'Look, I would like to keep the school open but there's only me and the deputy around. If you behave sensibly we can keep you here. If you don't we shall have to send you home.'

Treating them as adults.

> The other important job of the head is being on the boundary, working with the outside of school as well as the inside. That's something I was particularly keen on. I think it's very important.

In your RSA lecture in 1985 you talked about the fact that you didn't actually know everything that was going on in the school. You got over feeling guilty about that relatively quickly?

> Yes. You mustn't think you're overimportant. There's something wrong if you think that you're the absolute linchpin of everything. That said, the staff like you to show your interest in and your support of what they do; that's quite different I think. They would get offended if you didn't notice what was happening so they would invite me to see special projects and events.

How did you cope with the sort of backwoodsmen among the staff who felt that teaching was all about chalk and talk, and that all this outdoor stuff and projects were irrelevant?

> Well, it's a gradual process. Take my second school, Cranford Community School. When I went in 1981 I got the staff to identify where they were at, what were the problems and what we ought to be doing next. Then I asked them what they thought we should be doing over the next five years. And I put the staff into groups and got them to tell me what they thought – and what they thought was exceedingly sensible. We then involved the pupils in this same consultative process so that they were also committed to seeing certain changes in the school. I suppose I was lucky that what they came up with was what I would have wished to hear. But I didn't actually dictate policy, I just went in, almost to my first staff meeting saying, 'Tell me what you think we are here for, tell me what we ought to be doing.' I also interviewed each member of staff individually.

You kept your fingers crossed, perhaps, that what they would come up with would be something manageable?

> No, because if it had been something that I didn't approve of I would have known where I stood with them. I have learnt to work from where people are at. You have to work from where people are now, not necessarily from where you would like them to be. I believe people learn by doing and that they will also learn from their mistakes. In each of the schools where I was head, I have several times allowed things to happen that I was not sure were the best way forward. But for me to say, 'That's not the best way forward, you can't do that' is not going to be particularly constructive. When you give people their head they actually soon work out the common sense way forward, I find. I have never actually had a problem about that.

Do you have any explicit criteria for how far you would be willing to go in letting somebody do something that you really felt was a mistake?

There isn't that much you do that's so important that it's likely to cause damage – nothing that would harm pupils. Obviously you have to be very careful about health and safety at all times, and not breaking the law, but apart from that I think sometimes as teachers we think we're too important. I'm not sure that teachers are as influential, for better or for worse, as they are sometimes made out to be.

You are very keen that education should be rounded, you talked about education for the hands, the heart and the head. Does that mean that you have to use different learning styles for the things for the head, the things for the heart and the things for the hands?

No, I think they need to be integrated. One of the besetting problems of education and life in general is that people will keep saying, 'Are you a heads person or a hands person?' 'If you are a feeling person, you can't be a reasoning person.' That's absolute rubbish. What you want is to be in appropriate balance for the task that's being dealt with. So people say, 'You know, TVEI is about process and the national curriculum is about knowledge.' But you need both: the outcome of knowledge plus process is capability. And what we're about is capability in people – not just knowledge, not just process – but an outcome which is capability. It isn't an 'either/or' situation. People will polarise because it's more comfortable for the individual to take an extreme view than to struggle with the tension that you get when you actually understand the whole picture and span both ends. Then the result is more meaningful and really helps people. It's much harder to achieve, but it is worth working towards. Having said I would tolerate a lot of things, I'm very dogmatic about not being dogmatic!

Do you actually record for your own benefit what you are learning as you go along in order to convert experience into some explicit sort of step forward in your personal learning?

Not at all. I haven't ever managed to find time to do that. At various times in my life I've been lucky to have a sort of mentor. I do believe you learn best, not through writing something down, but through talking something through with people – though this may be a case of personal disposition. I am also capable of thinking things through by myself if necessary.

When I was a counsellor I had regular support sessions with a psychiatric social worker. I needed that kind of psychiatric supervision because I was dealing with very explosive situations. When I was a deputy and a head I got some support from the Grubb Institute. However, within the system I immediately began to work in teams and found I was not alone. For example, as a head teacher I used to have a weekly team meeting with my senior colleagues, and I used to see team members individually every week. We would reflect mutually upon what was happening and what we had learnt and then assess what we were going to do next. However, it would be done jointly in partnership. It wasn't me telling them or them telling me. You'd think together so that you would actually support each other as well as challenge each other and produce a better 'end product'. So I never felt unsupported as a head teacher. I always learnt from my experience by talking it through with my colleagues. I was never afraid to share my own anxieties, doubts or worries with my colleagues. I am told this is fairly unusual, but I think it's very important to level with people.

Some people have individual preferences in the way they learn, some like reading books, some people like going and seeing things, some people like trial and error. Is there a way of getting people to widen their repertoire of learning methods?

I think that can always be widened. People do learn in different ways, and you have to recognise that. To make them all do something very 'open-ended' if they really are more 'closed-ended' isn't the way. However, you can gradually help people to be more open.

With the help of senior colleagues, I did a lot of staff development at Cranford. We ran a lot of workshops where we put people into new and unknown situations which they had to resolve. So the staff took responsibility for their own learning. They learnt through doing things and then reflecting on that learning. They controlled the

PROFESSOR ANNE JONES

amount they went forward but, as they got more confident, they learnt more and more and had more trust in themselves and could let go of their need to control everything. Then they were able to help the pupils learn in the same way. With teachers a lot of the problem is feeling you have to control, and that's a very real fear because children can be exceedingly challenging. But the teachers who got confident about letting the pupils take up responsibility for the work that was going on in the classroom and doing less for them, spending more time encouraging them and facilitating them, did really well. And, most importantly, so did their pupils.

Do you tend to underestimate the amount of confidence people need to build up before they can become effective teachers?

Well, the Cranford transformation took five years to get from that initial staff meeting when we set ourselves targets. Some people didn't come along the road as actively as others, and some people couldn't as easily because of their basic nature. But nobody was written off. Everybody made progress and, in a way, some of the more 'old-fashioned' teachers made the most progress. It wasn't all going one way, because *all* the methods are very important, it's getting the right balance of methods. Sometimes you need to talk to people, sometimes you need to do group work, sometimes you need to remember things, sometimes you need to do it for yourself.

If a head teacher is trying to vary the management style according to what's needed in the situation, is it difficult to avoid sometimes appearing inconsistent?

It is if you haven't got your staff to understand what contingency management is. Once they understand it, they realise that that's what you're doing. I'm very much a 'learning from doing' person, but I do believe in theory as well. It's part of my theory of integration. Because I had read the theories I was teaching through, I understood. But I don't start with a lecture on the theory and then tell people they are going to learn that. They do something and then you can help people to see that it isn't just something haphazard, there is in fact a theory behind it. Some of the things I've done outside my main job have profoundly influenced my thinking. I got very involved with the Manpower Services Commission because I was very interested in the transition from school to work in the early 1970s. That led me to become chairman of an Area Manpower Board. Presumably my keen and active interest in that whole area then eventually helped me to get the job in the Department of Employment. I was very lucky to get those wider perspectives that I could feed back into my school. My school got the benefit of it, there's no question about it.

And as director, education for the Department of Employment, where you are in a tremendous influencing position but not in direct charge of vast numbers of people, are there frustrations in that as well as particular satisfactions?

I've long ago given up the idea of instant gratification. So I suppose I don't expect to get results for about five years. But I know how to recognise signs of progress, and I see those already around me. It's a blend of trying to keep a long-term vision combined with feet on the ground, taking little attainable steps towards a goal. Whether it's because I'm a woman and have run a home and all the forward planning that involves, but I think I'm quite good at doing both of those things simultaneously. Sometimes people are visionary without ever being very good at actually getting anything to happen, and sometimes people are awfully good at nuts and bolts but don't have any vision. I hope what I bring is a bit of both.

Tim Melville-Ross

❝ ... the nearer the top you get the more you need to be a strategist. You need to be far-seeing to get yourself out from under the day-to-day chores of running your department. . .**❞**

At the age of 30, Tim Melville-Ross's career prospects were unremarkable. Having declined a place at university he joined BP and worked in various departments without particular distinction; he then spent a short and unhappy period in a City stockbrokers. Joining Nationwide Building Society at the age of 30 as company secretary, over the next ten years his career really took off and by the age of 40 he was leading Britain's third largest building society.

He had moved through three assistant general manager posts in quick succession and took up the chief executive post with enthusiasm. He planned the merger which created Nationwide Anglia, and sets great store by face-to-face communication with its widespread staff.

He is still young enough to make a further career move at the highest level.

Director and chief executive, Nationwide Anglia Building Society, since 1987. Tim Melville-Ross is a member of council, The Industrial Society. His career has encompassed British Petroleum, 1963–73 and Rowe, Swann & Co., stockbrokers, 1973–74. He joined the Nationwide Building Society in 1974 and became director and chief general manager, 1985–87. Married with children. Educated: Uppingham School; Portsmouth College of Technology. Born 1944.

Chapter

12

What factor determined your original choice of career?

> I wish I could paint some sort of picture of a well-ordered and well-structured approach to beginning and developing a career, but in my case nothing would be further from the truth, because I went through a period just at the point when I left school of great uncertainty about what I ought to do. I had a place at university, but I decided instead to join the Navy. Much of my motivation for wanting to join the Navy was a desire to fly – I wanted to be in the Fleet Air Arm – but I discovered rather late in the day that I was too tall to be a pilot. So I decided not to join the Navy at all.
>
> So there I was needing to do some quick rethinking about my career. My father worked for BP at the time, so I had a number of connections there. BP seemed to have quite a lot to offer, particularly the process of beginning a career through a commercial apprenticeship involving a four-year degree course at a technical college on a sandwich basis, which was the route I took.

So although you decided against going to university, the way in which you entered BP ensured that you got the equivalent of a university degree.

Looking back do you think that was the best way for you?

Yes. It was the right way in pure career terms because I ended up with a degree and, by the time I qualified, I also had a measure of industrial experience, which was enormously useful. I would say that I was better equipped to handle my first full-time job for BP as a result of that initial training. However, I still regret to this day not having been to university. My two sons are just about to face these decisions and I am encouraging them to go to university because I think you become a more rounded human being: to put it bluntly, you have a lot more fun, you're more likely to build lifetime friendships and so on. I'm sad that I didn't go to university, but in strict career terms what I did was a good move.

The various jobs that I had done as part of my training course provided a very useful background for my career at BP. They were quite wide-ranging jobs: things like working with Air BP; working for six months on a refinery in Kent; I also worked for the supply division which organised the movement of crude oil around the world, and got quite close to how all that happened.

My first full-time job was in the agreements division. This happened because, at the same time as taking my degree course in business administration at Portsmouth College of Technology. I had also studied to become a chartered secretary. The job in the agreements division was, on the face of it, rather tedious, because one was simply involved in drafting various agreements that the BP Group entered into of one sort or another. But the labyrinthian complexity of those deals made the job absolutely fascinating, because the sort of things that we would be talking about were joint venture partnerships to build refineries, to explore for oil, to build aviation fuel delivery systems and so on. So it was all fascinating not just in a quasi-legal sense but also in a business sense, because all sorts of complexities like different exchange rate complications and different legal systems and cultures had somehow to be reflected in the deals that we were doing, which sometimes were with state-owned oil companies in the Third World and sometimes with US private sector oil companies. It was all quite intriguing.

I did that job for about eighteen months. With the benefit

of hindsight I can see how some of the management skills that are used nowadays were clearly not being used in BP at the time in that the division was overstaffed. I had too little to do, frankly. No amount of begging my superiors for more involvement in this or that seemed to correct the problem. So I started looking around within the Group, and made it very clear that I wanted to move.

Were you reasonably sure at this stage that you were on the right path, that you had picked the right company?

In the short-term, yes. I was still only 23 at the time and so it would be wrong to say I had formed a very clear view about my long-term career. That began to emerge towards the end of my time with BP. My career path in BP after the agreements division job was quite interesting and exciting. My next move was to go out to Libya where I worked as personal assistant to the operating head of BP Libya, which was an oil exploration and production company. We were there for Gaddafi's revolution which was all fairly hair-raising for a short while. It was formative of my overall personality in that clearly we were dealing with a situation of some danger and had to live very much by our wits. Maybe if there was any lack of decisiveness about my personality before, that was diminished by my time in Libya. You jolly well had to get a grip of yourself and of the situation, which was sometimes quite dangerous. So to that extent it was a helpful strengthening of my character.

Did it in any sense make up for not going into the Navy?

I think it might well have done because there was a military overtone to it all; one was having to deal with a military situation. People had machine guns and there was the insecurity of a very volatile political situation. To that extent I can see the parallel you draw.

That lasted for about eighteen months. My next career move was back into Air BP. This is the part of the Group that deals with the supply of aviation fuels to airlines. I spent the rest of my BP career with Air BP in different capacities, first of all dealing with the operational facilities in French-speaking territories. Later on I became more directly involved in the process of negotiating and hatching deals with airlines.

Broadly you were in the commercial sphere: the selling side, marketing?

Much more so than anything else. Primarily a marketing operation, although there was a degree of control over the operating facilities in different countries to maintain quality control, conditions of service for the staff and so on. Being involved with both of those was a very useful background to what came later, not least because, representing the central control authority, one of my principal duties was to ensure the efficient budgetary control and profitability of the various overseas operating arms of Air BP. I was quite surprised when I first joined Nationwide, which in those days was a very traditional building society, how lacking it was in the kind of financial controls that I had become used to in BP. The world is very different now, and Nationwide now has financial controls that are second to none, but not in those days. That was part of what I hope I was able to bring Nationwide all those years ago.

You say that you made a bit of a nuisance of yourself in order to further your career out of the agreements division of BP. What do you think would have happened if you hadn't made a nuisance of yourself?

It's conceivable I might have stayed in the agreements division, moving up the rather limited hierarchy there. I have a direct example to point to. In Air BP there is an individual who comes from the same background as I do. He was there when I was with Air BP in my commercial apprenticeship course. He was there when I rejoined BP four or five years later. He is still there twenty-five years later. So there is an illustration of what might happen if you aren't inquisitive and ambitious. I'm still not the sort of person who could have followed that career pattern.

Although BP didn't bring you on as quickly as you would have liked, nevertheless they seem to have responded and been supportive in developing you.

Very much so. It was a lot of fun, I met a lot of delightful people, I got a lot of different opportunities to see the company from different angles and learnt a lot in the process about basic business principles. Its very diversity and size are, in a sense, a disadvantage unless you are a real high-flier.

What was your goal at that point?

To try and fill in something that was clearly lacking from my make-up, which was a knowledge of how financial matters were handled in the broadest sense, in a business sense. It seemed to me that there was no way I was going to have the opportunity to correct that within BP, and so for the first time I began to develop what looked to me a fairly rational career move. For all that it was disastrous initially, in the long-term it was one of the best things I ever did. What I did was to leave BP and join a firm of stockbrokers with the specific intention of getting right to the heart of the financial system, finding out how money worked. My timing couldn't have been worse. It was October 1973 when I moved, from which point the stock market just crashed right through the floor. I had a difficult ten months personally because you simply weren't paid enough. All the bonuses that stockbrokers used to thrive on simply weren't paid because of the state of the market. I was aged 29, and already had a couple of young children. The short-term catalyst for my moving on from the stockbroking firm was personal financial pressure. Also, for all that, many would say my knowledge of the City was pretty superficial, I felt certain that I had gained all that there was to gain from the firm I was working for, and that maybe now was the time to move on to apply those lessons and those I had learnt in BP in a wider context.

There was also a realisation that I wasn't enjoying what I was doing. I have some major reservations about the way our financial system works in terms of the short-term attitude in the City, and the pressure that that attitude brings to bear on industry, which then behaves in the wrong way for its own and its customers' long-term health. I take a fairly cynical view of the process of intermediaries in the City encouraging principals to buy and sell stocks and shares and to move money around. An awful lot of effort by very clever people goes into generating transactions which are economically neutral and, in some cases, possibly even damaging. I found myself moving money around for no very good reason.

Having said that, I don't want to devalue the virtues that there are in the City, where a lot of very good brains act as a bellwether for the economy and give us a much better understanding of what is going on both economically and in terms of the behaviour of individual industries. That's all very acceptable and necessary, but there is an awful lot else that isn't necessary, in my view, and I began to feel that quite quickly. So for all those reasons I decided to move out.

As it happened, Nationwide was looking for a company secretary. As you'll recall when I was doing my commercial apprenticeship course with BP I had also become a chartered secretary, so that seemed quite a sensible thing to do.

Did you have a plan at that time, a strategy on alternatives to the stockbroking firm?

Not really, because of the short-term pressure I have to admit that all I did was scan the pages of the *FT* looking for a better job. That gives the lie to being part of any grand plan. I knew when I left the stockbroking firm I was not cut out to be a City financier, to be a partner in a firm of stockbrokers. I think by then I probably also knew enough about myself to feel that I was sufficiently strong in a number of respects to become a senior manager of quite a large organisation. It was at that point in time that genuine ambition was beginning to dawn.

What would you pick out as your main learning experience so far?

There are a few, but perhaps the most important was that formative time with the stockbrokers: disastrous though it was financially, it gave me the equipment that I find I now need, knowledge. Partly external knowledge in terms of a pretty superficial understanding of how the market works, but also partly self-knowledge in that it dawned on me that I was fairly adaptable, fairly flexible, I suppose with arrogance reasonably bright and able to hold my own . . .

Confidence building?

Very confidence building. Also, an understanding that I had a reasonable gift of the gab, which is a very important part of the make-up of any senior manager. You do get the occasional successful chief executive or chairman who is taciturn, but they are the exception. There is so much salesmanship involved in leading an organisation from the front that an understanding that you can stand up, make a case and think on your hind legs is a very important part of what makes a senior manager.

So now to Nationwide. How did your early career go there?

I have to say, reasonably well. It's been a marvellous time in my life and I still can't believe my good fortune because, when all is said and done, however capable or otherwise you think you are, a career is spiced with a great deal of luck and I have had a great deal of luck, there's no question about that. I spent the best part of five years as the company secretary which was a very useful formative time in two major respects. First of all, as the secretary of the board you are at a fairly young age and a relatively junior level, being three or four down from the top, but you are almost better placed than anybody to see the organisation as a whole, because you attend every board meeting, you attend management meetings and, over time, you begin to participate. So, more than almost any other individual you are able to take the broad view. It certainly helped me form a broad view of what the organisation was about.

The second important element was that we were just beginning through the latter half of the 1970s to realise that the previous rather structured and regulated nature of financial services in the UK was going to break down sooner or later; and we were starting to think of the time when all of those changes that have since occurred would happen. We would be much more diverse, getting into banking, estate agency and so on.

> So, especially towards the end of my time as secretary, I began to form some quite firm views of my own as far as that went, and was fortunate enough to be very close to the chief executive at the time, Leonard Williams, to whom I was directly responsible.

How did that closeness come about?

> Partly because that was the way the organisation was structured, my office was literally next to his. We have always got on famously and I owe a great deal to him. He helped me in career terms more than I can say. He knew that my thinking was developing in this way and, as my first move after the company secretary slot, he moved me into a job called assistant general manager (planning), which was essentially a role where I could begin to develop some of these new thoughts.

So he's a fairly key person?

> Very much so, very formative.

Did he recognise that you were going to go to bigger and better things within the company, or what?

> I think partly that. To suggest that at that stage he could see me as a future chief executive would be exaggerating, particularly because in building society terms I was unusually very young as a senior manager. But the other element was perhaps that, having done that secretary's job for quite some time, I was beginning to spend a lot of time developing new ideas and trying them out on him; we had an identity of interest there, I think. The housing strategy which the society began to develop around the turn of the decade was very much developed in dialogue between him and me and his immediate successor as chief executive, Cyril English. So maybe he reckoned that it would be helpful if my career were broadened. With the benefit of hindsight I can now see how what I went through over the next four or five years was invaluable preparation for the top job. I was given three different AGM posts. First was the planning job.

Secondly came a finance job, which was much larger in terms of its responsibilities. Cyril English gave me free rein in my third AGM job, which was to give a focus to the Society's emerging housing interests, as a result of which I established the Nationwide Housing Trust, which is a development company. I suppose I made a fair job of that. We had had a number of attempts in the past to set up a development organisation which had failed. I did it and succeeded, and so not long after becoming AGM (housing) I was then promoted to the general manager level and given additional responsibilities, principally over the lending book – the entire assets side of the balance sheet, if you like. As a general manager I had become part of the top management team.

That gave you responsibility for all functions within the housing area?

That's right. Not just our direct housing activities but more significantly, in terms of scale, the Society's lending activities, which is principally what a building society is here for. So there we were, a group of general managers, with the prospect of Cyril English retiring, and each of us regarded as a candidate to succeed him, as were a number of outside candidates. The board were very thorough about it and appointed a firm of headhunters. With uncharacteristic modesty, I had no real expectation of getting the job, more than anything on the grounds of age, because I was still only 39. Nevertheless it was valuable experience to go through the process of being a candidate – and, anyway, I did get the job.

What gave you the edge over the others?

I think experience, to begin with. For all that I was younger than the others, I had more outside experience, a wider experience within the Society and a fair grasp of financial matters – an essential ingredient. Also, though I say it myself, I was a reasonably effective, strongish sort of leader and had given evidence of that.

Did you wish when you took over as chief executive that you had had more of any particular kind of knowledge or experience?

Yes, I did. The one area where I felt I was very lacking in experience was in the whole retail-cum-marketing side of what we do. The great majority of our staff are employed in the branches, and the way we put our message and our product across to the customer hangs fundamentally on how we present ourselves in a marketing sense. I knew very little about that. I had spent no time at all working in a branch or as a line manager in the outfield network. I regret that.

I thought it was going to be pretty significant at the time, but now I've been doing this job for a number of years I don't regard it as that significant because of my own particular style of management which is to be pretty visible to the organisation. I spend a lot of time in the field with branches trying to understand how they are feeling, what are the problems that the front-line troops are having to cope with and so on. In some respects I probably get a better picture of that through not having been too closely involved in the day-to-day operations of a branch.

In a marketing sense, everybody thinks that they know all about marketing but I certainly don't. Nevertheless, marketing clearly has to be the means whereby you deliver your strategy and, as I have a fairly clear strategy for the Society, I have to have an understanding of how the marketing operation should work. Again, I don't feel that my own lack of marketing experience is, necessarily, a fundamental flaw, providing I make the right choice in getting good people in to do it for me.

Do you think there is a difference of degree or of kind between being a manager – even a very senior manager – and being chief executive where you go on to strategy – comparing management operations on the one hand with direction, policy and strategy on the other – or do you think the one flows from the other?

To a degree one flows from the other, but the very largest step of all is from the line of managers immediately below the chief executive to the chief executive slot. It's a lonely job: the buck stops here and all the rest of it. If you're to be worth what you are paid, you really have to develop a strategy and make it work – in consultation with a lot of other people, of course: with the board, your colleagues and with outside influences. If someone else has to present you with that strategy, then you're not doing your job properly. But the point of degree comes in by my including the very top management team in the process of developing the strategy; and, of course, the nearer the top you get the more you need to be a strategist. You need to be far-seeing to get yourself out from under the day-to-day chores of running your department, preparing the accounts, changing interest rates, programming the computer, whatever it may be. So some of what is needed in a chief executive is also needed in very senior managers in the organisation, but still the biggest step of all is to move into this office.

As one goes up the ladder one is usually motivated partly by the work, and partly by the people one works for. As a chief executive you no longer really have an individual boss as such. How do you cope with that? Is it lonely at the top?

I suppose statutorily you do have a boss in the board in general and the chairman in particular, but you don't have a boss in the formal sense. It is lonely as I've said. You have to have the sort of personality that equips you to cope with the loneliness and means that you are willing to take decisions quite regularly, without any further reference at all. I sometimes smile to myself because I get cross about the decisions that come across my desk: they're nearly all difficult. Of course, the reason is that the easy ones have already been taken!

But you mentioned a very close consultative relationship with your immediate team. You go so far with consultation, but at some point you yourself have to decide?

That's right, and inevitably very senior people in an organisation are, by definition, strong characters. For all that in an ideal world, if you talk things through, you would all come to a consensus view. It doesn't always work like that and so, sometimes, you have to take a decision which you know is going to be unpopular with some of your colleagues.

The merger between Nationwide and Anglia. How did that come about, and what part did you play? How different is it now to when it was just Nationwide?

It came about because of my thinking that in strategic terms Nationwide on its own wasn't big enough. As the barriers were broken down between one financial institution and another, it dawned on us that if we were to be a major player in the UK, competing directly with clearing banks and the rest, we needed to be larger. That meant a merger, because you can't buy a building society. In fact, immediately I became chief executive I took over the negotiations which had only just started with the Woolwich Building Society. That eventually fell through for all sorts of complicated reasons, but as quickly as possible after that I took the initiative to try to build a relationship with the Anglia. After due passage of time Nationwide and Anglia came together and the relationship has turned out to be a very successful one.

It's a different animal, not just because it's larger but more particularly because, even with the best will in the world, you are bringing two different cultures together. You have to spend a lot of time recreating an organisation, or effectively creating one from scratch. So that, perhaps, takes your eye off the ball in terms of running it as though it were an established, cost-effective, efficient organisation. Inevitably after a merger you go through a period of consolidation where you have to do quite difficult things like contain management costs and so on.

You're taking on a whole new set of employees. What do you find the most effective way of motivating staff – not just your immediate team but all the staff of the Society?

What we have used to great effect are what we call roadshows. We use them only very occasionally, partly because they are expensive, partly because they are hugely demanding on the management team, in particular the chief executive, and partly because you need to have a very important, specific message to put across. So since I've been chief executive we've had two roadshow programmes; one was attached to the launch of our current account, a very important development, and the more recent one was principally to launch our partnership programme – an internal programme to improve the quality of service that we give to our customers. The timing of the latter, immediately after the merger, was such that the roadshow provided a very useful way of reinforcing our new single culture.

In the case of the partnership roadshow, we had nineteen different events around the country. We put on a bit of a performance for any of the staff in that part of the country who wanted to come. Normally most of them came, which is a tribute to the organisation, and so you were dealing with probably five hundred staff at a time. They all arrived in this great arena and before dinner there would be a show which put the message across in an allegorical way about how we were trying to improve the customer service that we gave. That was followed by a pep talk from me and then we all had dinner. The senior members of management present moved from table to table during dinner, so that by the end of the evening one or another member of the senior management team would have been at every table and had twenty minutes with the people there to talk about their concerns and to encourage them to take the message away.

And the feedback on that sort of exercise is good?

Hugely positive – absolutely fantastic. Then inevitably the thing ended up with a disco, which 99 per cent of the staff enjoy more than anything. The roadshow is a *very* effective method of communication, and I can strongly recommend it to anybody.

Do you think leaders go on learning?

No question about it – absolutely none at all. However successful an organisation may look – and Nationwide Anglia is successful, although it still has a number of issues to address, like the cost base and so on – the chief executive himself and the organisation make mistakes along the way. I've made a number of mistakes that I hope I won't make again. They are often to do with people. It's very easy to persuade yourself that someone, who you know in your heart of hearts is not up to the job, should be encouraged, left where they are, let's see if he can't do better under good guidance and so on. I've learnt now that I need to be quicker off the mark and more decisive about dealing with people who are clearly not up to the mark. It's better for all concerned, including the individual, if you recognise that he's not up to it and should go and do something else. I suppose I've learnt the networking game. However strong a chief executive you are, even for a more autocratic chief executive than I hope I am, it is very important to network, to have a network of people around you; people who need to be influenced by you if you are to achieve what you want to achieve. They're not just within the organisation but outside: politicians, regulators, the media, stockbrokers. You need to build up a very effective network and to maintain it. It withers if you don't maintain it. I spend a lot of time making myself visible not only within the organisation but also outside it.

To what extent do you think that leadership of an organisation requires hard graft and experience either of that organisation or of a similar one? In other words, do you think that top leadership skills are transferable?

They are, certainly, and I would like to think that I could run another financial institution as effectively as I run this one. Possibly, too, there are other large organisations around that have some of the same characteristics – retail outlets like Boots, for example – that I could lead. But I do think you need experience appropriate to the chief executive slot that you're moving into. For example, Peter Birch, chief executive of the Abbey National, moved straight into that job. He didn't come up the organisation at all, but he had been chief executive of Gillette UK, so he had the experience already that equipped him for the job.

What I think would be very difficult to achieve would be for someone from a different career stream – say a barrister or surveyor or whatever – just to step into the top slot. You need to know about handling large numbers of people, the networking issue, about where the buck stops and about making decisions.

One thing we haven't mentioned at all is formal training. How important do you think that is?

> I'm a great believer in formal training for the staff of an organisation at nearly all levels. I have very substantially increased the training budget and resources within Nationwide Anglia. I've also moved it right up the organisation to as near the top as makes no difference. I've sent general managers off on top management programmes at the Cabinet Office, that kind of thing. I'm just not sure that chief executives should be formally trained in a formal sense once they have become chief executives. There is a lot of formative training in terms of informal experience and formal training that can be put in place before you become chief executive. My training people tell me about these splendid courses chief executives should go off to, to broaden their outlook and all the rest of it. I'm not convinced, partly because who the hell's looking after the shop when you're not there? So much of what you learn is from hands-on experience and from dealing with real situations.

Taking into account your own personal experiences and your views based on those experiences and your observations on the career patterns of other people, to what would you now attach the most significance?

> In personal terms, in the sense of outside influence – this may sound such a clichéd response that you may not accept it – you jolly well need a good partner and I'm blessed with such a wife who has kept me going through the whole thing. If you are struggling with a difficult family relationship you are just that much less likely to be able to cope with the stresses and strains of the top job and the process of getting there. She has been fantastic from start to finish.
>
> Another influence, in my case, was educational. I went to a public school and there is no doubt that it did something to me which made me more likely to become a chief executive. It's something to do with independence, the ability to stand on your own feet at an early age, and the whole surrounding culture of leadership – and even more clichéd – a sense of duty that you are privileged, and you bloody well ought to put some of that privilege back into the system.

Sir Leonard Peach

> **❝**I've always clung to the view that
> personnel is a major change agent:
> its job is to create the environment
> in which line managers can
> achieve whatever short-
> or long-term objectives
> they are aiming
> for.**❞**

At the start of his career, Len Peach 'devilled' briefly for Randolph Churchill. Learning how to handle such a temperamental character gave him the foundation of one of his main skills: influencing colleagues through a staff role.

Most of his working life has been spent in personnel posts in IBM. His professionalism was recognised by his peers when he was elected president of the Institute of Personnel Management. Not the least of his contributions to the personnel function has been his insistence that it operates at a strategic level, in the heart of a business.

When he was seconded to the National Health Service as personnel director, he proved so valuable that he was promoted to the chief executive position. He saw his priority as being to create a management culture.

In years to come his short period in the NHS will prove to have been of more lasting significance than his much longer stint at IBM.

Director of personnel and corporate affairs, IBM, since 1989. Sir Leonard Peach is chairman: NHS Training Authority; Skillbase Ltd. In 1962 he joined IBM and became director of personnel and corporate affairs, 1975–85. Seconded to the DHSS and became chief executive, 1986–89 NHS management board. Married with children. Educated: Queen Mary's Grammar School, Walsall; Pembroke College, Oxford. Born 1932.

Chapter

13

If I can take you back to your schooldays, you lived in the West Midlands didn't you?

> Yes, I grew up in the West Midlands. I came from a relatively poor home, I suppose. I was the eldest child in a family of five; I had a brother and three sisters. My father was a supervisor coremaker in a West Midlands foundry; it was a skilled job. We lived in Walsall.

What sort of place was Walsall at that time? Was it very much smoke-stacks and industrial grime?

> It was foundries and leather. At the end of every street there was a foundry.

What was the family attitude to education?

> It was one of pride, of great encouragement.

What do you think you learnt from school? What was the most useful thing?

In the last two years, in the sixth-form, I was quite a hard worker. During the sixth-form I moved from corporal to under-officer in the Combined Cadet Force, so I had the privilege of teaching what we called the 'Certificate A' platoon. In that capacity I got my first love for teaching of some kind. No one taught me how to do it. Essentially it was working through army pamphlets. There was no formal teaching that I'm aware of.

Did school include any formal careers work?

In the sense of career advice, no – absolutely not. I was always uncertain in my early days; my career was always looking at the next step on the ladder, never above it.

Who were you using at that stage as somebody to talk things over with?

No one. My family had very limited experience of the outside world. I didn't go outside Walsall until I was nearly 18. Horizons were very limited. There was no clarity about what I wanted to do, and very little advice. Careers advice is not good today, but it was certainly much worse then. The headmaster had faith in me so he put pressure both on me and on my parents.

You say you enjoy being busy. Is that a sort of puritan work ethic or what?

I find that difficult to answer. Every time someone has asked me to do things I've sought to do them, and that has resulted in a very substantial workload. I'm always longing to do something extra and something new.

But does that squeeze out leisure activities?

Eventually, yes. In those days it didn't because I was still a sportsman – I played soccer and cricket. When I went up to Oxford I captained the college soccer team. But as industrial life has gone on the pressure has increasingly meant less time, particularly in IBM, for domestic life. But I have a super wife who has been very supportive and the company is very good about drawing my wife in, which means she does get some satisfaction. She's not isolated.

Was it part way through Oxford that you focused on a career?

No. Again, it was all very last-minute stuff. I did nothing in the milkround. Then, after taking my degree, I was invited to help Randolph Churchill write a book on the life of Lord Derby. This was another interesting learning experience because I went to East Bergholt and worked as a member of the family from June to October 1956 – at the time of the Suez crisis. Randolph Churchill was a very good journalist and was able to use his sources, which were not so easily available to others. He was difficult to work with initially, and after the first morning I thought I wouldn't survive more than a couple of days, but in fact after two or three months he was saying, 'Won't you stay on with me?'

That experience of spending even a few months working with a tremendous character like Randolph Churchill, and the previous period at Oxford – did they teach you anything about the personalities of significant people? Did you have any tutor or professor you learnt from?

I had a very good moral tutor, Colin Morris. I think he was an important influence in terms of values as such. Talking to him, listening to him, and getting a greater religious background than I had acquired before was important. In fact I was confirmed into the Church by Colin Morris. The relationship with Randolph Churchill was one of learning how to live with someone who could be a very difficult character. He had enormous charm but he could also be extremely difficult; I had to learn how to handle him. This has stood me in good stead for the rest of my life, because many of the jobs that I've had have been staff-type jobs which have not had direct authority; you have to learn to exercise influence through other people who do have that authority. I got quite used to suggesting something on a Monday, seeing it rejected out of hand, and then it coming back as his idea on the Friday. I was very happy about this, because in the end I got my way. As you know that's not untypical of an industrial environment. So learning to work with a 'big' personality was an important experience in that very short period of time.

But by this time I had decided to try industry. The one piece of paper which I received at that time – after the milkround – related to a company called John Thompsons at Wolverhampton. John Thompsons were about to enter nuclear engineering. They were advertising for arts graduates to do ONCs and HNCs in mechanical engineering and to do engineering work. I thought, 'How interesting.' In October I joined them as a graduate trainee.

So you were beginning to earn your living for the first time. It sounds fortunate being able to get in from an arts background into an engineering company. How did that work out?

It didn't work out terribly well in the sense that the training programme was one of those 1950s' training programmes which were to be condemned. You were given a pair of overalls and asked to write a report on each department to which you were posted for two weeks. You stood around, did very little other than ask questions, and then at the end of the fortnight wrote a report. I was given a day off a week to attend the ONC mechanical engineering course at Wolverhampton College of Technology. It was becoming quite frustrating. Then, out of the blue, the training manager said, 'Would you like to go to the LSE at our expense?' 'To do what?', I said. 'They have a good diploma in personnel management and we want to build up our personnel department. You're the sort of chap who might do a good job.'

That was the first I'd really heard of personnel management. I thought it would be rather nice to go to the LSE for a year, and I was accepted. So my first contact with personnel management was not the result of a carefully discussed career progression. It was purely accident.

Off I went. It proved to be a very good year. It was very practical and down-to-earth. There were periods of training which took me to British Oxygen, Morris Motors and to Kodak, each for four weeks, so I was able to see other companies in action. It gave me a much wider background than I had acquired hitherto. All went well: I got a distinction and went back to John Thompsons. However, when I got back they said, 'Sorry, we've decided we don't want to build up the personnel department, we've just lost a million pounds on Berkeley nuclear power station and we want you to join an overheads group.' It was the traditional approach to cost cutting.

I was getting somewhat frustrated, having acquired skills I was not able to employ. Then a job came up in the West Midlands Gas Board and I became assistant education officer, responsible for management training. At that time the organisation was pretty go-ahead. The manager there was a man called Vincent Young, a good tutor and a good delegator. He gave me my head on management training. I trained West Midlands Gas Board managers and supervisors.

How did you learn about management development?

It was fairly simple teaching. I had acquired the management knowledge from the LSE course. I had acquired the teaching experience over a period of time, and I was able to modify some established programmes and learn from experience – from doing things right and doing things wrong. It was a very happy period. After I had been there about a year Vincent Young began to send me notes and advertisements with comments like, 'You should apply for this job.' Vincent took great pride in ensuring that his protégés made progress. He was great at fixing up arrangements in which you met leading personnel directors like Jack Scamp, for example, and indicating that perhaps you should pursue the acquaintance and move on to other things. After two years I was invited by Bill Breddick, my predecessor at the West Midlands Gas Board, to join him at the Solihull College of Further Education, teaching management. Then an advertisement appeared under the heading of MSL for a management training post in an unnamed company. I applied. The company turned out to be IBM. They offered me the job of assistant management development co-ordinator in London. The selection panel was headed by Parry Rogers, the newly appointed director of personnel. I was favourably impressed by the professionalism of what I saw. I liked him: he seemed to know what he was talking about. I was his protégé for a number of years thereafter.

Within a few weeks of starting with IBM in London, my boss left and I took over his job. One needs lucky breaks, although one makes the breaks oneself to some degree. I discovered that there was no succession planning in those days, which amazed me. So I formed a relationship with John Bache, director of service engineering, who was willing to experiment. Together we conducted a succession planning exercise for his division and presented it to the rest of the board. So within three months I was at board level, talking to the members, and once you have done it well with one group, hopefully all the other groups want to do it, so suddenly everything began to fit together. I was fortunate to have exposure at the highest level quite soon.

While we are on the subject of succession planning, cynics say one makes a lot of fancy plans but all kinds of things get in the way of them ever actually happening. They look good on paper and you think you've got it all buttoned up, but it never quite works out. Was that your experience?

It's true of all planning. Plans give you the opportunity to make decisions quickly against the background of a changing environment. The thought that everything is in concrete is a nonsense, and the same is true of succession plans. So you're quite right, things don't always come out as you would like them to come out. But succession planning is an important part of management, particularly of this culture in IBM, to ensure that you have capable successors. The great argument is that you make progress yourself if you have a good succession table, because you can then be moved on to other things and other people can replace you – otherwise you may become indispensable. So I'm a great believer in succession planning. I do believe it has to be done against a background of determining the requirements of any new job – that's often a flaw in the system. People are looked at against their performance in their *current* job, and the dangers are that that bears little relationship to the job for which you are considering them.

IBM always comes across to outsiders as incredibly fluid in the sense
that you move people sideways a great deal more than many organisations. You don't just concentrate on vertical promotion: you move people
from personnel to marketing, or whatever, quite easily. Is that a fair
comment?

> No, I don't think it's so. It's a very generous comment! You can move
> people in any organisation quite easily when they are relatively
> junior. For example, last year we moved twelve personnel officers
> into marketing, but they were relatively junior. Once people get
> higher in the structure it becomes much more difficult. First, they've
> got a salary base of some size and a job level of some size. Second,
> there is a degree of resentment in the receiving unit because the
> newcomer is seen to be occupying a job which they, from a
> professional point of view, felt was theirs.
>
> Over the years I've had to take great care with personnel because
> I like to bring some line management in from time to time to enrich
> the work of personnel. But it can be very much resented if the line
> management are seen to be staying for long periods and occupying
> posts which, in the minds of the personnel professionals, should be
> available to them.

But isn't it arguable that if you are developing all-round managers they
will become less and less specialist as they become more senior and,
therefore, you want to get to the stage where you could ultimately have a
total fluidity above a certain level. You could easily, for example, move
somebody from marketing into finance, because you wouldn't be looking
at their financial expertise but at their managerial abilities. You would
want to cultivate the 'learning organisation' in the sense that managers
would be constantly learning, and it would be expected that they would
learn.

> Well, classically I think that that's a very good argument: that's the
> Shell 'helicopter vision' argument, which says that if you've been
> through enough functions you can actually understand the totality
> and therefore come to balanced decisions based on looking at the
> facts and interpreting them. But it has its weaknesses. Often you are

so out of date in the function you once served in that you see it through rather old and jaundiced eyes. It's very difficult to stay up to date in any number of functions. After I had spent three years in the NHS and came back here, a lot of things had changed. So, if you're in finance for three years, then in personnel for three years, then in marketing for three years, you may begin to look at finance as it was years ago rather than as it is now. So it's a good concept, and I don't deny it, but it does have some disadvantages and it isn't easy to realise. In the civil service I saw their approach which is width but no depth. Industry as a whole breeds depth but no width. Those are the two extremes; the ideal is somewhere in between.

In your personnel career in IBM you have moved round physically – London to Greenock, Paris and so on. What was the most satisfying period of all? Was it Greenock? I've seen elsewhere that you have said you were rewarded at Greenock by being able to recruit engineers in Scotland when, nationwide, engineers were not ten-a-penny.

Yes, in terms of the job, that was one's own patch. There were a thousand people and what you did one day could be seen happening the following day. As you go up the hierarchy of management one becomes more remote. You simply don't see the effect of decisions you are making for a much longer period of time. So there was a great satisfaction in saying, 'We will recruit engineers' and being able to recruit one hundred and fifty engineers when it was thought to be impossible in that part of Scotland. It was tremendous to have the chance of changing the culture of that plant, because it had not been successful up to the beginning of 1962–3. It had a new plant manager, a Scot, a very competent man, and we formed a partnership together and, with some other functional managers, were able to change the culture.

So in the end it became – and has been reinforced by some very able management over the last fifteen years – one of the most successful manufacturing plants in the world – *very* successful, *very* good. And I hope that some of the building blocks that I put in helped in that process, but a lot of other people have contributed too. The plant manager had a sense of purpose which he communicated very clearly, and if you didn't agree with him he would say the same thing again but LOUDER. He knew what he was trying to do, and we were able to make changes. One, I'm sorry to tell you, was to make sure that those employees who didn't perform were dismissed.

The IBM system had really been prohibitive in the previous year because there had been a number of dismissals, and all of these people had been restored because of failures by the management to follow certain procedures. So management were rather poor because they simply didn't believe they could get rid of poor performers. So one of my tasks was to teach managers how to fire people successfully. In the first few months we actually dismissed about seven people. Managers began to have more confidence in themselves, not necessarily in firing people but in managing in general.

If you take those people at operating levels who may not have had managerial potential, what did you find was the best way of retaining their motivation and keeping them alert and feeling they could contribute something meaningful?

Well, we are experts at sideways movement. If people don't perform in a particular job we recognise that we have a shared liability: the employee has a liability through accepting the job; on the other hand, we appointed that person. It would be very rare for us to actually want to get rid of somebody because they had failed in a particular job. We look around to try to use the talents that that person has. So, in the situation you describe, we would almost certainly move the person into some sort of staff support job.

Does that mean you can, in a way, create a job for an individual who may be, if you like, a misfit? Don't you run the risk of inventing jobs that may not fit the organisation's needs at all?

I'm sure it has occasionally happened, by the way, but you are quite right. It's certainly easier to operate in that way when you are in a great growth mode – which IBM was in the 1960s anyway. We could create jobs quite easily. We grew from three thousand people when

I joined to twelve thousand nine years later, and we had a labour turnover in those days at 10 per cent plus. So we were recruiting a thousand to grow and a thousand to replace by the end of that period. That's a pretty big growth rate. So it was quite easy to move people sideways into jobs. But I have to say, despite my cynicism from time to time, I believe that most people want to do a good job and most are capable of doing a good job. The onus is on the individual and the employer to try and work out the area in which that person can contribute.

Also I have seen people relegated in terms of level and put into jobs where they have been superbly successful. It's the Peter Principle: they had reached their level of incompetence. But, put to the job where their talents were used, they certainly performed at a very high level. So I have great confidence in people's willingness, provided they get help and support from superior management.

How does IBM keep aware of what it can learn by looking at other companies?

Well, in two ways. First of all you have an outgoing group of people. Marketing is king in IBM. If you are serving different industries you learn from those industries. There is a tendency for marketing people to move round quite a lot anyway: they can spend three or four years with a pharmaceutical company, three or four years selling to British Aerospace and so on. Their learning is part of the process of dealing with these industries. Secondly, you also have to recognise that, in effect, I operate a small university. I'm in charge of education and training and my total budget is £39 million, which also has to cover buildings and machinery. I have to earn £10 million from customers. We do more than two hundred thousand training days a year. Every employee averages about twelve days a year; every manager has to do at least five days a year. So you have the external contact, which keeps people in touch with reality, and you also have the internal education system which is, I think, effective and efficient in the way in which it conveys knowledge. It has to be judged on that basis because it's a very expensive operation and we have to make sure we are achieving, in the minimum time, the maximum input and advance in skills and knowledge.

In 1985, I was ripe for a change. I had been doing a similar job – never the same, it's always changing here – but a similar job for ten years. I had been president of the Institute of Personnel Management and was coming to the end of that time when I was invited by Victor Paige to apply to be director of personnel of the NHS.

What was your view of the NHS before you joined it?

Oh, one of considerable admiration. I didn't see it as being a particularly welcoming institution from my experience of hospital waiting rooms. On the other hand, I had great admiration for the service.

The Management Board, of which I became a member, had been created within the DHSS but it had no thick line reporting to anybody – it was just there. But that didn't worry me because all my background concerned indirect authority. As director of personnel I think one wields very substantial power, but it is indirect. You wield it through other people or by influencing other people, and that was the position of the Management Board. I've always clung to the view that personnel is a major change agent: its job is to create the environment in which line managers can achieve whatever short- or long-term objectives they are aiming for. I built up, I hope, reasonable relationships with the regional chairmen and I strengthened the regional relationships to districts, much against the wishes of some district chairmen.

Was it possible, when you were chief executive in the NHS, to really build a team feeling among such large numbers?

It depends what you mean by 'team'. It was clearly possible to build that among the general managers. After all, there were only eight hundred and thirty of them. They were a group that had been appointed in a short period of time, and they were somewhat insecure. On the whole there was a camaraderie between general

management and the Management Board. We didn't always see eye
to eye, but there was a feeling that we were in it together. It was my
job to create a management culture, and hopefully we made some
progress. There were and are many competent people in the NHS.
The real problem was that the competence hadn't been given the
opportunity beforehand, and training was almost negligible. It
remains a major problem. The infrastructure is not strong. The
middle and junior management do not exist in the way that you and
I would like to see.

The reason I hesitate about the word 'teamwork' is because those
who work in the NHS are remarkably dedicated people, but the
dedication is a professional one. They are not well paid: they get
their satisfaction out of the job, and out of doing it in the way they
want. So the whole organisation is set up for a clash between
management and the professionals. Management wish to make best
use of existing resources, while the professionals wish to be
uninhibited and use the resources in the way they want to use them.
This occurs in industry too. You see it sometimes with computer
engineers, or with engineers in Rolls-Royce and so on, 'Don't bother
me, I'm building the best computer or engine in the world.' That's
the attitude which the professional brings – a tremendous
commitment to the profession and to his or her speciality, but not a
commitment to what the organisation needs to be effective and
efficient.

And when you are at the top of such a vast organisation as that, how do
you decide how to spend your time? What are the interventions that you
personally need to make to carry out the job best?

Of course, you need to sell the message, whatever the message might
be, and you need to carry the message out into the sticks. I must
have spent a great deal of time out there talking to people and being
talked to by people – I did up to six sessions a week. That was very
much part of my own style. You may call it 'management by walking
about', but it has always been my style to be out there talking and
explaining. I pride myself that during my time, for example, the
relationship with the nurses, which in the early days was difficult,

had begun to change; certainly the relationship with the doctors had. When I gave a radio interview after a few weeks in the job I was heralded by the *British Medical Journal* as 'The black shadow on the NHS' because I happened to say that in my view it would be rather better if most of our employees took their problems to their managers instead of talking about them to the media. This was seen as slightly threatening. It was actually meant in quite another way: if you tell us your problem, we might even be able to help you. I became the subject of attack. By the time I had finished with the NHS my 'obituary' written by the *BMJ* said, 'We are losing a friend at court.'

In taking that very big responsibility in the NHS you had a lot of experience in IBM behind you. What did you feel equipped you best to take that on, and were there any notable gaps that you discovered?

No, I didn't discover any notable gaps. I was helped by having worked by that time for twenty-four years in a very professional organisation, one which had had seventy-five years of fine-tuned management experience. IBM continues to examine itself quite regularly to see how it can improve its management. I entered into a world which was just discovering management, so I had an advantage of seventy-five years of accumulated knowledge. So the thing that gave me authority was the professionalism which I brought to the job and my experience. I was well used by the civil service, because they too were struggling to create a new form of management.

In the NHS I was able very quickly to do some of the basic work to introduce performance review and performance pay by driving it in – and I mean driving it in – to the resentment of some but with the great support of others. I had the advantage that I could appeal to their own basic instincts. You could drive in performance review on the basis that individuals need to know where they stand, what's expected of them. This appeals to the NHS mentality: the honesty and openness of the whole purpose of it appeals to their sense of values.

They weren't quite so easily persuaded into linking performance and pay because their style of management initially was very much, 'Let us sit down together with our employees and talk to them individually, but without quantifying.' Most of the opposition to what I did in the early days came from the personnel people themselves, who were all for the spirit but not for the quantification. To my mind the quantification is management itself. In the end you have to tell people how well they are doing, and the only way they understand it is by codifying it in some form – A, B, C, D, E or 1, 2, 3, 4, 5. When they see that, the messages begin to get over. If you just talk generally and vaguely the person on the other side of the table doesn't get the message.

It's interesting that some of the personnel group felt that we went too far, too fast. I don't think so. And it was only for the top ten thousand anyway – the managers. Below that level I gave personnel free rein down the line and said, 'You don't have to codify down the line. It's a very good learning experience and I agree that we just don't have the infrastructure to support it at this point in time.' So it was only the top ten thousand that got the real benefits of the performance review system in all its quantification and performance pay.

You then returned to IBM. Was it an easy transition, slotting back in?

It had changed and the vocabulary had changed, even in the short period of three and a quarter years. The vocabulary now is clearly that of a market-driven company. It's difficult to think how IBM could be more market-driven, but it genuinely believes it has to have greater contact with its customers. At the moment we are putting fifteen hundred managers through two-day courses and learning from each other how we can all be more market-driven, whether we are support or front line. Delegation is very much in the air. Having been accused of being a monolithic company for many years, there is a genuine attempt being made at all levels to force down responsibility and authority, and this is causing strains and pressures within the organisation. It's a genuine attempt. There are real changes being made in a very short period of time as the company seeks to adjust to a changed marketplace.

How do you judge how to spend your time, with so many things you could do and such a large organisation to work in? How do you make those priority judgments?

The easy answer is to say, 'I do what I like to do.' And that I'm afraid is what often happens, and some people make the wrong choice as a result of that.

It so happens that I like strategy. I have increasingly moved away from operations. I've become much more interested in total policy and total strategy. I'm certainly very much involved with the whole business strategy, so it's not pure personnel or pure education or pure corporate affairs. It's being a business man.

Increasingly, I hope, I have followed what Vincent Young and Parry Rogers did, which is to try to push out from me those things that other people can do as well if not better, and which they enjoy doing. You may have to modify jobs to suit the capabilities of the people involved but, much more importantly, you have to fit the abilities of the people involved into the jobs which are available. Some people are very good operators, and they should be in operations jobs. Some people are good strategists and they should be all-rounders so that you have your flexibility.

So, essentially, as far as possible I choose to concentrate on the strategic issues which I enjoy and can let the operators, the personnel managers get on with doing the job. I like to feel they know I'm here if they want help or advice, but otherwise I seek not to interfere too much.

Neil Shaw

❝Nobody can criticise you for having a high expectation level if they also know that your own expectation level for yourself is just as high, if not higher.❞

Before Neil Shaw's first general management appointment he had gained experience in finance, marketing, legal affairs and manufacturing. His strength lies in looking at a business in the round, which in turn helps him to set clear priorities.

Almost all of his career has been spent in one industry – sugar. His lack of staleness may well derive from the opportunity, while still in his twenties, to travel internationally on business and to understand the political and legal environment affecting the industry.

Some leaders seek a series of new challenges by moving from industry to industry. Neil Shaw, by contrast, appears to find endless stimulus in a single business, but operating on a global scale.

Chairman and chief executive, Tate & Lyle plc, since 1986. Neil Shaw is chairman of Tate & Lyle Holdings and Industries; Tunnel Refineries; vice chairman, Redpath Industries. He is director of a number of companies including: Smiths Industries; Scottish & Newcastle Breweries; United Biscuits. He is chairman of Business in the Community and a member of Council of The Prince's Business Trust and the London Enterprise Agency. He became president, Redpath Industries Ltd, 1972–80; group managing director, Tate & Lyle plc, London, 1980–86. Twice married with children. Educated: Knowlton High School; Lower Canada College. Born 1929.

Chapter

14

You are now chairman and chief executive of Tate & Lyle. What were the most important learning experiences that brought you to this position?

I went to work at age 17 as opposed to going to university, and I think that started me on a learning curve at an earlier age than some of my friends who went to university and had an enjoyable time for three or four years. So I started working at a fairly young age, but in the long run I think that has benefited me rather than hindered me. My first job was as a bank clerk in Montreal, I did very well there. I got transferred three times in eleven months. Then I was offered a better job, and I left.

What did you move on to?

To what in Canada is called 'a trust company': it settles people's estates and does a lot of income tax and corporate finance work. In my time there, and at the bank, I started taking the equivalent of a university degree through night courses at McGill and by correspondence at Queens University. I remember many hours of night school work, and I must say I don't recommend it to anybody!

I learnt, at an early age, that I had to concentrate and to use my time as best I could.

How did you progress in this second job?

I developed significantly in my second job. I worked hard and I was maturing and finding out what was going on in the financial world. I was young, but I was doing work that was probably five to ten years more advanced than my actual age. The interface which I had in my early twenties with a lot of people, some of whom were quite influential, did me an immense amount of good, because I was able to see what they were doing. I was able to say, 'Some day I can get there.' I began to understand how the whole financial sector worked. A lot of people still don't grasp it.

I'm a very straightforward, no-nonsense person. I tend to put things in their perspective quite quickly. I don't like to masticate a subject to the point of getting bored with it. I like to talk about it, make the decision and move on. I think that was maybe born from the kind of lifestyle I lived at the time. So perhaps Canada did shape me a bit.

Let's talk now about your move on to the Canada & Dominion Sugar Company, when you were 25.

My first job there was to work as an assistant to the general sales manager in Montreal. I had assumed that was the job I was hired for, but I soon found out that the chairman had decided I was going to work for him as an executive assistant. So within six months I was transferred to another town having been told I would not be transferred for two years, and having just bought a house which I could ill afford. That was probably a very significant factor in my life, because I started to appreciate that there were other places in Canada where things actually happened, and that change was going to be the order of my life in the future.

How did you progress with them?

Very well. I worked for this very hard-working and rather eccentric chairman for five years, I did a variety of special jobs, a lot of them dealing with government and with legislation dealing with the sugar industry; also with a variety of individual concerns in the community. A lot of our business was in sugar beet. We were very heavily involved in bringing a lot of immigrants into Canada, so I travelled to Europe. I was bilingual, which helped.

This hard-working and eccentric chairman – what was his style of management?

He was a bachelor, very dictatorial. He had a very strong character and had a profound influence on all the people he interfaced with. His way with people was very much that he was the boss.

Did you learn anything from him – either about how to do it or how not to do it?

I learnt a lot of how not to do it. He was a hard taskmaster, which was good, but in the final analysis he really wasn't happy with people and didn't have a lot of permanent friends. He didn't have the kind of life that appealed to me.

What was the first major development for you within Canada & Dominion Sugar?

Well, towards the end of this chairman's reign I went into the marketing side of the company. In those days you didn't have a lot of training in marketing but, if you liked people, knew financial figures and got along with them, the tendency was for the senior executives to move you into the marketing side. That was fascinating for me, because I opened up two or three new marketing areas for the company, both on the east coast and in the Midwest, and I enjoyed that. I liked doing something that was new, something that the company hadn't done before. I couldn't get any advice from anybody because it was the first time. Nobody was criticising me because they didn't know themselves. I had to do the innovating to achieve the company's marketing goals.

How long did that go on for?

> A couple of years before the controlling interest in the company had been acquired by Tate & Lyle. The dictatorial chairman retired and one of Tate & Lyle's directors came over to run the company: Joe Whitmee, a very fine man. He was succeeded by Saxon Tate. During Saxon's presidency the company started to diversify into non-sugar activities and I was made the first president of one of the companies that we acquired in 1969. That was my first general management appointment.

What is your view of the timing, experience and so on that are appropriate for someone in a general management position?

> I was probably wrongly chosen to be the general manager of an industry that I knew nothing about, which was plastics and aluminium – one of the non-sugar interests. It was a very risky appointment to have made, because I didn't have the background in those industries. Today I would advise people not to make the same appointment! Go outside and get someone knowledgeable in the plastics and aluminium industry – maybe somebody quite young, maybe a number two or number three – and put them in as the general manager of the division. But in the late 1960s people didn't know much about managing. We were doing it rather by the seat of our pants.

If you take the main managerial functions: production, marketing, finance – how many of those functions do you really need to have under your belt in order to be an effective general manager?

> If possible, it's extremely valuable to have a little bit of all of them, and quite a lot of some of them. To understand the problems and the feelings of the manufacturing vice president you have to know what it is to go in on a Saturday morning because a machine hasn't worked and people are counting on sales, and you start working on the margins that people worry about in manufacturing. I personally benefited tremendously from being exposed, in a real way, with

responsibility for the results: when somebody holds the noose above your head and says, 'You're responsible' you apply yourself and you learn very quickly. I was very fortunate in that I did get experience in manufacturing, finance and marketing.

So, when you became a general manager, the only thing you lacked was knowledge of the particular products you were dealing with. Did that prove to be a disadvantage?

In the event, it wasn't too serious. The biggest challenge that anyone has in going into a new industry is the terminology. The toughest learning curve is to know who the competitors are and the words that are used in the business. It takes a little while just to get the feel of it.

Can you look back to the time before you became president of the non-sugar business and identify your most significant learning experience?

Probably the political process, which I learnt to understand during the period I worked for the chairman. We were constantly travelling down to Ottawa or Washington to press for changes in legislation. Sugar beet was a very highly protected crop. There was a lot of politics involved because of the farmers. I became knowledgeable in the mechanics and requirements of the political system in a democratic country. Before that I didn't really understand how you could influence those kinds of things. I then became involved in a lot of trips to see influential people, up to and including the Prime Minister.

What were the main challenges and tasks once you became president?

The primary challenge was to confirm that the diversification of the company was going to be a success. We went through some very rough years making the diversifications work. We had started them in the late 1960s. I became president of Redpath Industries in 1972 and the jury was still out as to whether it was going to be successful or not. So, in addition to running the basic business – the sugar industry which I knew well and understood – I had to make sure that the non-sugar side was successful. The biggest challenge was on the people side, because now I was the boss, as opposed to division head, and I had leapfrogged a number of people. There were discussions among some of the older people as to whether Shaw was the right fellow to be running the place. So for a period of time it was getting the people side straightened out.

How did you deal with that problem?

I wasn't the kind of person who said, 'You either follow me or don't.' A lot of it was working with them and trying to gain their respect. I think you earn respect over time. You can't do it by winning the popularity contest. You do it by working hard, by making decisions regardless of the fact that people will like or dislike some of them, and over time you find that the troops start to fall in behind you – though there may be one or two who never do.

So it's doing it by example rather than by diktat?

Yes, and showing your expectation level is high. Nobody can criticise you for having a high expectation level if they also know that your own expectation level for yourself is just as high, if not higher. You work just as actively and hard to achieve your own objectives as you are asking them to do if they are to achieve theirs.

We gradually moved into a proper planning system of running the business, which helped tremendously. Of course, by this time it was the early 1970s and we were talking about significant changes in management style. We started going to a lot of the seminars of the American Management Association. The revolution was on. Competitiveness was increasing. Outside influences were starting to have a much bigger impact on my life.

How did you modernise?

Prior to my appointment as president of Redpath (which is what the Canada & Dominion Sugar Company became), Saxon Tate had started a very significant amount of management work in the company – basically an analysis of where the industry and the company were going, both in Canada and worldwide. I continued the process and expanded it so that in a fairly short space of time – three or four years – we had developed a fairly sophisticated planning system. We knew what we were trying to achieve, and it was relatively easy to report to the board on our progress.

Were you more concerned with strategy than with day-to-day management?

No, there was a strong mixture. I was very heavily involved in day-to-day management. I hadn't reached the stage – I'm not sure that I've reached it today – when I really think just in strategic terms. Maybe it was two-thirds week-to-week and month-to-month problems to one-third on the strategic scale.

Before joining the main board of Tate & Lyle, while you were still in Canada, what were the most telling experiences?

Being made the chief executive of our non-sugar activities was certainly one of them. I was faced with the challenge of trying to make one or two of the companies successful. We didn't have the product lines or the people, and the only answer was either to get out or to get in even deeper. I gained a tremendous amount of experience and knowledge about acquisitions. They were tiny by today's standards, but I learnt a lot from the process of dealing with people, of negotiating a merger, of putting the new companies together. In fact we saved our non-sugar activities by bringing in two or three more companies which had more qualified people than we did and we were able to join them together, and two and two did become five. We did become much more successful.

Moving into the United States was also very significant. We were in the sugar business in Canada. In 1976, with the support of Saxon Tate, I acquired a sugar company in New York because we thought a significant opportunity was being missed by the sugar industry in the United States, and we were right. We had a couple of tough years to get the company straight; it had already been closed down. We walked into the company and opened it up and received tremendous support from the union employees. The customers wanted someone with a good reputation in the industry and after that started we never looked back.

You spotted an opportunity and took it and it proved to be the right move. Where did the ability to make that kind of instinctive judgement come from?

I think it is experience. In my role of working for the autocratic chairman I spent a lot of time in the United States learning what was happening in the big octopus of the American market. That was one factor. Another was that I had learnt a lot about the legislation and I understood the American political system. The third point, which is important, was that customers – and I knew this from my marketing experience – really do like to have two or three very good suppliers. It was obvious to me at that time that the east coast of the United States had one excellent supplier whereas the rest of the companies had poor reputations. They were badly run and financially unstable. I took a few visits to six or seven major customers to ask them the question, 'If Tate & Lyle came into the eastern market would you buy from us?' They said, 'If you come you'll have orders right away.'

Confidence is obviously something else you have. What do you think breeds confidence?

I'm an optimist, which gets me into trouble quite often. But I'm also fairly realistic because of my training in the various sectors. Confidence is critical to success, and a lot of it stems from simply doing your homework.

Between 1972 and 1980 you were Tate & Lyle's senior man in Canada. You were made group managing director in 1980, and since 1986 you have been chairman and chief executive. Unusually, these days, you got the top slot through having worked your way up within the company.

Presumably because of expansion there was always plenty of scope for progress within the organisation, or did you ever think of moving out?

> I only had one period in my life when I really didn't think I was getting anywhere in Canada & Dominion Sugar, and that didn't go on for too long. When I was on the marketing side I worked for someone whom I felt I was just not going to get past – a very conservative, very old-fashioned type of manager. The then chief executive transferred me to England and I worked for two and a half years here as the export sales manager and became quite well known to the middle management group in the Tate & Lyle organisation.

Was that a planned development move in any sense?

> I think it was. There was a chap here who I knew in the sugar business in Canada who had become a director of Tate & Lyle, and I knew Joe Whitmee who had been sent over to be chief executive in Canada. So first they had a problem over here and second, I was considered because of my association with the chap over here and it was felt that I could probably handle the job. It was good for both sides. I became more knowledgeable about Tate & Lyle's activities and also became known to a wider group of Tate & Lyle executives.

So it was an important building brick in terms of subsequent development?

> Yes, it was.

Let's come on to 1980, when you become managing director. Was that expected?

> For me, no. I wasn't expecting anything of that kind to happen. It was a pleasant surprise being asked to come over, very much so. In Redpath Industries, which was 55 per cent owned by Tate & Lyle, the 1970s had been quite good to us. We made steady progress. Tate & Lyle on the other hand was going through a dreadful time because

the UK joined the Common Market in 1974. The cane industry was being sacrificed to a certain extent to sugar beet, a strong political issue on the Continent, and to the desire to expand it in the UK. The need for change was causing a lot of problems. Also, you have to bear in mind that Tate & Lyle was a family company, so it was much more difficult to make executive changes at a time when such changes were urgently needed. Tate & Lyle's future was in jeopardy. We were lucky to survive.

What were the immediate tasks and longer-term tasks that you were confronted with?

The immediate task was survival. Tate & Lyle could have been taken over for a very very small amount of money at that time. Maybe one reason I was considered as the person to take over was that the then chairman and managing director – Lord Jellicoe and Saxon Tate respectively – knew that I thought I could raise enough money in Canada by selling off some of our subsidiaries to give us (the Canadian subsidiary) enough money to take over Tate & Lyle.

Something was wrong, and we had to make some moves, otherwise somebody else was going to do it. I had been on the board since 1975, and I had seen these difficulties. I didn't understand them all, because I hadn't really been involved in the European side, but the need to act was obvious, otherwise we were going to drown. It was a period when management was going through a love affair with consultants, and Tate & Lyle was inundated with consultants.

When you took over did you change that in any way?

They all had to get out within one week! I felt that the issues that needed to be dealt with were simple – the answers weren't but the issues were. The answers required a lot of hard work, a lot of action, and putting in a plan that said, 'in twelve months' time we will have achieved the following things'. It was a question of survival, and a lot of it was cutting out things we were doing that were not paying off and getting back to the fundamentals of our business. I had a lot of support from the chairman.

Because of a shortage of management talent in their organisations, some chief executives recognise that they have got to their position too quickly, and they lack some essential bit of experience. Were you ready for the Group MD job, or was there anything that you could, with hindsight, have done in terms of career development?

> When you are given a very big step up, you probably always feel you could have done with some more experience. But at the same time I think that, if you believe in yourself and can reduce the basic problems of the business down to three or four well-understood problems, you will then be able either to deal with them directly or turn them over to people who do know how to deal with them directly. By identifying the issues and talking about them, explaining them and obtaining confirmation that these are indeed the issues, you gain a lot of support, because clarity about what needs to be done is the most important management attribute.

You mentioned that, when you took over as president of Redpath, there was a bit of a people problem. Did you have any managerial challenges in terms of people in Tate & Lyle?

> There were, I'm sure, people who really didn't think it was right to bring a fellow from the colonies and put him in charge. That's natural, that's human nature, and I knew who they were, I could tell very quickly. Being very clear about what you expected, setting down the plans and being fairly simple about it, getting rid of all of the extraneous material that was floating round and getting back to basics – that was the most important first thing.

What were the next set of challenges?

> It was a major job to move the company up from a very low level of profitability, based on a very large turnover. The next objective, from my point of view, was to start the company on a modest acquisition programme where we would expand very specific areas we had decided to concentrate on. I was a very strong believer in the business we were in, sugar refining. A lot of people felt there was no

future for it, which I thought was wrong and I still do think is wrong. We had a business that we knew well and were well steeped in. It was growing on a worldwide scale. There was no reason why we couldn't move out of the UK and expand, as we did. It all started to take shape. The same thing happened in the non-sugar activities. We started to put money into activities where we were gaining knowledge. We were working to a performance standard that said if you keep performing this way you start to get a better and better return. We started to have a company that had some thrust in it, some growth and dynamics that were a little better. A little more money was coming in.

Becoming chairman was another major step. What is your comment on the breakdown between strategy and policy on the one hand, and management and operations on the other, and how do you divide them?

The whole issue of whether a chairman can be a chairman and a chief executive at the same time is one which we will be talking about for many years to come, I'm sure. It's also one that I don't feel that strongly about. I do feel strongly that you must deal with situations as they exist at the time. In the case of Tate & Lyle it was right to have a chairman at a time when we had to go through a massive transition, and Lord Jellicoe masterminded that transition very well, although he didn't get involved in the business. He brought me in to do the business. But knowledge of the business was going to promote the company. The next chairman, Sir Robert Haslam, wasn't here that long but was also a very strong supporter of what we were doing and what was in progress. It was at his recommendation that I took over as chairman: I had a lot of confidence about where we were going; I was running the company; I was deciding where we were going to go. The chairman was chairman of the board of directors, but really couldn't say very much about what should happen. I'm not a strong believer in bringing in a chairman who doesn't know anything about an industry and expecting him or her to do anything other than chair the board. To have him or her make announcements about what the company is going to do is rubbish if he or she doesn't understand the business. You can announce the financial results if that's what you want, but really it's the chief executive that does it.

So in our stage of evolution I think it's right to have one person as chairman and chief executive. I'm not a great chairman, I'm much more a chief executive, but I'm gradually learning that I've got to make a few changes. Time is going to run out and it's time to start looking for a new chief executive in the next two or three years, then, maybe, I will move on as chairman for two or three years. I can be a reasonable chairman because I know the industry well, but I have to be careful I don't try to manage at the same time.

So would I be right in saying that you don't think that skills are that readily transferable at the top – jumping from one industry to another. You think that previous knowledge or experience of an industry is pretty important?

My personal belief is that, if you're going to strategise in the pharmaceutical business, or in the chemical business, or in the sugar business, you need a fundamental knowledge of that worldwide business. I don't think you can bring in a total outsider to the industry, make that person chairman, and then expect them to lead in strategising in what that business should do. You might as well bring in a consultant and say, 'Tell us what we should do.' If you want a disaster, that's the recipe for it!

I firmly believe the best way to avoid being taken over is to keep looking ahead, not backwards. Keep performing well. If you do that, you will have a group of shareholders who will support you and anybody who comes after you is going to have to pay a tremendous premium for you. Of course, at some price any company can be purchased. We don't spend very much time worrying about who is going to take us over. We have a black book and all that sort of thing but we don't spend time on it. We do spend a lot of time on whom we would like to take over on a primarily friendly basis. We've only made one hostile takeover. Generally speaking it is mainly what we do to grow our business on a global scale that makes us a low-cost producer in a highly competitive industry.

What importance do you attach to formal management training? What courses have you yourself been on?

> I've been on two or three marketing courses in the United States. I have not been on any of the business school courses, but we do use Henley, Harvard and others for our middle and senior managers, especially the ones that we think are high fliers. Of course, some of them very much like to do those kind of courses. I'm not sure that sometimes we don't let them go too easily, because some people really enjoy being a student as opposed to running the business. But in general we encourage it. We do a lot of in-house training and we use a lot of outside courses for our own group.

Can you sum up your views on what goes into the making of an effective manager?

> My ideal manager . . . I start with a person who is disciplined but likes people. He must have charge of himself, but he must also be able to be a good listener and to receive what other people are sending him. He must have sensitivity to his environment. Being a good manager is being aware of what's happening around you, both in your department and in the outside competitive world. He must not be arrogant.
>
> Obviously a good manager has to have the basic skills whatever his function, but he also has to have a love of the work that he's doing. A good manager wants to get at his work every day. He never has to cajole others to get their work done. His people are doing the job because they like to work with him.

Steve Shirley

Photo by Sandra Lousada

'Even today there are stereotypes of what people can and cannot do. All of us as managers have to attack the ongoing basis of these mind sets that say, 'This is the way the world goes, and it's never going to change.'

'Single-minded' describes Steve Shirley in a phrase. At school she had to battle with her teachers to study maths, which was not regarded as a 'feminine' subject. In her first job, under 'a beast of a boss' she learnt the discipline of achieving good standards in uncongenial work, 'To me this is one definition of "professional".' Her second post, in ICL, gave her an appetite for the commercial aspects of business.

A determination to develop her own management philosophy led her to found her own company, F International, which pioneered new work patterns especially for women. She saw the enormous scope of information technology to liberate people's creativity.

She has been repeatedly exasperated by what she sees as the insularity and lack of imagination of British managers, but with great tenacity has not only exhorted others to develop people's talents but has shown them how. She will be seen as one of the key influences on flexible patterns of working.

Founder director, FI Group plc (formerly F International Group), since 1962. Steve Shirley's career has encompassed: the Post Office Research Station, 1951–59; CDL (a subsidiary of ICL), 1959–62. She was president of the British Computer Society 1989–90. Married with children. Educated: Sir John Cass College, London. Born 1933.

Chapter

15

What ideas about a career did you have at school?

I certainly wasn't going to go into business. I was going to be the world's greatest research mathematician. My love of the new and of research in its purest sense still pervades a lot of what I choose to do rather than what I have to do. It was a hard fight at school to be allowed to study what I was interested in as distinct from what my teachers thought I could excel at. I was interested in mathematics. At the ages of 7, 8 and 9, that was what I really enjoyed. But the science subjects – except biology – were then not considered things that girls were expected to do.

So the clarity of life's route march was that I was going to be the world's leading mathematician. Then an overnight switch to computing led me into the FI Group and thus very solidly into management. The joy is that the intellectual gymnastics which are the grounding of today's teaching can be developed so that you become a mature manager spending your time growing a culture in which others can develop themselves. I do not see myself as the traditional entrepreneur: I'm not interested in making money *per se*. I'm interested in achievement and helping people to excel, and allowing myself to do those things at which I can excel.

At what point did that develop?

As the technician in me developed into the technologist – starting to see a bit wider into the markets the ways in which high technology can influence the way in which we live in society – I became blocked by the hierarchical business world in which I was working. So, in order to be able to go on working while I brought up my own family it seemed necessary to found my own business. So the FI Group was grounded in my pure personal requirements with an enabling culture responding to change which could allow people, particularly women, to develop within a flexible work style and pattern which also matched the demands of the technological marketplace. I was surrounded by technical people offering technical solutions. But I was not just meeting people's actual requirements for the way in which they lived or their need to add value to their organisations or to use high tech in any strategic way. I think, in a very amateur way at that time, I was groping towards the concept of being effective rather than just efficient.

How would you distinguish between effectiveness and efficiency?

There's quite a lot of the Teutonic in me. I admire efficiency a great deal: without it you can't start to concentrate on effectiveness. I see effective people as leaders who, with a very small, focused and dedicated effort, can make a lot of things happen. For example, this year [1989-90] I have the honour to be the president of the British Computer Society. Because of its position – it has the largest group of information systems engineers in Europe – it has enormous status as the national, indeed global, chartered organisation of the industry. From that platform I hope I can, over a short period of time, build a permanent infrastructure into the business world, because that's my world – I'm no longer a computer person. If those bridges of understanding can be made during my year I will feel that I have achieved, that I will have been effective. Even if I've not been very efficient I will have been effective. That's a sensible use of my time.

What was most formative before you started the FI Group?

> Because of my family background – I was a child refugee from fascist
> Europe – there wasn't money for me to do anything else except start
> working. I stayed on at school until I was 18, so some of the work
> environment had been pre-set. The influence of family environment
> is totally underestimated, in the same way that today many managers
> are not conscious of the impact of home events on the work
> situation. One thing about the FI Group is that it sees people as
> whole people. They are not just the secretary, the mother, the lover
> or the husband. People are whole and have skills and personality
> traits which can be developed or they can be blocked, they can be
> exploited in a positive or a negative way. Our style of networked
> organisation is very clearly one which enables the added value to
> come from training and education and the proper management and
> marketing of scarce skills.
>
> The early disciplines of excellence, quality, persistence, continual
> improvement and opportunism – all those things that make me one
> style of manager as distinct from another – those were set long before
> I left school. I started work as a backroom boffin in the Post Office
> Research Station where there were some very good disciplines of
> performing adequately at things at which I had no skills. To me this
> is one definition of 'professional'. The professional is not someone
> who gains and achieves heights in something, but, equally, the
> professional's performance never falls below a certain acceptable
> level. I learnt that in my first job. I had a beast of a boss who made
> me do things like drawing in the old style, on a drawing board. I
> haven't any talent for that. I had terrible trouble producing drawings
> for which I just didn't have the aptitude. But I learnt to actually do
> such tasks and realised that, given the tools and the training and the
> education, you could perform adequately in something for which
> you have no flair.

Did the unpleasantness of this man act as a challenge to you?

> I suppose he was an example of the sort of manager I didn't want to
> be.

239

He clearly wasn't an enabling man. Did anything redeem him?

> He had high standards. He taught me to be more assertive. It was he who taught me some judo so that, as a young girl in London, I could physically protect myself.

I assume the Post Office was not a commercial environment?

> No. It was very much the cream of the research establishment. In my activities today I still have to push back the urge to pursue, to a ridiculous level and at an unacceptable cost, the last element of perfectionism. I do this in all sorts of things. I had a battle against the special commissioners of the Inland Revenue over grants to our employee trust. The battle was about amounts of money that were significant, but I was in danger of spending more in battling that issue through, all because I feel very strongly and see issues very clearly on things like right and wrong. One has to temper that sort of drive and perfectionism with the responsibilities of heading a large organisation, because a lot of people look to me. Now, I am pleased to say, I am strongly supported by a second generation of professional managers that is jointly responsible for the organisation's future. To pursue some chimera where I think that that last 'i' needs to be dotted or 't' crossed sometimes just isn't practicable, and so I have learnt to compromise. You could talk about the iron hand in the velvet glove, and one does learn to have more finesse in business, but there's a hard kernel in me which is inviolate.

Going on from the Post Office, you had a spell with an ICL subsidiary.

> That was a very interesting time in the industry. The rate of change technically was as fast as it has ever been. I was changing from being a backroom researcher to a commercially oriented, practical person with responsibility for delivering significant parts of a major project for my employer. During that eighteen months or so I was deliriously happy with my work and my life in general. I was moving quite clearly out of the technical area and asking questions like, 'What's

the strategy behind this?', 'How does one price it?', 'What are the economics?' and 'Why are we doing this?' I was trying to break out of the typecasting of myself as a technologist and as a woman being the subservient supporter of other people's targets.

Did you have any management responsibilities with ICL?

For the first time I was responsible for heading a small team of five. What I wanted to do was consultancy and selling. With FI now a major service company, people always say I must be a marketeer. It's not true, I'm not a natural marketeer: I'm a natural sales person. I wanted to move into sales, but ICL did not then have women on the sales side. Even today there are stereotypes of what people can and cannot do. All of us as managers have to attack the ongoing basis of these mind sets that say, 'This is the way the world goes, and it's never going to change.' We're all guilty of it.

In the IT industry the rate of change is fantastic. The demands that that makes on people and the way in which we have to hone our abilities is really quite enervating. There's a continual drive to retain control over a business world which is turbulent. There is too much that one has to do right now – 'I've got to do this, I must do that.' You learn increasingly with experience to concentrate on the important things.

How do you learn that?

I learnt more during the 1970s' recession about concentrating on the important things than I had in the preceding ten years, because it is the survival instinct that actually brings out the recognition of what is important. There is no future for British industry unless we get the focus right. We have to look to what is happening in Europe – the extended Europe. Hungary and Poland are coming out of the economic cold. I'm very lucky because in the IT industry we're forced to look to the left and to the right, to America and to Japan, because that's where things are coming from. I believe it's the survival instinct in an organisation that, if you're at all sensitive to what's going on, forces you into that focus which is so important.

What kind of person were you professionally and managerially at the point when you began FI?

> I was certainly blossoming during the ICL days because I was very happy. Neither at work nor domestically do I think it's possible to divide people up into parts. I had got over the chip on my shoulder of not having gone to university. I was challenged enormously. There were no more patches of boredom as I had had in my previous employment. I was learning quite a lot and I really enjoyed every minute of my work. For the first time I was earning at a reasonable level so the pressure of, 'Have I got warm shoes to wear in the winter?' had gone away.

Do you think that not having been to university made you try harder? I'm surprised that it took you to your late twenties to get over it. Was it a driving force?

> I still am occasionally attracted to academe. One sees so much of British management which is pragmatic, craft-ridden, so stuck in the past. I expect as a manager to have a tool kit of skills, and one of the tools I miss, and will never now achieve, is that academic sharpness which a Ph. D. or its equivalent could have given me. So you make up for it by achieving in quite different ways. It is intellectually so satisfying when an academic approach can be used in a business environment: hence, of course, the importance of business schools. I expect all leaders to be studying or dipping into all the key management texts, because without them you are reinventing the wheel. From them you learn how this organisation dealt with a restructuring process, how IBM have done this and how in Japan they do that – you're taking ideas from a whole variety of sources.
>
> As the years go by the craft skills of the job become less and less because there are professionals to do it for us. What a joy that is! The emphasis on the real education issues becomes more important. The things that never go are, first, the need to lead people by persuasion and example and, second, the conceptual ideas: writing, talking, debating, modifying, enunciating – all very dynamic.

Somehow the same questions in business come up over and over again and you think it must be very easy, but the answers are different because the environment is different: questions, which at one time would have seemed quite simple, now acquire layer upon layer of complexity as you try to balance people issues, market forces, the economics, national and global issues. Even though it becomes better supported, because you've got data gathering and analysis going on, the actual decision making is still surprisingly intuitive. What you're balancing is the one hundred and eighty-seven different things that have gone into making that decision.

I like doing new things and making new things happen. In my business life my prime achievement is undoubtedly the formation of the FI Group and achieving a level of professional management. It is very easy to have an idea, but it's the implementation, taking it through the various stages of growth, of which I am most proud. There are other new things which I feel I have achieved. They are all wrapped up with the use of information technology as an enabler for other things. Around about 1979–80 I began to be conscious of how information technology could be an enabler for disabled people. Since that time, starting with some very key presentations in the House of Commons, computers are now being used not just as robotics in the factory or the hospital but as a communications aid for people who have difficulty speaking. And who are these people? I started off being interested in enabling the 'traditional' disabled, and then realised that the majority of the disabled are, of course, the elderly. It started as an idea of just communicating, and then it became a matter of taking disabled people more into the work environment.

I have also realised that information technology is the enabler for the whole of the rest of industry. It is the thing that will enable business to tackle some of the strategic issues: not just to do things more efficiently than before, but to do new things, perhaps things previously considered impossible, and in particular new things that will capture customers and suppliers and distributors in an information net. These are amazingly powerful concepts. I have spoken on British Computer Society platforms using a series of case studies showing how information technology can be used successfully to reposition organisations in their markets. The excitement of when you get the IT strategy really linked into the business strategy is very very satisfying, intellectually as well as from the bottom line. There are still too many chief executives and MPs who think of information technology from the efficiency point of view, rather than from the strategic – there's a long way to go.

You spoke with justifiable pride of what the FI Group had become and about some interesting stages in its development. What were the milestones, the turning points as you built it up?

It has changed from being the efficient producer of quality software, which we were for the best part of fifteen years, to being a market-led sales-driven organisation run by professional managers – with all that that implies. Once you become market led, you are tracking what your customers are doing. For me personally, the fact that I head an organisation that has customers means that I'm continually refreshed by the case histories of the work that we do; I am regularly looking at ways in which our customers are using information technology or considering new directions in which they might like to look in the future.

The three sectors in which we concentrate are, firstly, the financial services sector and its retail end, building societies and insurance. Then, secondly, the distribution and logistics side where we're working for companies like Tesco and organisations where they're using IT to do something completely different, including the control of their suppliers and distributors. And, thirdly, we service the public sector, which is my natural environment.

Would you describe yourself as entrepreneurial, or as someone who has adopted entrepreneurial methods in order to achieve something bigger?

Clearly I'm not a conventional entrepreneur. I'm more interested in achievement than power. A traditional hierarchical organisation has among its workforce the younger variants of entrepreneurs, and it must somehow hang on to that innovative drive so that they don't do as I did and take it outside the organisation and develop it on their own. You notice this particularly with women. The proportion of women going into business on their own is, pro rata, much higher than you would expect. It seems there are still women who feel blocked within conventional organisations and take themselves off. That is a tremendous loss to an organisation because it is the innovative people who question, who rethink, who don't just do what they did last year and do it more efficiently. They actually think, 'What are we trying to do, where are we going?' They are the ones who grope backwards to determine what has to be done. It's all to do with the timescales on which people think. Entrepreneurs believe one can pursue several goals – not necessarily conflicting goals – simultaneously; we think on a timescale that's sometimes overlong. My natural way into the market is always too early, always! Every time I've done it I'm way in front. Today networking is considered to be just starting to come in, yet I started the networking concept in 1962, and was planning it even earlier. So the timescale in which leaders operate can be quite different.

But the basic saws about what one is doing I'm sure are indeed basic. They are things like, 'If you stop learning and trying to improve yourself, if you stop getting any better, then you stop being any good at all.' The perfectionism that I had at 18, while being tempered perhaps with experience and a little ability to compromise, is still there.

As well as your involvement with the British Computer Society, you are involved with the National Council for Vocational Qualifications, the BBC Consultative Group on Business Affairs, the Open Tech, the Industrial Society and other bodies. Can you comment on some of those and how you manage all that?

There's a common theme, though perhaps it's not immediately obvious: it's of the line manager as trainer. Most of what leaders do is coach and train, and we do that *en famille* and with our peer group; the interchange of actions and experiences is one of the most valuable things that we can do for our fellow man. So, the Open Tech is an extension of seeing not work but learning as something that can be done at a distance, and again that is an enabling thing.

There is a lot of distance learning happening now. It is just one example of bridging across and acting as a catalyst. It is not a joke when I say that my corporate role is non-operational; my colleagues cringe when I say, 'Nothing happens here.' Yet somehow there is a seeding of ideas which I hope I let others implement.

There's a fair link between the NCVQ, the Open Tech and the Industrial Society?

Yes, it's all to do with people, growing them and helping them to do excellent work. It's not work that we enjoy, it's being *good* at it. When we enable other people to do good work the synergy is so strong that there's a tremendous satisfaction.

Do you think that being a woman has anything to do with your mission to help people, to provide the framework in which they are going to flourish and thrive?

To use an Industrial Society phrase, I think of myself as a gardener: it gives me tremendous satisfaction when one of my colleagues achieves wonderful things. The joy is of having younger, very energetic and much better trained people, taking others forward in a professional way. I refer again to that tool kit of skills which every manager needs to have and without which they don't have my respect; but I myself still lack some of those professional skills! British management is not as well trained as it might be. If you look at the German competition, the rigour, the better training, the more numerous business schools – the British love of the amateur is ridiculous.

What do you see going into that tool kit that every manager should have?

Obviously you would expect me to say the ability to use computers on a day-to-day basis, including their use for access to databases both inside and outside the organisation. It is nonsense to be wrong-footed by some of the things that are happening in the world.

Then think about our board meetings. The majority of our

discussion is about people, restructuring, communication, dealing with organisational interfaces, actually improving things flexibly because we, like everybody else, have built up a hierarchy that's got a bit rigid. There's a continual attack on costs and productivity but the discussion is invariably about people: management, team-working, how to select people, picking high fliers and succession planning. It's always about people, so it's the human spirit that you come back to in the end. I know few key people in industry who are not people managers.

Do you find that there is an important difference between being head of the business and being chief executive?

Oh yes. They are very clearly separate. I'm delighted to be out of the chief executive slot. You get stale after twenty-five years, and you also get very tired. The role of the non-executive director on the board is to support the person in today's hot seat. The only people who really know what it's like to be in the hot seat are other chief executives who have been there, and so I now cast myself, not only as the titular head of the organisation, but also as a very experienced manager supporting the executives in what they are doing. I know what it's like to be under pressure, balancing, juggling in order to get the bottom line response and to resolve conflicting issues.

How, over the years, did you get your team to be as people-minded as you clearly are? Is it something that you have deliberately fostered in them?

An enormous amount can be done by example. I do not believe in a management style where you point and say, 'Go thataway.' But if you say, 'I'm going this way, please come along', you can achieve a great deal. As the organisation got bigger, all sorts of myths – not necessarily helpful ones – grew up, and in about 1981–82 I decided to try and set down what I believed the company was all about. I spent eighteen months – I was doing a lot of other things as well, of course – preparing what we now call our Charter. It was to set out what we were about. It doesn't mention anything specific about making a lot of money, but it sets out our value system. It shows training and education as the things that we will rely on to develop our human capital. We say very specifically that our people are the asset of the company; although it is the buildings that are in the balance sheet, it's the people who are the asset base that we train and develop. In FI we spent over a million pounds last year on training, about a quarter of a million on what we call strategic training. That's a lot, but without that we're not going to get anywhere.

So it's a high priority. Can you comment on the kind of training you provide?

We use the work centre concept and high tech to deliver and allow people access to training on a flexible basis in very specific skills that they will need in order to do tomorrow's jobs. We also do a fantastic amount of management development. We do assertiveness training for our sales force and we have professional sales training. Our marketing people are supported by consultants. We really rely on the personnel and training managers to do the human resourcing for tomorrow, because the people will be obsolescent unless they're retrained and redirected.

Does an organisation in which the vast majority of the people who work for it are home based require different management skills?

In 1985 a survey showed that our workforce really wanted to come into offices very much more. What they wanted was flexibility and so the historic home based thing was transient. Well, we are very flexible and what they wanted, and we have since provided, are neighbourhood work centres. The new head office in Hemel Hempstead's business park is symbolic – it's quite a large office. It too will have a work centre in it where people can come in and out to train and work in teams.

Everything today happens in teams. What I do, what you do – they are important to team achievement. The FI culture actually co-ordinates things in quite a different way. I believe the emphasis we have on communication among our distributed workforce, and on working in a flatter environment in a more holistic organisation, are things that every company should develop. They are not peculiar to FI as a thrusting service organisation.

How long do you think it will be before the vision you have for British business will really take off?

December 1992, unless there have been some major changes in approach among some of the traditional companies in Britain. I think sheer competition will shake out many of the dinosaurs. It's going to happen fairly fast. If we are actually to survive, watch out, out there!

Dr Brian Smith

6The more computers come into business
the more opportunities there are for
businesses that rely on people...
Competence comes from computers.
Basic competitiveness requires that,
but the ultimate competitiveness is
when someone smiles at you...9

It was in the unlikely setting of ICI's polyester development department that Brian Smith first learnt about what he calls 'the emotion of a business' – the endless challenges of working in a team to solve problems and respond to customer needs.

Moving up through ICI, he worked closely with and learnt much from personalities as different as Robert (now Lord) Haslam and (Sir) John Harvey-Jones. He then moved to Metal Box as chairman. Here he took bold decisions and devoted considerable effort to defining strategy and to clarifying the roles of the main board and the operating businesses.

By the time he retired from Metal Box it had become CMB, a truly international business through a merger with the French company Carnaud. Brian Smith is a warm, emotional man – 'You laugh, you cry, you don't care if you are wrong at times' – with an infectious enjoyment of his work.

Chairman, BAA plc, since 1991. Brian Smith is a director of: Lister & Co. plc; Davy Corporation; Cable & Wireless; Yorkshire Chemicals; Mercury Communications; Beresford International. He joined ICI Ltd in 1954 where he held various posts and was on the main board, 1978–85. He was deputy chairman of the MB group (formerly Metal Box plc), 1985–86 and chairman 1986–89. Married with children. Educated: Sir John Deane's Grammar School, Northwich; Manchester University. Born 1928.

Chapter

16

Had you any particular career ambitions very early on?

I had a negative career ambition. My father was a bank manager and he used to say to me, 'Now listen son, whether you work and get through the exams is your business, but if you fail, I'll have you in the bank.' Plainly not the best message, but I think he was only leg-pulling really. No, I went to a fairly traditional grammar school in Northwich, Sir John Deane's. It had some excellent teachers and I attribute my becoming a chemist to T A Muir, my chemistry master. I was the sort of child who, until the age of 14, was generally about twenty-four out of thirty in the class. I've not got a great memory; I find it much easier dealing with concepts and ideas. But by the time I was in the sixth-form, I was in the top half-dozen, among the brightest ones, and that was because I was meeting people who encouraged you rather than leant on you just to learn by rote – encouraged you to try thinking. One of the problems for youngsters is knowing what they want to do. You don't know so you go where a leader takes you and that applies with a lot of life, doesn't it?

When I was in my thirties, with a young family and an exciting job, I wrote to T A Muir and said, 'Things are good and this is due to you.' I got a nice letter back from him, but two years later I got one from his wife and it was a rather different letter – it said, 'Sadly, my husband has died, but you should know what your letter meant to him.' One of the things I've noticed is it's hard to say 'thank you' at times, but I've always been pleased I did so that time.

Did you find chemistry exciting to learn?

Oh yes, it became the natural thing. It's like anything else, if you become interested and feel that you're good you start getting pleasure out of success, your own personal success; most people like to feel they are winning.

After six years at university which I enjoyed I went to ICI and joined the new fibres operation in the textile development department at Harrogate. That was in the very early days of synthetic fibres. When I joined, the first polyester plant in Europe at Wilton, was just starting up around Christmas 1954. The department had a rather dour but very perceptive Scotsman in charge. He took the view that if he just recruited textile people who had been brought up on wool, cotton and silk, they would spend their days trying to make the new fibre behave like wool, cotton and silk. But if he recruited a number of bright people of different disciplines and mixed them together, he would have people who weren't prisoners of their experience – and they would just try to make it work. It was an interesting and highly successful gamble. He was also the sort of person who if you didn't challenge him every now and again wouldn't have anything to do with you. He would throw things out to see whether you were prepared just to say, 'Yes sir' or whether you said, 'Hey, hang on, I don't think that's right; I had thought of it this way', and he would say, 'Ah, have you? That's interesting.' Then he would walk away! You knew very well that he was trying you out. He wouldn't have anyone who didn't *think* for themselves. Now that's a great environment to be in when you join a business. We had a young group of people, all of us learning and all of us creating.

I always remember when my boss gave me my first section to put together. As I was walking out the door he said, 'By the way, just choose your successor now, won't you', and I said, 'Hang on, I've not even . . .' and he said, 'Just listen to what I'm telling you.' As always, he was right. All too often people try to make themselves indispensable, whereas if you do the opposite and train your successor you can then be given the next challenge. That way your career develops.

Is management training wrongly directed towards macho management and not enough to the more sensitive skills?

I'm a negative macho person. I have a great antipathy to the godlike figure who drives the world or the business – the charisma man. Instead I believe you have to choose a nice balance between giving enough of the 'godlike' qualities for people to believe in you – people love a leader who does that, everyone's comfortable then, someone's in charge – and actually making sure people recognise where their responsibilities lie and then giving them credit for their achievements. Then you can bask in the glory a bit. But if a business looks too much like a one-man band, then it contains the seeds of disaster, no matter how good that person is. I believe that after five or six years you have to start worrying about *any* leader because in general, when running a business, if you haven't done the things that you think are important within that time, then you're lying around but if you have then, if you're not careful, you settle back into a comfortable aura thinking everything's all right. There are a number of examples where a powerful leader has done a marvellous job of creating and growing a business, and then it's slowly started to fade and in the end has collapsed. Very often because there is no alternative leader in the company either.

So I worry about the entrepreneur style. It has a flair and it does mean many good things – initiative, getting on with it and so on. The danger, at times, is that it's like a skyrocket with a marvellous train of sparks and beautiful stars but then it goes black as the stick falls back to earth. Very often what you need is for a genuine professional manager to move in who can take what's been created by the entrepreneur and run it well or even do better with it. In too many cases the entrepreneur who has built something starts to believe that because he was a genius on one thing he is a genius on everything. The stronger he is, the more he gathers people who agree with him. There are so many examples around, and that's sad when it happens.

The danger is then that it's so easy for the entrepreneur to say, 'Oh shut up, just do it my way' and of course people will do just that, right or wrong. But if you want things to be done *very* well, the art is to get the person who is going to do it to want to do it, and then let them get on with it. The whole art of management is to get someone else to tell you what you know you want them to do, so when they tell you and you can agree, then you've done everything. All you then need to do is offer them help and resources, knowing full well that you've got a common purpose and that they are going to be the vehicle whereby it is achieved.

The other way of doing things, by edict, I don't like – you have to tell them what to do every day and their great cop out is, 'Well, you told me what to do and it's wrong isn't it?' And the answer is usually, 'Yes.'

Are there some leaders that you particularly admire who perhaps are of the more modest type?

Well, you don't have to be *too* modest because if you're too laid back and modest then you've got problems – the outside world doesn't think anything is happening because it thinks you should be the man that carries the message.

I have worked with a lot of people and watched their different styles. I learnt from men like Bob Haslam. Bob's style is to listen carefully and then persuade people to do what he thinks is right. Look at his track record at British Steel and British Coal. That is quiet but highly effective management. Bob is not a guy who goes out beating big drums and waving a big flag, but he's a very powerful leader and people recognise that.

The contrast in styles is with someone like John Harvey-Jones. John is an extrovert, even flamboyant, but he believes passionately in people and in people doing it their way and not having to be told what to do. When he became our chairman at ICI a number of us believed that we had to achieve a change of culture within the company, and if you are going to become a revolutionary you have to put on a front for it, which he did.

John believed that, at that time, British industry in general had a reputation for incompetence, dullness, greyness and stupidity. He believed that if industry wanted to compete with the media and politicians, it had to get out and say what it stood for, and to do that you have to attract attention. So he quite deliberately went out to do that and speak for industry, and I do believe he had a profound effect on people's image of British industry. It was no longer filled with grey, faceless people like me. It was full of oddball characters with hair and those terrible ties he used to buy. I always remember the ICI butler coming in one day and saying, 'Chairman, I've found this perfectly horrible tie and it reminded me of you so I bought it for you' – it became a bit of a thing with us, but it was a deliberate thing. It was part of John's natural character, but he also felt it was a necessary part to achieve two things. One was anarchy within the company, so that you broke down tradition and a bureaucracy that had become sterile, and the second was to give the outside world a view that industry was not like that.

So a leader has to respond to these things. I go round a business and into the factories and talk to people about today's realities. When I go to the City, I have to put on a somewhat different style because I am the man they see as chairman and from whom they expect a positive message. When I go back to our troops and say, 'Hey, you ought to hear what I've promised out there, which you lot are going to deliver, aren't you, and for God's sake tell me if you're not, because then have I got a problem! So you tell me what the realities are and we'll talk about where we're going. Don't let me get too far away from you' and so on. People don't mind that sort of challenge, particularly when I say, 'I'll carry the can if things go wrong, because that's what I'm paid for.'

So the chairman is at the interface between the company he is leading and the outside world?

Very much, nowadays. You see it all the time as the corporate battles are fought. At the MB Group we spent six months putting a merger together and fighting off Elders. If you're going to lead in that sort of situation you had better be doing it both inside the company and outside talking to shareholders. You have to go out and persuade people why you believe you are right. People will understand all the logic but, in the end, they are only convinced by the passion and the belief you bring. I don't think people work for logic. I don't work for logic – people work because they believe in things. People don't go into an office on the basis of doing ten letters a day, but because there are challenges which they are going to enjoy overcoming. If we don't we'll have a bad business and unhappy people. So the art is to try and communicate the dreams and enthusiasms. You can't do without the logic, but that alone won't motivate people.

You learn a lot, I imagine, by going round and talking to people and listening to them and thinking up ideas?

Oh yes, yes.

Do you codify your learning in any way – do you keep a diary or do you write notes to yourself?

No, I'm not disciplined enough for that and I'd be afraid to do it because it implies a sort of analysis of a database. It doesn't work that way for me and I'm not a great believer in reading lots of management books and trying to follow what it says in chapter three. I think a lot of things are done instinctively, you can pick up techniques from other people, but the techniques are only the means to an end. You have to be quite clear about the end, and you have to have basic beliefs which you can measure against.

You have said, in another context, that directors need to stand back and not get too involved in the day-to-day business. How do you put that into practice?

It was one of the things that we did when I joined the MB Group. I think, putting it at its simplest, I distinguish totally between (a) where a company is going and (b) running its operations as they are today. Of course, one depends on the other. You can't indulge in imaginative visions of the future if the business is an absolute bloody mess, but if you have got a business that's in fair shape then the worst thing to do is to keep grovelling round its entrails. If you are in a boat off The Lizard in a Force 10 gale and it's filling with water and everyone's bailing like hell and someone says, 'Are we aiming for Barbados or Rio?' You say, 'Shut up and just bail!' But later, when the boat's getting under control and the storm is dying down, you have to start saying to someone, 'Just go look at the chart and we'll set a course now.'

When you're getting out of trauma, then it's hands-on – everybody's involved and the chairman is digging in deep with the rest of them. But all too often when you've survived trauma, and most of British industry has, it's such a relief that you stop. But once you've got a business into shape then what you should do is to hand it back to the management and start to concentrate the effort of the top team of the company on its future direction. No one else can do that job but the board. People in the operations can't tell the company where to go because they're each running a piece. The big danger is that the people on the board, who have all come up through the operations, find it far easier to spend all their life going down talking to the guys running today's business, giving them gratuitous advice, like giving your grandchildren chocolate.

Now what did we do in the MB Group? The first thing we did was to take a big head office, with six hundred and thirty people, and disband it. And we said to all the people who were running businesses in the head office, 'Out.' And they said, 'Where shall we go?' And we said, 'We don't care where you go – just give us your telephone number when you get there', and they all went off and we pulled it down to about eighty people.

Now there were another fifty to sixty people who were doing central tasks like running the pension fund, or central purchasing, and I wouldn't have them in head office either because I didn't think they were head office – they provide a service to the operations. The danger was that, if they were all in head office, all the operations would do was to moan about overheads, so I put them all out and said, 'You're paying for them. You can either use them or not – it's nowt to do with me.'

Once we got the businesses out and shaped up, we then got each of them to put their budget together and went through with them what they believed they were going to achieve. I wouldn't change any of the budgets. I said, 'No, if that's what you said you will achieve I just want to understand it. *You* go away and do it. I don't want any excuses about not doing it, because *I* haven't changed it. I haven't told you I want £5 million more here or £2 there – now *you* go out and do it.' And they said, 'Oh!' because the usual thing had been for head office to ask for more and then make a provision against failure and everyone knew there was a backstop so they did not feel committed. I don't like that.

Then we said to them, 'Okay, now we know where you are, where are you all going? You've each got your own business, your own resources, your own markets, so during this summer you can come and tell us where you are going.' We then had a whole series of strategy reviews, and asked them to be ambitious. At the end of those reviews – Christmas time it was – we got them all together and said, 'We've added up the sum total of your ambitions and it actually equates to the sum total of our resources. It's also the dullest, most unambitious thing we have ever seen. It doesn't seem to take the company anywhere, so if that's all we can do with this business, we will strip you all of all the cash we can and go and do something else with it.' That acted as a motivator.

It sounds to me a slight understatement . . . !

Well, you have to recognise that for five years those guys had been shutting down and cutting back. The company had gone from thirty-five thousand employees in the UK to fifteen thousand. When you ask people with that background to have ambitions, the whole psychology is the other way up. It's bound to be. So we went round the circle again and we finished up with ambitions that needed two or three times our resources. Now we were talking! Now we could (a) select where the strengths are and (b) we could go looking for resources. So we did that. Now we'd got each of our businesses with a clear pattern of where it was trying to get to – and we didn't tell them, they came and told us. We would argue with them and we might sometimes say, 'We're not happy with that. Go away and have another think and come back in a month's time.' But then we had a commonality that we wrote down. We had the meeting, we had a very simple summary which we agreed, and that was the covenant between us and each of the operators.

They then had the task of achieving the day-to-day operating budget and also the task of starting to look for and creating change for the future. That took us a year. Then we said, 'Now we've got all those individual ambitions flying, where is the company going, because the company is the sum of those parts and what are we adding on top of that?'

So we then started to look at where *we* were going. Europe was the obvious place where we had to fill a hole: we had the UK, Italy and Greece but not Germany, France or Spain. We bought a company in Spain; we were negotiating for one in France, but every time we went round the circle it was obvious that putting ourselves together with Carnaud, the leading French packaging company, filled the gap beautifully because they were in France, Spain, Germany and a piece of Italy. So I rang up the head of Carnaud: we knew them well – they had been our licensees for twenty-five years.

And his reaction was – 'About time!'

Yes. He said, 'We've been thinking the same way' . . . so two weeks later I went over and saw the main shareholder and the company director-general and I said we believe if we can put the businesses together it will be the greatest thing since sliced bread. They thought the same and we said, 'We think we've got a way of doing it; if you are prepared to give up your sovereignty and we will do the same, we'll do a marriage where we share responsibility. Are you prepared to do that?' They said, 'Yes.' There followed a period of intense but secret activity leading up to the public announcement on 25 October 1988. The night before we signed the deal we had our senior managers here waiting to hear the details of the agreement. They wanted it to happen because they had all done their own strategy thinking and knew what they needed. So, instead of having a group of managers feeling worried, nervous, uncertain – they were walking around saying, 'Hey, that's *our* dream isn't it? To be part of a truly pan-European, world-scale, packaging company operating across the world.' Now they're all away enjoying themselves, learning French like crazy. That was what we built.

I took a five-year job at the MB Group, and I said, 'That's it, I'll start at 57 and finish at 62.' And I was asked what was my ambition for the business. And I said, very simply, 'I would like to have the business knowing exactly where it's going and not give a damn that I have left', and if I have done that, that's good.

The great advantage of someone coming from outside is that you start without any preconceived ideas, but you have to work on a few simple principles about responsibility and take risks because you don't know anybody; you don't know who are the optimists and the pessimists or the fools or the geniuses. So all you can do is give people responsibility and watch their performance and you watch some expand and sparkle and others who are not able to do that. Then you have to make the changes.

Do you do that by allocating out around the boardroom table who you are going to look at between all of you – or is it more random than that?

Well, at the MB Group we had a small group at the centre responsible for the direction of the company. This group was detached from operations so that they were impartial. Each of them had a sort of grandfather role; so the first call for one of the businesses if they had a problem or wanted money was to talk with the grandfather, who could polish it up so they didn't come in looking too amateurish. We had two other executive directors who, for pragmatic business reasons, continued to run operations directly and hence were not part of the head office group.

Does that device get over the difficulty of directors being too close to the businesses? Is it a happy compromise?

Yes, but it's uncomfortable for the directors. When I introduced it I believe that most of the directors felt that I was doing it to take away their power so that they could be got rid of – because if they didn't run operations what were they going to do? And I said, 'You're going to be amazed how difficult your new job is' – and they were, because it's easy to go and run an operation, but it's hard to build the concepts on which the successful future of a business depends and then make them happen.

It's a tremendous watershed, isn't it, between being an operational manager, however senior, on the one hand, and being a main board director on the other? You are moving into a totally different league. Do people realise the difference?

No. The trouble is you put the best manager on the board and then suddenly you ask them to change or, even worse, you don't ask them to change. An awful lot of boards consist of a group of operating managers and the boss. The trouble is that every operating manager shouts his own corner – he knows damn all about the others so he's got no opinion on them – and the boss adjudicates. That's fine if the boss knows it all and can adjudicate, but it's a one-man band again. The advantage the other way round – and we found this in ICI – is that when you are divorced from the operations you became more dispassionate about them. At ICI we found we were no longer defending building another enormous cracker at Wilton – we were really looking at whether we should put any more money into that type of project and amazingly, after a while, people said, 'Let's talk about it more.' We weren't defending or attacking in a group; we were having a total view overall.

Is there any way of preparing a manager, who is clearly brilliant as a manager, for this completely different role as a main board director?

I remember one of our senior guys coming in to have a strategy review and saying to him – because we were all very busy – 'I seem to have caused you an awful lot of work, and I'm sorry for that.' He said, 'All you've done is made us think for the first time what we're trying to achieve rather than just managing today.' All too often a business just manages today. If you challenge the people at the top of a business as to what they are trying to achieve or where they are trying to go, then the thinking starts, and you can stimulate that challenge deep into the organisation.

I divided the MB Group into five and within a year we divided one of them into two and then one of those divided itself into another four. When I went up to one of the factories in Scotland they told me they were dividing themselves into three within one factory, because they believed they'd got three distinguishable businesses within it. What they like to have is the salesman and the production man and the technical man in a little group, a project group, which starts to worry about the future of its own unique business. Are we getting it right with the customers? Who are the competitors? All the questions that the outside world demands and which you never get if you're at a big head office.

Big head offices love talking to themselves in an incestuous way, like an ant hill. They are so busy having internal meetings that the reality of the outside world can be ignored. We believed in delegating responsibility down the company and making each unit as small and outward looking as possible. I went to one of our factories, talked to the girl who did the order handling on the computer screen, and *she* went out to see customers, not to sell anything but to talk with their purchasing people to make damn sure that what we were delivering was on time, what they wanted, and if there was a problem she knew about it. Now that was her job. Three or four years ago she would never have gone near people like that. It would have all come in over the top when there was a problem. I said to her, 'Well, what sort of first time delivery do you give?' She said, 'Every time, because I know exactly what they want rather than what the order says.'

The more computers come into business the more opportunities there are for businesses that rely on people. You have to have the quality, the logic, the systems, the stock control, the MRPs. Our factories were full of the latest techniques, but I went round and said, 'What are you doing to make this a good business? What are you doing with the people; what are you doing to enthuse them, train them, motivate them, run with them, have fun with them? Have you said "thank you" to somebody today?' All sorts of things like that – they're the things that turn a business from being competent to being excellent. Competence comes from computers. Basic competitiveness requires that, but the ultimate competitiveness is when someone smiles at you, whether it's the guy at the airport or the woman who's doing order handling.

And when you spot somebody who you feel has got the message – how do you pick this up and do something with it?

I went to Anheuser-Busch, the big brewers in the States, with whom the Group has a good relationship. I went to one of their factories outside St Louis and was welcomed like a bosom friend by the works manager, who had been there a year. The factory had been up to its eyebrows in problems with another manufacturer's equipment which they couldn't fix so, in desperation, they asked if we could help, and we sent one of our supervisors out from our factory at Shipley. He spent three days there, identified the fault and cured it. As you can imagine, they were impressed and grateful. So when I came back I sent our supervisor a crate of wine and said, 'Thank you' and I got two messages back – one was that the guy was delighted, and the other was the management saying, 'You caused us a rare problem, because others who have done special things said, "What about us?"' I said, 'Well, you had better think – you've got the problem, not me. You should do it as well.'

It has to be spontaneous, but the word gets around?

The word gets around, and it doesn't need to be fair. It's funny, when we went round the business talking about this sort of thing you found all sorts of ideas crawling out of the woodwork. They said, 'Well, of course, if one of our guys did rather well we would take him and his wife out for dinner – but we never dared let on in case head office said, "You can't spend the company's money on that."' Times have changed. I was talking to the guy who runs the unit in Southport, he took his team off to the Lake District for a weekend, the guys, their wives, their kids, the lot. The guys worked all Saturday while the wives and kids enjoyed themselves. Saturday night they had a dinner and the following day it was all the families together. Now that is how it should be if you're going to have a little team that will do things for each other. Success in business depends more and more on having people who will cover for each other, do things for each other and not live in organisational cages.

We did other things. We had a system whereby each of us had five key tasks. I don't like to think of it as management by objectives, because that tends to be a numerate thing and the tasks were to do with creating change in the company, so the basic logistics of the business were not usually in our key tasks. To do this, I wrote down key tasks for each member of the board and they did the same thing independently, then we put them together to see if they were the same. If they were, good – and if not, you had better talk about it. It was against the judgement of success with those tasks that the money generated by our bonus scheme was allocated to individuals. If one person got more than the average, somebody else must have got less! We started with the board and senior managers as an experiment. Before we had actually completed a year, they insisted that we spread it to all nine hundred management staff, including the new people coming into the company. That meant that young people coming in got specific tasks to achieve and could rapidly see their unique contribution to the business.

So it is then fair to measure?

Yes, remembering the tasks are agreed and progress is reviewed. I stated one of my tasks for the first year was to improve the commitment and morale of the people in the company. I wrote that in April, and when I came back from holidays in September I realised I had actually done nothing about it. So I immediately did what any good chairman does. I went to see Mike Kirkman, the personnel man, and said, 'I've got a key task and you're going to help me do it.' Between us we then came up with a plan to make things happen which involved my visiting the factories and talking about our 'Climate of Change' programme. The technique of defining key change tasks is a surprisingly powerful weapon. It separates the guy who talks from the guy who achieves and it's amazing how clearly it does that. The board as a whole recognised and agreed the individual key tasks and the outside directors then used them to determine each director's performance. It's a very powerful weapon – surprisingly so. It was done in the first place to change a culture and it certainly makes people recognise the things for which they are uniquely responsible.

How far do you find the job of being chairman of a sizable company a lonely one? You have talked a lot about teamwork. In the last analysis is it lonely or do you always feel that you are part of a team of people moving in the right direction?

It's only lonely if you become isolated. You should go out and get people to tell you the realities of the business. Challenge issues that drop on your desk – and sometimes quite big ones. Take the ultimate decision – do we or don't we do it. If you cop out of that the whole place will find out and judge you accordingly. Now if you take that aside – that in the end there is a 'buck stops here' responsibility which you mustn't avoid – then the rest of the role is building a happy, challenging and dynamic team.

The job can be tiring and it can be stressful. If a problem is caused by an outside world event or something that's either totally unforeseen or out of my control, I recognise it as a challenge and start reacting to it. If it's something I should have foreseen, I can get very upset with myself. It's a measure of failure if you haven't set up a business in the best possible position to win. When you know you didn't read something carefully enough or didn't think hard enough at the time, there are no excuses. It's no good saying you were tired, when the truth is that you were lazy.

I suspect people can become lonely because they're afraid to let people see their emotions. If people realise you laugh, you cry and you don't care if you are wrong at times, then you don't need to be lonely. You're only lonely if you get in a birdcage and keep the world away. If you don't want your judgements to be questioned or analysed or argued about, you will get lonely very quickly because people will be afraid to tell you. You've got to encourage the guy to come and say, 'Hey boss, it ain't right'– and he's the hero, not the fool. He's the man you want around.

Don't shoot the messenger!

Yes, don't shoot the messenger: welcome him in. And if you do that you will have a business that will tell you the problems early on and then you have the best possible chance to do something about them before they become a crisis. The great thing about the MB Group when I left was the shape it was in and the quality of the people who created that shape. When I first joined, the great feature of the board report every month was the number of loss-making factories. There weren't any when I left and we hadn't shut any of them. I hadn't told people what to do but had given people tasks to get each of the operations clean, hard and tight and then had to be quite clear where we were taking it.

I guess we were lucky but you don't get lucky unless you start to make things happen. If you sit there moaning that life's difficult you will be unlucky for the rest of your life. You may not get lucky even when you do try but at least you give yourself a chance. I talk to kids sometimes and say, 'If you stand on the touchline shouting the odds and not joining the game, don't ever moan if you don't get lucky because life will not care about you. But if you do join in it's amazing to see what happens.' I think the whole essence of education and training is getting the kids to join in – and enjoy it.

Sir Peter Thompson

❛Management is a relatively easy job in
an environment of employee willingness
to change, so how do you create an
environment of willingness to change?
You try to make sure everybody believes
it is their company, and that they have
an input to decisions being taken
both globally and locally.❜

As a graduate trainee Peter Thompson soon found his metier in transport
management, with its constant decisions and visible results. It proved a fine
learning pad for broader management, and a spell with nationalised British Steel
gave him a thirst for industrial democracy.

He attacked his first general management challenge, in British Road Services,
with gusto and transformed the company from an 'ugly duckling' to a highly
successful business. As part of the change, he introduced meaningful
consultation into a traditionally 'macho' industry.

Sir Peter is in his element as a managing director rather than as a chairman.
He possesses a rare ability to formulate a vision of what a company can become,
and to lead its employees to that goal.

---

*Life president, NFC plc, since 1991. Sir Peter Thompson is chairman: Community
Hospitals plc; Child Base; FI Group plc. He is a director of: Pilkington plc; Smiths
Industries plc; Meyer International. He is a member of the National Training Task
Force and member of council, The Industrial Society. In 1975 he joined National
Freight Corporation as executive vice chairman and became executive chairman,
1984–90. Twice married with children. Educated: Royal Drapers School; Bradford
Grammar School; Leeds University. Born 1928.*

Chapter

17

Could I just ask firstly about how you decided to go into industry. You were brought up in Yorkshire and lived much of your time in Bradford, had that much to do with it?

> My first instinct was to be a teacher, but during my year of teaching practice at university I realised that it really wasn't my bent. The problem was that I hadn't got the patience. The satisfactions of teaching are fairly long-term. You don't get a kick every day from instant decisions you have taken or things that you have done. So, half-way through my university career I changed over from reading history to economics. I decided that if I wasn't going to be a good teacher the next most sensible thing to do was to go into industry, and economics, I thought, was a more relevant discipline.

What was industry's image like at that time?

> It was shortly after the war and the image among the basic industries was one of massive change. Nationalisation was all the rage. There was hope about that the problems of industrial strife which had existed in the 1930s were going to be resolved by the motivational

forces of public ownership. But there was not a lot of glamour to making a career in industry; it was seen as dark and satanic, particularly in the heavy industries. However my interests were not really at the heavy end, they were more in consumer products. The nation had had all the shortages of the war and clearly there was tremendous pent-up consumer demand. I said to myself, 'There's a growth scene ahead for consumables and it's going to take us a very long time to get rid of the shortages' – remember in 1945 there was still rationing. So I judged that in the consumer world the prospects were enormous.

Did you get any advice, either at school or at university, about whether industry would be a sensible career?

No, I didn't. There was a careers office, but it did not have particularly enterprising staff. A few companies visited the university to interview graduates in an early form of the 'milkround', but I think in the main you were left to find your way into your career as best you could.

How did you come to choose Unilever, or how did they come to choose you?

Well, if you wanted to go into consumer goods there were two companies that were quite outstanding at the time, particularly in regard to the training they were prepared to give. Firstly, there was Thomas Hedley which became Procter and Gamble, if you particularly wanted to go into marketing and selling. Secondly, there was Unilever with their central general management development scheme. I applied to Unilever because I wanted to go into general management, but feeling that I had precious little chance. The best I could offer was an upper second degree in economics from a red-brick university which was not backed up with much achievement outside. For example, I did not have a very distinguished army career.

Did they in those days have a sort of Cook's Tour? Did you go around all the parts of the group and spend a little time in each?

Yes. The training system, by today's standards was a bad one. It was all about rubber-necking for two years. I had been in the army for three years where in the main I'd been trained rather than done much fighting; I then had four years in university in which I'd been educated academically without really doing anything very much; then, on top of that, I had two years in Unilever where you just sat looking over people's shoulders. The frustration was enormous. I used to break out occasionally and try and do things and get myself into trouble for doing them. But it was essentially a scheme of rubber-necking. I was allocated to the shipping and transport side of Unilever. Part of the time we spent with outside companies who were providers of transport like British Rail, the Mersey Docks and Harbour Board and the Port of London Authority. In that respect the breadth of experience was very wide.

Was it then that your love of transport really began?

Yes. I had originally started with the intention of going into the marketing side of Walls Ice Cream and, rather unusually, was fired on the first day. I went to them as the first trainee recruited by the centre and was actually imposed on a subsidiary which had previously recruited its own trainees. Anyway, the chairman rejected me on my first day at work. So then I had to go back to the centre where I was offered a traineeship in transport. Since then I've never really wanted to do anything else. It is the instantaneous nature of transport I think that appeals to me.

Where were you based as a transport trainee?

I was based in London, but I travelled all over the country. I stayed in digs and hostels and so on – never in one place for more than perhaps a month – so for the next two years I was literally living out of a suitcase.

Were you fulfilling a series of troubleshooting roles, or were you in a fixed job for a period?

No. As a trainee you were really just observing. I spent six weeks going around the depots just seeing how they worked and learning about documentation and administration. It wasn't about troubleshooting. Occasionally the more perceptive manager would say, 'Look I've got this problem, would you go and try and sort it out.' It would usually be a fairly micro problem. The whole emphasis of the training programme was upon being a recipient of experience from other people.

When was your first opportunity to get into a management role?

After the two years of rubber-necking I went to a major soap works in the North West, a company called Joseph Crosfield. One year I was the assistant transport manager and the next year the assistant manager of the warehouses. That was really the first opportunity that I had to practise any kind of management. Unilever used Crosfield's for graduates' first management experience because it had a very good cadre of foremen and managers who took a pride in training people and bringing them along. I felt it was probably a bit like the army, where the second lieutenant is nominally in charge of the platoon but it is really the sergeant-major who commands the men. It was a bit like that. However, I was given meaningful projects to do. It was a sensible phasing into the process of learning the art of management. There was nothing formal about the learning there – there was no requirement to take exams, although I did in fact take the Institute of Transport exam. It was learning on-the-job, particularly how the foreman handled lateral problems and how the manager tried to sort out the longer-term problems.

And who would you talk over your problems with if there was something bothering you at work? Would you talk it over with your immediate boss or with one of the foremen or somebody at home or what?

It depended on the nature of the problem. If it was a straight business problem then I could go to one of two bosses. They were both very receptive, they took a lot of interest in me and were willing to talk if I had problems.

Another good thing about the Unilever system is that there were about ten management trainees scattered about the huge soap works – guys in the same position as I – trainees in their first jobs. So we had a kind of little club there: a number of us lodged together and we went out in the evenings together. There was somebody to share a problem with. In a sense it was like an extension of university.

And you later became transport manager at Birds Eye?

That was the next move. It was an important move for me to make because, in a sense, Crosfield's had been rather cloistered. It was still formal management training. We could influence what was happening a little but in reality we all knew that it was the permanent managers and foremen who really made things happen.

Birds Eye was a small company. Unilever had bought the rights to the food plate freezing process from a man called Clarence Birdseye. It was in its infancy, but clearly had a huge future. I was there for about nine years, and during that time Birds Eye doubled its turnover every year. It was a company full of aggression. We had a good product. 'What's opposition?' 'What's competition?' We had 75 per cent of the market. We were increasing our market share, and the size of the market was exploding so it was a period where much authority was devolved upon the individual – a relatively young individual – simply because it was expanding so fast. We weren't in a situation of filling dead men's shoes, or people being protective of their own patches. It was a very exciting time and I was given a lot of authority over an expanding section of the business. Without the logistics support, growth in sales and growth in production could not have taken place. It was a very good time.

You would have been learning a great deal about transport then, but were you also learning about marketing, production and other aspects of the business?

Yes. In the transport warehousing and logistics area you sit alongside people who are concerned about production: so we had constant meetings with the production people about transporting peas from the field to the factory, the raw materials that had to come into the factory from the UK or shipped from overseas. But you also sat alongside the marketing and sales guys for whom the actual physical distribution was a very strong part of their marketing weaponry: in the shops in those days the frozen food cabinets were tiny and whoever got there first filled the damn things up! So marketing was about the quality of the physical delivery as well as all the other things, like sales promotion.

At the time I was absorbing the customer-led marketing philosophy. We had a great marketeer as chairman, a man called James Parrot, a great leader. He inculcated into all of us that our only reason for being there was to serve the customer. Here was where I learnt how a market-led company worked.

Did you, at that stage, record what you were learning? Are you in the habit of keeping a diary for your own learning?

I've never gone through that discipline. I sometimes wish I had. But I've been blessed with a very good memory so I've never felt the necessity of writing a lot of things down.

You moved on after quite a stint with Unilever. GKN was your next port of call.

Yes. I moved out of Unilever simply because, at the end of the day, I'd got a wife and three kids who needed feeding and a mean boss – in terms of salary. So, for the last time in my life, I actually scoured the situations vacant column and looked for a job. GKN were just setting up a new central transport and shipping department and I came in underneath the chief buyer to give professional input on transport systems.

In that middle period of your career you worked for GKN, for British Steel and for the Rank Organisation. Can you draw some parallels or some contrasts between the styles of those businesses?

I joined GKN at the wrong time. The board hadn't really made up its mind whether it wanted to have a centrally controlled business, or whether it wanted to have a series of devolved businesses which it allowed to flourish, each in its own marketplace. Half of the board felt that it was sensible to have fairly centralised control, the other half that it should all be devolved. The half that said 'centralise' really saw, for example, that there were enormous economies to be made on the transport side by putting together the distribution activities of the nuts and bolts division with the screws and fasteners division. They were going out of factories which were very close to each other into the same kind of outlets. To do this, somebody had to make a central policy decision. In fact, within six months of my being there, the battle had been won by the decentralisers. We were trying to put together a common distribution system for all the GKN companies, but the parts were saying, 'We don't want to join' and their right not to join was upheld. So I finished up acting as a transport consultant for the individual companies. There was no possibility of getting a grand logistical system accepted for the Group. I spent my last year to eighteen months looking at particular factories and seeing how you could improve their logistics performance. This didn't satisfy me because I'm not by nature a consultant: I'd sooner *do* things than advise on *how* to do things. So that was GKN – an interesting mistake!

The Rank Organisation was a fiefdom: it was John Davis – what a man! It was management by minutiae, by diktat. He had about five secretaries to whom he would dictate about everything to everybody. He had a ruthless management style: if you didn't perform you were out. If you captured his attention with something you wanted doing, it would happen. A totally different management style to anything I had experienced in Unilever or GKN. He came in for a lot of stick at the end of his career, but in reality he did do a good job for the Rank shareholders. He did have the vision to recognise Xerox after it had been turned down by some five or six major groups.

I was paid a lot of money to go to Rank – that was their style – but the scope of the problems in my world of transport wasn't there. I didn't like the management style much. I didn't feel that I was learning much or increasing the sum of my knowledge. All I was doing was taking what I'd already got and applying it in a different situation.

I know that when you went to British Steel you were frustrated there too, because the managers weren't prepared to give you enough authority to get on with the job. It wasn't a question of grading that was worrying you – it was a question of being allowed enough scope. Is that right?

I think there were a number of things about British Steel that bothered me. Firstly, I still believed that nationalisation could conceptually work: that it should be possible to run a people-focused, efficient business when you are all working in common for the good of the nation. This sounds naive stuff, but I believed that was possible and desirable and British Steel was being put together to do just that when I was asked to join them.

It was a huge managerial problem. There was massive scope for improvement in the movement of raw materials – they were spending £250 million a year (this was back in 1960) just moving things around. So it was a huge managerial challenge, and one which I felt was also a huge conceptual challenge. If we could all get it right, we could make a nationalised industry work: if the workforce and the management were in harmony and all working to the same goals we could achieve great improvement from rationalisation and applying technology.

I suppose I expected a different style of management to that which I had experienced in the private sector, yet it didn't work that way. There didn't seem to be any concept that the company should be managed in a different way to a private sector company. There didn't seem to be any vision of 'trying to create something which is different'.

So, there was huge job satisfaction in the sense of the scope and responsibilities – shipping fleets, fleets of lorries, railway wagons, port developments – tremendous learning and intellectual challenge, but not much vision. We then went through three reorganisations in the space of five years. No business can or should stand reorganisation at that pace. Each reorganisation seemed to be taking away from the individual the right to show any enterprise or to have any authority. In transport and shipping we wanted to do a good job, and in many ways we saved British Steel a lot of money, but there was a reluctance to give you the authority to do the job. If the business at the top hasn't the imagination to understand that running a worldwide shipping fleet is actually different and requires different authority from running a steelworks in Scunthorpe, you know there is something wrong. That, coupled with three reorganisations in the space of five years and the missed opportunity for a breakthrough in human relations which should have been possible within the umbrella of government ownership, didn't happen. New initiatives were not going on at the workplace. What was going on was at board level in discussions with the powerful unions. The directors seemed to think the important action was at this level when the action for improved human relations should have been down in the works. So I became disillusioned with British Steel – sadly, because as a student I was a socialist, and I still felt there must be a better way of running businesses than the capitalist system.

So the move to BRS (as it then was) was quite a natural one. It was an opportunity to get hold of something and really do things with it?

Yes, it was two things really. It was the opportunity to actually run a business. Although in part I had had executive responsibility, I was really providing a service to the guys who were actually running the business. Here was a chance to try and put some of my thoughts about what motivates people and how to run a business into practice. I was the boss of a very significant business, although it was a division of NFC. The organisation had twelve or thirteen thousand people in it and was spread all over the UK in some one hundred and fifty locations. It was also in the public sector and I still had a feeling that somehow we could make the public sector work.

What was morale like when you went into BRS?

I followed a very good tough MD at BRS, who was an accountant and who recognised that there was a need to reduce the cost base.

He did that job; a job I wouldn't have relished. He brought to the business the guts to tackle overmanning. So I took up from there. He had given the BRS management the will to become profitable. That's what I found in BRS. It was fortunate for me that what was now needed was something I was interested in, growth and development.

When you started at BRS, did you sit down and think to yourself, 'Am I adequately prepared for this tremendously wide-ranging job, with thousands of people to be in charge of?' Did you mull over a plan of campaign or did you take the job as it came along?

The uppermost emotion was one of fear. Remember, I had never actually run anything. I had been an improver and a service provider, but I had never actually run anything. So, my first stance to the guys who were running the business was to say, 'Look, I've come in from outside. I don't know anything much about BRS. I don't really know what it's capable of. I don't know what its people are like, what its strengths are, what its weaknesses are. I'm going to spend the best part of six months just walking round the patch. I'll run the board meetings, but I want you guys just to continue as you are.' I hadn't inherited a disaster scene. They weren't making good profits, but they weren't making losses either. I set myself the task of visiting every location during that four to five months, meeting every one of the depot managers, spending a lot of time talking to drivers and fitters and trying to get the feel of what were the strengths of the business, where they themselves wanted to go and what their problems were. The frightening thing was that many of them had problems which had proved intractable. As you walked round and talked to them, they would lay them on your plate and say, 'Come on Guv, you're coming in from outside, what are we going to do about this?' My reaction was, 'Well, what would you do?' And in reality I found in that six months that there was much recognition among them of what their real problems were and what the solutions were. All they needed was somebody to say, 'Right, this is how we – you and I – have diagnosed all the problems; these are the strengths, these are the weaknesses, this is the way we will go.'

It was a very centralised business and I instinctively felt that that wasn't right. More and more it was trying to serve local markets and that needed a devolution of responsibility. So I took my time and then decided. We split the company down into seven pretty autonomous operating companies and we had a central policy group which I chaired. We developed a clear-cut product strategy which said, 'Until now you have spent 95 per cent of your time on areas of the business we haven't any chance of making any money out of' – which was general haulage. 'Where our future lies is in long-term relationships with customers, providing them with fleets on contract hire with long-term contracts. That's our future world. You guys have all your training, experience and fun playing about with lorries in general haulage. You keep on doing that if you must. I'm not going to talk about that. I'm only going to talk about the future products and the future motivational packages.' So I said, in effect, 'I'm turning my back on 75 per cent of the business. I'm sensible enough to know that just because I've turned my back it won't go away, but we've got to refocus you, retrain you so that you become branch managers, local businessmen in your own right. You will have your own profit and loss account, you are responsible, and you have to understand the new product range that we want you to sell and how to sell it. So you need to be trained as businessmen on the one hand, and in new products on the other.'

And what do you feel that the managers a couple of levels beneath you were looking for from you? What role were they looking to you to perform?

I think all the people down the line want is a guy who seems to have a purpose and that, whether he's confident himself or not, he is expressing confidence about which direction the business is going to go and that he actually trusts them – the branch managers – to get there. They were looking for leadership and vision. How to take this business, which had been a pretty tatty performer, and make it proud in its new marketplace? The middle management argued against the need for a new vision – nobody likes change. They thought it was wrong, with all the experience that they had of general haulage, that we should just abandon it. We took all our branch managers through an intensive training programme, almost on a one-to-one basis, bringing them together in groups, then training them individually. We said, 'Look, here is our vision of what BRS is going to be about: it's going to be 60 per cent in contract hire, maybe 20 per cent in warehousing. We'll introduce a new product, truck rental. Now you go and design a corporate plan for your depot which will achieve that. We will train you in how to do that. Then come back and each individually present your corporate plan to the board.' It worked. There were some who were incapable of making change, but slowly they gradually began to change and attitudes altered. I guess it's like everything else. You need to have people who are responsible for the church, the business, or the shop, or whatever, who have got views and places where they want to take us.

In your experience, is it important to consult your people about *everything*, or just about the really major issues like the direction of the business?

It's wrong to exclude them from involvement in the global corporate plan. In NFC, when we bought the company we recognised that the new worker shareholders needed to have, and indeed had the right to have, more involvement in the major decisions of the business. We realised we needed a vision to take us into the twenty-first century. First of all you need to consider, 'What do the existing employees and shareholders want?' So, the first thing we did was to carry out a MORI survey in which we painted a whole variety of scenarios about what the company could be like; what its values might be. Then we asked them what kind of company they actually wanted? We sent out thirty thousand questionnaires and we got back fourteen thousand filled in. Now their input into the global strategy obviously isn't anything like as direct and as powerful as the input of a group of drivers who sit down to solve an operational problem like, 'Here, we've got a task to deliver these parcels to this address, how best do we do it?' There it's direct, their knowledge is relevant. The input into strategy is more about their feel. When we complete the strategic review, before the board endorse it, we take it back to them and say, 'Look, this is what you were saying. You may have got it right, but we think you may have got it marginally wrong because of these reasons. . . .' Take it to them – have meetings all over the country and get them to endorse the plan – and then make it known that they've endorsed it, that the board has endorsed it, so that the workforce are now part-owners of the plan. Then the actions that you subsequently take in line with what the strategy requires – for example, it required that we held back investment in the UK in order to grow the overseas subsidiaries – are ones they will understand and approve. All the questions that we used to get at the AGM and at the local meetings with the shareholder employees used to be, 'Why are you holding back investment?' And we could always say, 'But you agreed to this, it's part of the strategic vision which flowed out of your input.'

Probably they won't remember at all what they had said. But human beings live at all kinds of levels, and part of living is about how they feel. If they feel they have been involved, that is a motivation for improved implementation. There's no question that if you say to some clerks, 'Look, we're going to change your office around. Before we do so, I'm going to take the decision because I'm your boss. But how would *you* do it?' That kind of decision is more immediate and the impact is more meaningful in the sense that they know the problem. To get them to have joint ownership of that kind of solution is marvellous but for God's sake don't believe that people work only at that level. They also want to feel it's their company.

So the involvement of employees is not just to create one big happy family. It's because you genuinely believe, and you know from experience, that it helps the business to make ultimately better decisions?

Certainly that. We have to consult with them: they are our owners. I think the decision-taking process is better. We take better decisions at the centre because we've got more inputs – much broader inputs than we ever used to have – but we also recognise that in our industry what will give us the marketing edge is a motivated workforce. If our drivers actually smile when they go into the customer, and they feel happy and content with the way they are being looked after and managed, and they feel they are part of it, that can be our unique selling point. We go to our customers now and say, 'Look, the guy who is going to deliver your goods to your customers if we take over your contract will have a large financial stake in the business – so he's not going to foul it up.'

Management is a relatively easy job in an environment of employee willingness to change, so how do you create an environment of willingness to change? You try to make sure everybody believes it is their company, and they have an input to decisions being taken both globally and locally. That they have a right to be consulted about anything that affects them. And finally, if the company makes money they share in that. A lot of the senior managers have never managed in any other environment. I remember what it was like back in the 1970s when there was a constant resistance to change. Now you have an environment in which people accept change – they want change, they recommend change. Strategies are important; they require vision. But, put a great strategy with a reluctant workforce and some poor implementation and you are unlikely to succeed.

You are also a director of various other companies: Pilkington, Smiths Industries and so on. Are they interested to learn from NFC's experience, and are they picking up some of the flavour of what you have been doing?

One asks why do companies like that approach me and say, 'Would you like to come on the board?' I assume it's because they have seen what has happened to NFC, the way it has come from being an ugly duckling to be the highest-rated company in its market sector, and that the change has been something to do with this world of involvement and sharing. So I assume that is what they are looking for from my input into the board. When plans and budgets come forward, I never fail to say, 'What about the people?' The environment now, in almost the whole of British industry, is much more towards involvement and sharing and trying to build employees' personal financial stakes in the business. They are all interested in it and all the companies I am associated with are taking steady steps in that direction.

The concept needs much longer to mature and for there to be many more examples of success before management accept participation as a right value. It is an uncomfortable style to live with; it slows up decision-making; it reduces the number of weapons you've got in your armoury – for example, it's bloody difficult to sell a subsidiary company if you hold these values. You can't on the one hand embrace people and say, 'You're part of the family, we respect you, we want you, we want you to be more involved, and we listen to what you say, and by the way we're selling you!'

It is a bit more uncomfortable at the AGM which we encourage people to come to – you get three or four thousand people there at a weekend. They don't all come because they want to applaud the board. Often they are critical, 'Why the hell did you do this?' You have to stand up there and justify what you are doing. It is not easy, particularly if you have to make somebody redundant. So it isn't a comfortable style. You are very accountable to your workforce and very exposed. But despite this I'm sure that most companies are moving down the line of recognising people and putting them more into focus.

What do you see as the main difference between operating at a management level and at board level?

Operating at management level is to me the most satisfying thing that there is. It is about making things happen. Whereas operating at board level is much more about making sure that the direction the whole ship is sailing is right. That is much less instant; it's much more about gut and feel and analysis. Whatever you do doesn't happen overnight, it's a slower grind. I contrast it with the first management job I had where I came in in the morning and had a warehouse full of Persil, and I had a loading sheet, and during the course of the day that could be changed, but at the end of the day all the trucks were loaded. The job had been completed; the warehouse was empty. I had been effective and done something in the short-term. Of course the further up the management scale the longer the timescale becomes. At the very top level, the chairman level, my world is all about longer-term decisions and the unquantifiable things like values. Nobody really listens too much until you see what happens when the values in a business get confused. The County

Natwest problem over the Manpower acquisition was an absolute tragedy because the merchant banking values were very different from the clearing bank values. When you see values becoming confused like that, you understand why it is terribly important that the chairman or the board should be working in the world of values on the one hand and longer-term strategy on the other – but it's not as satisfying as loading Persil!

Clive Thornton

❛ *. . . the most important thing I've learnt about top management is that you are in danger of over-managing.* **❜**

Being disabled through a road accident as a teenager only heightened Clive Thornton's determination to make the most of his abilities. He gained a law degree by private study, and became chief solicitor of Abbey National. On taking over as chief general manager he shook the organisation hard. He particularly enjoyed 'bouncing it along' by making daring use of statements to the Press.

For a few months he led the Daily Mirror Group but was outmanoeuvred by Robert Maxwell. Since then he has never run a really large organisation but has spread his considerable energies between Thamesmead Town, an innovative housing project; the Catholic newspaper 'The Universe'; and farming.

Ebullient, combative, self-disciplined, decisive, his greatest ability is that of reducing problems to their central core and tackling them with irresistible vigour.

Chairman: Universe Publications, since 1986; Melton Mowbray Building Society; Armstrong Capital Holdings. Clive Thornton was articled to Kenneth Hudson, solicitor, 1959 and admitted as solicitor to the Supreme Court, 1963. He joined Abbey National Building Society, in 1967 and became director, 1980–83. He was chairman, Mirror Group Newspapers, 1984 and chairman of Thamesmead Town Ltd, 1986–1990. Married with children. Educated: St Anthony's School, Newcastle upon Tyne; College of Commerce, Newcastle upon Tyne; College of Law, London. Born 1929.

Chapter

18

At school, had you got a career plan sorted out?

No, I hadn't. At 13 years and 9 months I had started evening classes in shorthand, typing and bookkeeping, which must have meant I had ideas of being in an office rather than in manual work. Most of my classmates on Tyneside would be thinking of a manual job. I left school the day after I was 14 and went along to the Juvenile Employment Bureau. They sat you in a line then called you in and offered you a job. When the boy next to me was called he was afraid to go in, and said, 'You go in first.' So, I went in and they said, 'Here is a card, you go along to this firm of solicitors and be interviewed.' I learnt later, when I met up with the other boy, that he had gone to a woodyard, so that was how hit-and-miss it was. I went to the solicitors' office and was taken on. The solicitor was described as 'the poor person's solicitor' because in every town there was one firm that had to take on the job of giving advice for little or no cost to people who couldn't afford it. That attracted me – handling those sort of cases.

But at 15 I lost my right leg in an accident. I managed to recover in four weeks and went back to the office on crutches, and the solicitor said to me, 'We've been reviewing your case, Thornton, and we've decided to keep you on.' This apparently warranted partners sitting down to decide whether they should dispense with my services. I was then being paid one pound a week. I had started at fifteen shillings a week and had a rise after one year, so it wasn't a great deal out of their pocket. I resolved from that moment I was going to be professionally independent by qualifying as a solicitor, and financially independent as quickly as I possibly could be. It was that that drove me on.

Was the attraction of the law a double attraction – that on the one hand you were helping people who desperately needed help, and on the other there was also the intellectual challenge?

Well, latterly it became that, but initially it seemed to me that I found myself in an environment that suited me quite by accident. The training was what I would describe as 'sitting next to Nellie'. It was a very primitive form of training and I had to pay for my own evening classes and my own studying. The idea that the solicitors would have participated in that would have been farcical. If I had asked them there would have been outrage at the mere suggestion that they would have benefited by advancing my training. So you really had to learn it the hard way. But, in some senses, that was part of the thing that drove me on.

I had such a hard tussle to get to the point where I could begin to qualify that I resolved that, when I myself qualified, I'd take on anyone I could as an articled clerk without preconditions, giving them every possible help and benefit to achieve professional status. And it came as something of a shock to me later when I identified three or four such people and had a talk with them about doing it and they said, 'Yes they would like to do it' and then gave it up. I realised that they didn't value it – I thought they would immediately jump at the chance. So I learnt that you shouldn't think everyone is going to value having something handed to them on a plate. You are going to be disappointed if you think they should. Don't expect people to feel that they owe you something just because you've given them an opportunity.

When I eventually qualified in London I was managing a department during the day and working in the evening. I organised my life so that I did at least two hours studying every evening between seven and nine o'clock – every evening, every Saturday morning and every Sunday afternoon – that was the pattern, and there was no let-up. The schooling I had had was very elementary. I didn't find learning shorthand very easy, although eventually I got up to teaching standard both in that and typing. I still do shorthand and typing. I've always found it very helpful, but I didn't find it easy. All the time I was conscious of being determined, as if I were struggling with some obstacle. Once my daughter was talking to me about losing my leg, and she said, 'You would have lost it anyway because you need to make life difficult for yourself. Whatever you do, it can't just be an ordinary thing.' And some of the things I have done and am doing now, I'm sure I'm doing because they are exceptional. No one has yet achieved something like Thamesmead.

So you are always looking for a new mountain to climb?

When I had the leg removed I resolved that, as the prognosis was poor, I would have to pack as much as I could into life, to make sure I wasn't missing anything. If anything happened to me now, I don't think there is anything I haven't wrung out of myself. I have a supportive family around me. I married when I came to London and my wife has always fitted in. We've always worked together as a team and we do an enormous range of things in which we are both very interested. We are both committed to the idea of doing as many things as possible.

People who qualified with me often said that they studied for four or five hours at a time. I suppose there are people who can sit down and engross themselves for that length of time. But my experience has been that you should try to keep a balance between your family life and your work. You can only do that by arranging a programme. If you know you can enjoy the day or the part of the day that you have set aside for recreation, it makes it much easier to sit down and do a stint. I found that after an hour and a half to two hours it was the law of diminishing returns: the quality of what was done after

> that, when you added it all up, wasn't really worth thinking about.
>
> Just to prove this point, I have a degree, but I only took that degree in 1977. I said to someone, 'I think it would be possible to take a degree if you spent a concentrated one and a half hours a day on it. Since I arrive in the office at half past seven and everyone else arrives at nine o'clock I am going to secure some books and enrol for a law degree. I will concentrate purely on the reading for one and a half hours every morning for five days a week and see whether it's possible.' And it was.

And it's possible that, in your case, because you quite like working alone, you don't need a tutor to inspire you or egg you on. So getting this balance and variety has been an important feature?

> I think it has. When I first got married I said, 'We've got to have a family life as well as business and we must have a balance to it.' Studying should be organised around that. When I used to mark examination papers for the Building Societies Institute, it was obvious that the majority of students had not progressed in an orderly fashion. They had left it all to the last couple of months. I thought that strict application to a balanced programme which at first might seem to be far fewer hours would, in the long run, be the better way to study, and it paid off.

So you were working as a solicitor and doing more and more work in banks and building societies. Was that the way through?

> When I came to London the solicitor who gave me articles happened to be solicitor to a large company, the Co-operative Building Society. He said to me, 'You'll be managing the legal department. I don't think it will be very easy for you to qualify by evening study, but you wouldn't have to pay for your articles, and if the Law Society will allow you to do that I won't stand in your way.' I said there wasn't going to be any other way of my doing it. I was managing a legal department which was quite a big job in itself and I've never seen people work as hard as they had to at that time. They stretched me to the full. But it also made it possible for me to order my

affairs. I identified quickly what was important and what wasn't.

In fact, many years later, when I was going through a selection process for the job of chief executive of the Abbey National, together with the other candidates I was sent to a psychological management consultant called MacKenzie Davie. He produced a dossier on me and I found it uncanny that he identified even the smallest quirks of my personality that I had to acknowledge were right. Two of the things he said were, 'Your attitude to everything is to identify quickly what is important and what doesn't matter, and concentrate on the objective. Then, once you have achieved it, you move on to something else and forget about it. You don't allow anything to put you off your stroke.' The second thing he said was, 'You can stand an enormous amount of stress.' I honestly didn't believe at that time that I could stand stress. But he was right.

When I qualified with the Nationwide – it was then the Co-operative – I felt I owed them something: they had given me the chance to qualify, and so I remained for two years. Then I left and joined a merchant bank. The reason behind that was the second part of my ambition; I had become professionally qualified and now I wanted financial independence. The merchant bank immediately paid me two or three times as much as the building society. After a short while my boss came to me and said, 'You have an enormous capacity to cope with a large volume of work expeditiously, which I find quite remarkable.' For the first time I realised that what I was doing was out of the ordinary. People at the Nationwide had never said it was – all I knew was that I had three secretaries working for me and my desk was always clear. I couldn't do any wrong for four years with the merchant bank. I went from one step to another until I was at the elbow of the boss. Then one day someone said, 'You remember you were interested in a job with the Abbey National? They're now advertising.' So I applied for the job, but they were offering £3,500 and I was then earning £6,000. I said to them, 'Before we go any way with this interview I have to make it clear that my attraction in coming here is because I think your legal services are long overdue for a radical sort out. You have an extraordinary amount of documentation. I think the whole lot could be condensed onto one form. I have been able to manage for the past few years and proceed through courts with documents that are much simpler.' This rang a bell with a few of them.

When I took the job at £3,500 I didn't disclose to them that I was earning £6,000. I had already got to the point when money didn't matter. I had made what I needed. When I went to the Abbey I was on my own and with a secretary we changed the whole lot. The Abbey National's legal affairs were in such a terrible mess. They had two hundred different forms of mortgage deed. Even the documents were not designed to go in a typewriter – it was thick parchment! They were long overdue for a radical rethink of their business practices, particularly on the legal side, and that attracted me. They were the second largest building society. If we radically changed the way they did their legal work it would revolutionise the profession. Two or three months after joining the Abbey National I was at a social function and the chief surveyor's wife said to me, 'My husband keeps commenting on the remarkable degree of confidence you've got in yourself. He says you can sit there and change something on which the whole worth of the Society has previously been placed, and you've argued your case with everybody.' In fact it took me six months of arguing to get things through. But once we introduced it everybody copied, so it did in fact change all the documentation of the building society industry. But I wasn't troubled in the slightest. I didn't lose any sleep at all at the time about the importance of what I was doing, nor have I done so since.

As chief solicitor you were on your own, you had a secretary but you were not in charge of a great tribe of people.

That's right. I was on the management floor and I had the status of a general manager, but not the name. Eventually a small department was set up, but it never consisted of more than a dozen people.

So by the time you became chief general manager of the Abbey National your experience of managing large numbers of people was still very limited?

I had no experience at all.

Did that mean that your style as chief general manager was to get a lot of things done yourself, and not delegate?

> I worked on the 'clear desk' principle. When I had been with the Society for a couple of years the chief executive sent for me and said, 'Look, there's going to be a reshuffle at the top. You've got the legal department but I want you to take over the mortgage department and departments dealing with the administration of the title deeds.' That meant three departments; one hundred and twenty people in all. I immediately went into each of those departments. The managers had all retired. I went into each office and found that everybody's desk was heaped high with paper. Everyone had a trolley-full of files in their office. I called all the people in and said, 'Why is the room like this?' They said, 'Well the procedure he followed was that as he was the department manager he insisted on overseeing everything we do. We brought the work to him and he put the final endorsement on it.' I said, 'How often do you get the thing handed back to you as unacceptable?' and the answer was almost never. I said, 'Today you will clear this office. You will take back all the files that you brought in here. From now on you will decide matters yourself and you will only bring in something if you cannot decide it yourself. If I come round here and find anybody working late I will assume there is something wrong with the way he is doing the job or he is doing it from choice and I will want to know why.'

Did people welcome that change?

> Yes they did. I said to somebody, 'For God's sake, treat each day as an adventure and not as a day of drudgery.'

How far is it important for somebody leading a very large team of people to carry people with them, and how far is it perfectly all right to say, 'That's what we're going to do, I don't care whether you like it or not, just do it?'

> Being a person without any management training I acknowledge that. I had indicated that the whole industry was due for a shake-up,

and a change at the Abbey could lead the way by example. Mackenzie Davie said to me, 'What does a man with your background find interesting about running the Abbey National?' I said, 'So you think it's a great dinosaur of an organisation?' He said, 'Yes' and I said, 'It won't be.' The attraction is to do something about that.

But you don't mind ruffling a lot of feathers in the process?

No, in fact I would rather do that. I've thrived on that; there's a time when that treatment is necessary. The board will say, 'What we need to do now is consolidate.' That, to my mind, means we go to sleep. But a successful organisation must have constant birth and rebirth, and part of that process must be at the top.

So if you're not moving forward you're actually moving backward?

That's right. You need a constant birth and rebirth of ideas and it cannot come from the same individual. Most people kid themselves that there's no one who is ready to take over. No one ever sees the full worth of the person beneath them. They always think, 'Well, they've got some way to go and I had better stay on until they're ready.' You've got to allow for the fact that the right person will have about 40 per cent growth untapped. So much turns on people at the top. They should set themselves a time to finish. The art is knowing when you have outstayed your welcome. Very few people seem to learn that. I set myself five years. It's an odd individual who, having been in that position, can then sit on the sidelines of that organisation and think well of their successor, unless he or she is doing exactly what they would have done. That's another reason why you should get the hell out of it. I could have remained on the board of the Abbey, but I didn't.

How do you delegate?

I try, very quickly, to find out what people are made of, and then chuck them in at the deep end and see. You shouldn't ever expect more than they are capable of giving, which is often more than they believe they can do. But once you're getting that, I would leave someone completely alone. If I were suddenly let down more than once I would take a different attitude towards them.

But if you leave them completely alone, does that assume that they are roughly your sort of personality, which thrives on being allowed to get on with it? Do you not need to spend any time encouraging them and guiding them?

I used to go round branches of the Abbey National. My wife and I visited four hundred out of the seven hundred branches. We held functions regionally to draw all the personnel together when we couldn't get round to their offices, and I saw all I could see in that space of time. And I thought it was important to meet the wives as well, and bring them into the fold. So as far as it was important for me to tell them what I was trying to do, I did. I also realised, even before I got the job, that it was impossible to change a culture without using some exceptional ways of doing it. If I had just sat there I would never have done it.

On my first day I was up in the south-west of Scotland and a reporter said to me, 'Do you see anything in your approach to this job which has particular reference to this part of the country?' I said, 'Yes, I have worked out we have raised £25 million in south-west Scotland in the past year, and yet we've only lent £1 million. From now on you can be sure that whatever amount we raise in any community, that will be the amount that we put back in mortgages delivered there. So we're not going to lend your money to the South East, which is what's happening now. I am going to inject £25 million into south-west Scotland.' So that then appeared on the front page of the *Glasgow Herald* and someone said to me, 'You have not met the board yet, you have not cleared that with the board. Don't you feel you will be in trouble from the staff?' And I said, 'Well, it's what I would have said to them had they asked the same question. It's what we must do. It would have been better had I told them first, but that's not the way it came.' By the time I went into the board there were so many words of congratulation on this initiative that I wasn't aware that any of them thought it was a bad thing: they thought it was a damn good thing.

And did you in fact put £25 million back into south-west Scotland?

Yes. I then said, 'The same applies to all the inner city areas. We should earmark a sum of money that I can put into six pilot schemes. If I put money back into the middle of the cities, where we raise it, it will be the best form of advertising.' Well, of course, everyone was interested in this.

You changed 'red-lining' into 'green-lining'.

That's right, we did. I said, 'Our policy is that we draw a green line around' and we promoted that. I then said to them, 'We'll have to change the way the management is run here: there will be a meeting every Monday morning where we look forward to the week. On every other one you can please yourself whether you come, it doesn't matter one way or the other and I won't take it unkindly if you're not there. But I expect you to be at the meetings in between because that's when I expect decisions to be made.' I used to write down on a piece of paper what I wanted done and I wanted it done quickly. I abolished fifty-one committees in the first week of taking over. The previous style had been that if a decision had to be made you formed a committee to address the problem. I knew that if I was going to change things it couldn't be done that way. So I used to say to them, 'I want a product of a certain kind' and of course it never came. And I would say, 'I asked you at the first meeting for a product. No one has shown me anything at all, so I have worked out something. Don't tell me it can't go on the computer because that has been the excuse so far. We've got enough experts. I want to know whether you can *do* that.' If there was any delay in them doing it, I would then tell the newspapers that I was going to bring out a new product on 1 September. That bounced them into it. They had to do it.

You used the Press as your marketing department?

I used the Press because I'm not very happy with marketing departments. I think it's possible to have a marketing man who has the skill, but the idea that you can have a department full of such people in my experience is nonsense. What you have is an advertising department who call themselves marketing and then they use outside agencies! You might as well get rid of the marketing department and keep the marketing man. When I didn't think things were moving quickly enough I used the Press to market the product and bounce the organisation into doing it. And I was lucky – it was always attended by a lot of good Press comment.

You obviously wanted to get a much more innovative and creative feel into the Abbey. It's a very large organisation with lots of branches all over the place. When you were moving around and visiting all the branches, how did you actively encourage the spread of good practice from one branch to another?

Well, first of all, whatever you do in one branch the grapevine operates immediately. I used the grapevine. If I wanted something spread around, I would make a casual aside to somebody – it wasn't so casual. I found the chauffeur was usually the best man for doing that.

I made it known that I was available to the Press and the media twenty-four hours a day. They could ring me day or night, and they did. So that put a permanent intrusion into my privacy. I recall going down in the early days to a branch at Eastbourne and I said to the manager, 'What do you think of the Huddersfield & Bradford Building Society's new product?' He said, 'I've never heard of it.' And I pointed across the road and said, 'It's in their front window. If you are going to be one of the new style of building society managers that we require you will not sit here and listen to what head office tell you. When I come here next time I'll expect you to know what products are on offer up and down this High Street, and what you're doing to counter those products. That is what selling a service is about.' The next time I went to that office he had a board at the back of the counter area on which he had hung the brochures of all the societies.

I eventually found that the most effective way of communicating, in my case, was to use the Press and the media. Sometimes staff complained that they heard it first from there, but they didn't in fact: I only did that when I was being obstructed. Communications come to a halt somewhere just below the top level. The people at that level think, 'Knowledge is power. If I tell him as much as I know, then my power is diminished.' So you have to break through that. I told all the branch managers, 'You are to cultivate the Press, and you must be your own man on the spot. Don't worry that you'll get it wrong.' On one occasion, I found myself mentioned on page three of the *Sun* and the manager was terribly worried because he had used somebody's wedding photograph as a local promotion and it happened to be a couple he had turned down for a loan. He was unlucky – he got the photo from an agency. He rang me up, terrified that I was going to jump on him. I said, 'I've given you the right to speak to the Press. I can't do that and then jump on you for getting on page three of the *Sun* – it's no bad thing, anyway.' But that was the way to try and encourage them to do it and the way to bring pressure on the movement. Most people think Press relations are to paper over the cracks and to defend you from unpleasantness. What you should do is to cast caution to the winds and be upfront. You would be surprised how they will respect that. That was the main thing I learnt.

Isn't it arguable that, since leaving the Abbey, you've not been able to use your ability to get a large organisation to change fundamentally? You were with the Mirror Group for a little while . . .

Well, somebody said to me afterwards, 'Just think – that energy isn't being directed towards a serious national problem.' I said, 'Well, yes. But I left to direct my energy to what was also a serious national problem: the fact that all of our communications and media are drifting into a few hands, and hands which one may not always be able to trust.' I regret the fact that I wasn't able to remain there very long, because I think I was beginning to bring about some changes there.

I started full-time on the *Mirror* on the first day of January and I left on the twelfth day of July and it was all high-profile stuff for those months. I thought I had achieved a rapport with the unions that no one else had, and I had no experience whatever. When I first met the chief executive of the *Mirror*, I was invited to go over the problems. They were part of the initiation process, they weren't resentful of that. He said in a matter-of-fact way, 'You had better leave the union side to us, because we've got thirteen unions and sixty-four negotiating chapels and we could eat you for breakfast when it comes to dealing with these guys.' I said, 'Well, if you don't mind, it's something that I've got to learn and if we're changing this company into something they don't understand, they'll understand it better from me. I will go round and meet the unions. I will see them about anything that comes along, because I want to know face to face what the score is.' There was a dispute about two weeks after I arrived – it had been smouldering before I got there – and the minute I saw the pickets out at the front, I stopped the car and got out and went and talked to all of them and found that they had a complete misunderstanding of what the dispute was about. I set up a relationship with the unions that they had never had before. It was not built on animosity. I said 'You will see everything face up.' I think I was making great progress, so I was sad that what I was started on, stopped.

You have been chairman of companies and you have also been a chief executive. What is the major difference between those two posts?

I remember having a discussion with Campbell Adamson at the Abbey National who said to me, 'What do you think my first duty is as chairman?' I said, 'To hire or fire the chief executive.' He said, 'Yes, that's probably it.' I said, 'I would expect you to act quickly if I was not the chief executive required here, or if I wasn't matching up. On the other hand, I would expect to explain to you what it is I'm trying to do and I expect you, if you agree with that, to shape the policies and bring about a framework within which that could happen. That is what I see your job as.' We both assessed each other's role and we worked very happily to achieve what we did. I don't think in the end he was quite happy about the amount of attention I got from the Press, and that's probably why they went for a completely different individual after me.

I think the chairman must see that the board is united and backs the policies, so that there is a proper framework within the organisation. I find that, very often, you can get things blurred at the edges when there isn't a proper team working in tandem or something is going wrong. A successful organisation requires a chairman who is not managing director, and a managing director who doesn't believe he is chairman. They are distinct roles and one must see that the board is united in its policymaking and that the management are given a proper system to implement those policies to make them work. It's when you get a blurring of that that you have trouble.

In Thamesmead we have succeeded, because I regard my role as one of welding together a team of twelve people. Nine of them are elected from the council estate – the largest in Europe and have no previous experience of being part of a board, and they are the best board I've ever worked with. They learn quickly; they all contribute. I think the chairman should also see that everyone round the table speaks. Far too many chairmen neglect to do that and they allow people to come along who don't say anything, who don't read the papers but collect their money. A chairman should make sure he has got a board of active people and should bring about change when they have had their day. He should see that the board has constant birth and rebirth.

I see my job in Thamesmead as being upfront with the community in creating the framework within which the chief executive can get on and do a very difficult job.

As chairman of this company [Universe Publications] I have learnt two very important lessons. The first is that you have to be prepared to take over executive responsibilities in order to protect shareholders when the occasion demands it. The second is that you must be very careful to avoid over-management, or interference when you have capable people under you. I had not been here long before I found myself without a managing director. The company was in an extremely difficult situation and we were unable to secure a replacement. There was no alternative but for me to take over the executive role as well as that of chairman for a short period to turn things round. The problem was that I had commitments to other companies. However everyone, in my experience, is immediately replaceable by their subordinate.

So, within a short space of time, I found myself taking over as executive chairman. I called the whole lot in and said, 'This is the problem; this is the balance sheet; this is what's at stake. You don't need anyone else to achieve success, you can do it yourselves. I cannot be here every day because I can't ditch my other responsibilities. I imagine I will be here about 40 per cent of the time and the difference will have to be made up by each one of you doing something extra.' After a while one chap piped up, 'What are we going to get out of it for all this extra work?' All the others looked horrified and I said, 'Well, in your case I won't expect you to do any more than you are paid to do, so that is what you will get out of it. That applies to you.' Within four months we turned things around, and by September we had turned in a record profit, so they had done it. Then I handed over to a new managing director. I said to him, 'You may believe, certainly if you talk to the previous guy, that I interfere at all levels. I do not. If I believe you can do the job, you are free to do it. You will see very little of me, but I'm here when required.'

If I trust somebody, and if I've assessed that they are reasonably capable of doing the job, they will be trusted. But if I know they are not, then I have to do something about it. I have learnt that you might as well face unpleasantness straight away. But the most important thing I have learnt about top management is that you are in danger of over-managing. When we were talking about appointing a managing director, I said, 'My difficulty in recommending someone to you is that I realise a good man would only need 40 per cent of his time to do this job as managing director. Because I have been doing the job myself on a part-time basis, I've had to refrain from going in and asking people how they are getting on and going into it too deeply. Whereas had I had only this job to do, I would have thought that it was absolutely essential to do that.' When you are paid to do one full-time job, you do a lot more calling up of people than is ever warranted. You fill the time, and I realise now that a good 50 per cent of my time in some of the jobs I have done could have been spent on other things with no detriment – and probably advantage.

Tim Waterstone

‘I try hard to make life fun for people. The work ethic beats hard through all of us. We all enjoy work, we all need work, we need the comradeship and the sense of achievement.’

Very early in his career, Tim Waterstone was personal assistant to the managing director of Allied Breweries, Derrick Holden-Brown. He learnt a great deal from watching him run a major business by delegating to local managers but also being highly visible.

Moving to W H Smith, he started well but lost spectacular amounts of money launching an American subsidiary. He was dismissed and badly shaken, but bounced back by starting his own company in direct competition with Smith's. He has built this up so successfully that he has now sold his business back to Smith's at a profit of £10 million.

He sets his own stamp on his company, taking great care over the selection of managers and the control of stock. He believes in keeping commercial principles simple; he loves the cut and thrust of negotiating, and regards it as essential that business should be fun.

Founder and chairman, Waterstone & Co, since 1982. Tim Waterstone is chairman: The Principals Ltd; Priory Investments Ltd. He is deputy chairman of Sinclair-Stevenson Ltd and director of Classic-FM Radio Ltd. Formerly he worked for: Carritt Moran, Calcutta, 1962–64; Allied Breweries, 1964–73; W H Smith, 1973–81. Six children. Educated: Tonbridge; St Catharine's College, Cambridge. Born 1939.

Chapter

19

Have you always been attracted to books and in particular the book business?

> I have always loved books. I read English at Cambridge and have read avidly all my life. It's difficult once you've joined the book industry not to be quite fond of that as well. It's a deeply complex, very ungentlemanly, very commercial business, and very great fun. I'm a marketing man by training and I regard my prime skill as identifying markets and going for them.
>
> From Cambridge the Appointments Board popped me into Allied Breweries, and I had ten very happy years there. I did a sort of graduate trainee job for the first three months. Great fun! We worked in wine cellars with the draymen on the brewery lorries. The famous Cook's Tour. It was a very congenial bunch of trainees. They made quite a lot of fuss of us and made us work awfully hard.

What do you think you particularly learnt from it?

> A certain amount of humility. This was 1964. There was quite a lot of social unease in terms of the relationships between management

and staff. Allied was a good democratic company – unusually so in those days – and we were encouraged to get our coats off and work, to join in with the ranks, to have breakfast with the brewery drivers in their roadside cafés and really join in. That was a very good thing indeed. Any vestiges of Oxbridge conceit were knocked out very quickly!

And do you think the draymen enjoyed it too?

The liked making fools of us, and I don't blame them. They used to make us stand in a line and pass down barrels of beer. Half an hour of that was absolutely exhausting.

What sort of company was Allied Breweries at that time?

One merger had just taken place. It was slightly unformed, a very big business, and I worked for Derrick (now Sir Derrick) Holden-Brown, the managing director, as his personal assistant and subsequently marketing manager on the wine and spirits side. I worked very closely with him and found him the most remarkable leader. It was a business which, although large, was deeply entrepreneurial and I learnt a lot there.

It was a very marketing-led company, and I was thrown very quickly into the world of market research, market planning and so on. I knew nothing and had to learn an awful lot very quickly. I loved it. I enjoyed analysing opportunities, market segments – those were quite heady days. I also learnt from Derrick Holden-Brown all sorts of things about financial overview. You need to *be* with somebody of that quality to learn. I don't think you're going to get that out of a management textbook. It's a process of looking down at a business from above and sorting out the wood from the trees and seeing what matters and what doesn't. He was a man of such deep numeracy that, if you had any feel for numbers yourself, he was the most wonderful if unconscious teacher.

Did he stop what he was doing and talk you through things, or did he expect you to absorb it all?

No, he could be impatient, and quite often rather cross. I don't think he consciously taught; I just watched him.

So you were very fortunate having access very early in your career to somebody at the very top of a very large organisation.

Yes, I was. I had a good relationship with him.

Allied came about as a result of mergers and had a large number of employees. Did the board try hard to communicate to people right down the line, or did they leave it to the grapevine?

It was a very informally run company and very delegated. People were given profit responsibility very quickly. For a company so large it was relatively informal in its structure, and worked well because of that.

How did they go about spotting talent? They had clearly spotted you, but did they have an effective system of picking out good people?

I do not recall a personnel department of any sort. Derrick Holden-Brown was a tremendous spotter of people, and one or two of his director colleagues were similar.

When you say Holden-Brown was good at spotting people, did he walk about a lot and visit factories and look out for people?

Yes. One of the things that made an enormous impression on me was going to France, to a large factory. I remember being struck by the way their managing director went round and shook every hand and knew every name. The contrast with normal English management factory behaviour at that time was profound.

I thought how similar Holden-Brown was: he had a clever way of remembering people's names, always smiling at people, shaking hands busily. In those days the British didn't shake hands very much, but Holden-Brown always did. I'm a great believer in shaking hands, perhaps catching it from that.

So you got some very good experience under your belt with Allied. Was the move to W H Smith a natural one?

> Well, I never had any money of any sort and I was attracted by the offer they made. I did it terribly on impulse. To begin with, I didn't enjoy it at all. I thought I had made the most ghastly error of all time. It was a very well-run company but very structured – everything was done by committee. In those days, people with flair were not the most popular at Smith's. Smith's is a completely different animal now, but then it was somewhat a caricature of itself.

Were you given your head a bit?

> They took me in to start up a new division. I was always an outsider, though, and I sensed I was unpopular because I wasn't part of the mainstream. I had been brought in from outside, and I went to the USA with Smith's in 1978 to do a greenfield start. It was the absolute banana of all time. It lost considerable sums of money and the knives really were out for me.

You had had this tremendous learning experience of working directly under somebody running a very powerful business. In Smith's, were you trying to develop a team under yourself?

> Yes. I feel I'm good at leading teams because I give people a sense of clarity and a sense of fun and aspiration. I enjoy clarity, vision, goals and striving towards them. What I'm much less good at is managing established businesses which no longer need great clarity of goal, mission and achievement, but which need quiet supervision.

Do you like setting objectives yourself? Do you draft things on paper and say to your team, 'This is it' or do you consult the people around you?

> People always caricature me for being a non-consulter. I don't think people who work with me closely would agree. I am definitely a leader

of the things I do. I hear opinion well and I have a sense of consensus, but I'm not terribly comfortable being a member of a team answering to somebody else's directives.

So if this was a team meeting around this table and you were leading your team, would you expect them to answer back and to fight or . . ?

I enjoy all that. I enjoy debate. I get very pumped up by adrenalin almost every day in my office. I like the fun; I like the comradeship; but I do like being number one. I don't behave well on charity committees. I get so impatient at the lack of clarity.

I had a very moderate academic career but I do have a clarity of mind which is enormously helpful. Derrick Holden-Brown does have this astounding clarity. I think clarity is everything in business. Business is a simple thing and the simpler you keep it the easier it is for everybody.

You find that that process is best done in writing, in drafting something, looking at it, being critical about it?

I clear my own mind first of all by analysis on paper. I've always been a very heavy communicator in the written form. I've always enjoyed using inter-office memoranda, which other people hate. I like it as a 'mind-clearer'. I'm also very uncomfortable without numbers. I find it astonishing how people can have a business conversation without numbers. People talk about opening that site, that site or that site: until we've wrapped numbers round it you can be subjective and artistic and aesthetic but, at the finish, you must have a numerate basis. I find it very difficult to work with people who are incapable of framing their thoughts arithmetically.

Do you believe in using psychometric and aptitude testing when you are taking people on?

I do, deeply. Something which I am more and more convinced about is that none of us can spend too much time being careful about appointments. Getting the right people into the right jobs – there is a tremendous unkindness in inviting people to expose themselves in an area in which they are unfamiliar or unskilled. The more you test them and make absolutely certain they are able to do the job you want them to do, the kinder that is.

So when you had ended up in the USA, and had a not-very-successful period there with Smith's, was that the turning point for you in deciding to have a go on your own?

I was 42 when I was fired by Smith's, and it was a fairly colourful firing. We were pretty cross with each other. I was badly shaken by the lack of good quality job offers I received. I was afraid and I had no money. But it didn't really matter because venture capital is easily raised. If you have a totally clear vision of what you want and powers of persuasion and a huge amount of self-belief and are prepared to be brave when doors are shut in your face, almost inevitably you can get money to do anything. Initially I didn't want to raise huge sums of money. Since I had no money of my own, I wanted to put it together brick by brick, so we worked the share price up and up and by borrowing money I managed to retain a decent stake for myself. So I went the weary way, but I'm very glad I did. We've made mistakes in Waterstone's, but in all honesty I think the financial strategy was absolutely brilliant. We went the dangerous way, which is going back into the market every year for more funding but, mercifully, at an ever-increasing share price.

And you didn't compromise on quality?

Once you compromise on quality, you are lost. The whole thesis of Waterstone's was very heavy stock per square foot – twice if not three times the industry average – plus very good sites, good design and the best staff. I felt that once we started to wander away from a deliberate unique selling point we would have lost our clarity.

You must have taken a lot of trouble over choosing the managers of your branches.

The greatest fun, of course. We had six people on 1 September 1982, all of whom I had recruited: now we have six hundred and something, and they were all hired by me. That does create a huge amount of personal loyalty and friendship.

How did you go about picking your managers?

I had the most enormous stroke of luck. Of my first six, five came from Hatchards. They were of a very high standard and knew everything. Four of them are still with me. I never really advertised again. We've done a certain amount of local advertising, but the word spread and people approached us.

How important is it to have a *rounded* manager? You may have somebody brilliantly knowledgeable about books but not numerate enough to handle the finances, or you may have someone who is marvellous at design and not good enough with the people.

I believe our real responsibility is to have someone who is very good with books. One would love to find a beautifully rounded manager – the most literate person in the UK, also highly computer literate, and very conscious of security. If that person exists, I would love to meet him or her! The most important thing for us is to get managers who are highly literate and then make sure they understand the need for proper control. Shopkeeping is not that tough a thing to learn. You can't teach book knowledge. People have to teach themselves book knowledge. Bookselling is the most skilled retailing at the product level in the way we do it.

Are there many women managers among the team?

Oh yes. Well over half. The men all think I'm so attracted by women that I always give them the jobs! Women make terribly good booksellers. I don't mean it to be patronising. Bookselling requires attention to detail and a sort of steadiness and quiet drive, and women are so good at these things. We have some absolutely wonderful women managers. A good woman manager is a joy to work with;

they are so loyal and so determined. We've just brought our first two through to the board.

You've mentioned several times that work is fun. Can you do anything to create that?

I try hard to make life fun for people. The work ethic beats hard through all of us. We all enjoy work, we all need work, we need the comradeship and the sense of achievement. I try hard to make Waterstone's a thoroughly pleasant place to work in. We are a deeply delegated company, so the branch managers control their own staff and they are responsible for their own profits. One of the things I watch for most of all is staff disaffection. I try to smell it very early on. I do a lot of branch visiting – certainly two days a week. I'm very careful when I go to branches to talk to every single member of staff, to read their file and look them in the eye. You can quickly pick up staff disaffection. It's always the same reason – bad branch management – and I'm very quick to get on to it.

How do you tackle that when you've got a manager who just doesn't have very good people skills?

If we simply can't make it work, we fire the manager. We've done it several times. I feel as much responsibility to a bookseller of 22 just down from university as I do to the manager aged 28. They're all part of my family, and I'm not going to have one misleading the other.

Can you do much about retraining or putting people on a new track when they get to, say, 50-plus, and they're not in a particularly high-level job?

It's an interesting question. We haven't met it yet. One of the problems we are going to have is that, sooner or later, growth is going to stop. I'm not quite clear what is going to happen after that. The heady days of new branches opening every quarter of an hour, people applying to branches and so on, are going to come to an end eventually, and I don't know how we're going to tackle it. We'll find a way, but we are going to have a new problem in four or five years' time: the problem of retraining and remotivating people who are not going to go further in their jobs. Though our decision to open branches in the USA does certainly add a new career dimension for our people.

How do you keep the balance between your own working hours and your family hours?

I don't take work home. I'm just turned 50 and I find I can work like stink from eight in the morning till half past seven at night. I can't work after that successfully. If I have my children with me, I very much like the whole process of family life. To me the whole spiritual dimension of life is enormously important. For me to be balanced and happy in all my dealings with people, for my feelings of contentment and fulfilment and peace, I need to work all the time at the spiritual side of life as well, though essentially not through organised religion, with which I grew increasingly uncomfortable.

There's no difficulty in squaring that with the business ethic?

I've never had any difficulty in that at all. I also like to apply a business ethic to my private life as well. My impatience with charities and Parochial Church Councils and things of that sort is their muddle and lack of clarity, and good intentioned ineffectiveness. That leads to a muddled human situation and quarrelling and scruffiness and anarchy. I cannot separate my business life from my private life. I like to behave in exactly the same way in both.

So the voluntary sector needs to learn some management skills?

Absolutely overwhelmingly.

In looking over your management career, one of the things that is very clear is your resilience. You've obviously been able to bounce back when something has gone wrong. How far can a leader in charge of a large organisation assess his own effectiveness?

I do it alone. I think I'm pretty honest about myself, and as I grow older I'm increasingly clear about what I can't do as well as what I can. I do try to construct an arithmetical framework around my own life and to take decisions on a very numerate basis. Sheer scorekeeping helps, and I certainly expect Waterstone's by 1992 to be not only the cultural success it is, but a financial success of absolutely first division standard. In our own business, one of the great drives we are having over the next few years is that if I do come out of the business in 1993 and it has my name, one of the things I want it to carry for generations to come is a reputation for superb stock and staff quality. I'm introducing a system now where, every time I go to a branch, I have this absolutely childlike thing – I hand across a list of a hundred and fifty titles which to me are key, and I check the stock and they get a percentage marking each time. At the end of the year, that branch manager is very largely going to be judged on the quality of the branch's stock and staff.

How far can you learn from other companies outside the book business?

I think about the business world all the time. The *Investors' Chronicle* is one of the high points of my week. I just love the whole process.

Do you have a network of contacts?

Yes. I have friends dotted around throughout my own industry and outside, and I have telephone acquaintances. I've made friends on the telephone with somebody from Laura Ashley whom I tend to ask if I'm doubtful about a town.

Do you get involved in advising young people who want to make a business career?

Yes, I do a lot of that now. I like doing it, and I try to see as many people as I possibly can. I try to lift from them what their aspirations are. The people I find most difficult to deal with are people who will not engage with life, who will not attach themselves to life at any level. Life should be very good fun; you should love everything you

312

do and you should love your work. If you give me somebody who is engaging in life I find them exhilarating to talk to. And if they will take advice from me, I find them exhilarating to advise.

Chapter

20

Most of the leaders we interviewed are at the summit of their careers. One or two have just retired; others are close to retirement age; some who are now managing directors or equivalent may move on to become chairmen; a few are young enough to contemplate one more major appointment in a different organisation. So all of them are able to look back over a substantial number of years in increasingly powerful positions.

By examining what they have revealed in these interviews we can find important messages about three stages in the career of a leader:

- **The hill**   Climbing the hill towards a top position. This includes their education, early jobs and the period in middle to senior management. What were the main influences on their performance and on their learning? How did they cope with success and failure?

- **The high ground** The crucial stage when they were selected for the top job. Why were they chosen, and what was their reaction? In the period immediately after appointment, when a leader is expected to set his or her stamp on the organisation, what actions did they take?

The Learning Curve of Achievement

• **The horizon**   In their role at the top of the organisation, what vision are they working towards? How do they make decisions, what do they delegate and how do they develop the next generation of leaders?

This structure has emerged through reading and re-reading the transcripts. Themes gradually appeared which we have grouped under these three phases. What do these leaders have to tell us?

The hill

There is no clear message here about the kind of formal education a leader requires. Most, but not all, went to university. The most striking feature is that the two leaders whose formal education was shortest (Clive Thornton, who left school at 14, and Sir Peter Imbert, who left at 16) took immense pains to make up for this later on.

> I have a degree, but I only took that degree in 1977 . . . I am going to secure some books and enrol for a law degree and concentrate purely on the reading for one and a half hours every morning [7.30–9.00a.m.] for five days a week. (Clive Thornton)

> I was very conscious almost immediately after I had left school how much opportunity I had wasted. So during my time as a police officer and throughout my career until about ten years ago, I went off to night school to learn whatever one could . . . (Sir Peter Imbert)

Early exposure to responsibility has been much valued.

> [As a young accountant] So my experience was of being exposed almost every month to situations of which I had no prior professional experience. (Brandon Gough)

> Experience in the army was obviously enormously valuable. At the age of 25, I had had experiences which very few 25-year-olds have had now. (Lord Donaldson)

Where this responsibility was not forthcoming, they pushed for it.

> I had two years in Unilever where you just sat looking over people's shoulders. The frustration was enormous. I used to break out occasionally and try to do things and get myself into trouble . . . (Sir Peter Thompson)

> [In BP] I had too little to do, frankly. No amount of begging my superiors for more involvement in this or that seemed to correct the problem. So I started looking around within the Group, and made it very clear that I wanted to move. (Tim Melville-Ross)

All these leaders are thirsty for challenges, and thrive on them.

> [In Canada & Dominion Sugar Company] I liked doing something that was new, something that the company hadn't done before. I couldn't get any advice from anybody because it was the first time . . . I had to do the innovating to achieve the company's marketing goals. (Neil Shaw)

> [At IBM, Greenock] There was a great satisfaction . . . in being able to recruit one hundred and fifty engineers when it was thought

to be impossible in that part of Scotland. (Sir Leonard Peach)

[When a job move to Canadian Pacific was suggested to him] . . . I was not being intellectually satisfied. I was doing well in what I was doing, but it wasn't testing me or pushing me any more. I believe I've always needed some intellectual stimulus. (Sir Graham Day)

I went through several interviews of the kind, 'Shall we take you as a management trainee?' But they concentrated far too much on, 'Come-and-make-biscuits' or '. . . ceramics' and no one said to me, 'Come and be a manager.' And then along came the civil service and said, 'Come and run the country.' (Sir Alex Jarratt)

I wouldn't have been happy on the outskirts so I joined the Metropolitan Police and found myself patrolling the West End. I wanted to be part of the action. (Sir Peter Imbert)

Few of these leaders had a clear plan for their career worked out more than one jump ahead. But they made decisive moves when necessary. Having reached deputy secretary level in the civil service, Alex Jarratt was offered a complete change – to move into industry with IPC. 'I sat down that Wednesday with a sheet of paper, I drew a line down the middle and listed pros and cons. The things against leaving were getting longer and longer . . . As I walked down Pall Mall I said, "I'm going." It was a gut reaction.'

I also nearly became a television star. I was auditioned for *What's My Line* to take over from Barbara Kelly as a permanent member of the panel. I got a contract for just a few weeks. It was absolutely fabulous . . . But . . . I then made a conscious decision to turn my back on the lights, the fame and the glory, and to do something really solid. So I then went into teaching thinking that this was what I really wanted to do. (Professor Anne Jones)

Then I took a long hard look . . . I really began to take my career seriously. . . So when I was offered a job at Garland Compton to run

> the entire research function, I took a step sideways out of the
> specialisation that was getting me into a box . . . which greatly
> broadened my base. (Ann Burdus)

Sir Richard Attenborough is the only one among our leaders who
experienced instant revelations about his career path. 'I remember my
father taking me to London to see Charlie Chaplin's *The Gold Rush* when
I was 11. I thought that it was the most devastating occasion I could
remember . . . I suddenly felt, "That's what I would love to do".' And
again later, on his move from acting to directing, 'Then some madman
sent me a biography of Gandhi and suddenly – it was like a blinding flash
as I read this extraordinary story – I knew I wanted to direct.'

Being given real responsibility comes across as more important than
formal management training as such.

> The firm had the very attractive style of pushing people up to, and
> maybe beyond, their capabilities. It was very much a sink-or-swim
> environment but with a safety net. There was a great willingness to
> allow people to demonstrate their range of capabilities; it was a
> stretching environment. (Brandon Gough)

> [In the Central Policy Review Staff] Well, it's an amazing
> opportunity for somebody of 32 to be given, to get right into the
> centre of central government, to be able to see the Cabinet minutes
> when they come off the presses, to be able to establish a network all
> over Whitehall. (Baroness Tessa Blackstone)

It is no surprise to find that people who thrive on responsibility also show
an unusual degree of determination.

> If you have a totally clear vision of what you want and powers of
> persuasion and a huge amount of self-belief and are prepared to be
> brave when doors are shut in your face, almost inevitably you can
> get money to do anything. (Tim Waterstone)

> [After his accident as a teenager, when he had to have a leg
> amputated] When I had the leg removed I resolved that . . . I would

have to pack as much as I could into life, to make sure I wasn't missing anything. If anything happened to me now, I don't think there is anything I haven't wrung out of myself. (Clive Thornton)

[When Capital Radio started] Unfortunately we went on the air at the time of the miners' strike and the three-day week . . . we had no money, we had no listeners, and we had no advertising. In fact we hadn't got any of the three ingredients . . . which are absolutely vital . . . I had to go to the bank and say, 'Look, I have no money left. You've backed us so far. All I have is my art collection. May I put it in the vaults? Please, I need some money for Friday.' The Bank of Scotland were magnificent. They didn't take the pictures. They said, 'Your conviction is enough. You are sure it's going to work.' (Sir Richard Attenborough)

Several of the leaders (for example, Donaldson, Gough, Melville-Ross), acknowledge that luck played its part in their advancement. But for the majority of them, the most important single feature in their development appears to have been one or more mentors. These fall into three groups:

• a teacher, either at school or university
• an immediate manager
• a much more senior person, not necessarily in the same organisation.

There were also a few managers who would by no means fit the definition of a mentor* but who were powerful personalities. Among the teacher category, Brian Smith spoke movingly about his chemistry master. Sir Leonard Peach described his headmaster's faith in him as, 'putting pressure both on me and on my parents.' In the category of immediate managers, Sir Peter Thompson mentioned the 'very good cadre of foremen and managers [at Crosfield's] who took a pride in training people and bringing them along.' Tim Melville-Ross worked under Leonard Williams at Nationwide – 'I owe a great deal to him. He helped me in career terms

*Mentoring is a system, often formalised, of pairing a senior manager with a junior colleague not in a line relationship. The senior acts as confidential sounding board, adviser and guide to enable the junior manager to understand the culture, opportunities and power bases in the organisation and see how best to develop his or her own career.

more than I can say' – who moved him through three jobs in five years, giving him an ideal jumping off point for the top job.

Tim Waterstone was personal assistant to Allied Breweries' managing director very early in his career. Sir Derrick Holden-Brown was 'the most remarkable leader . . . I don't think he consciously taught; I just watched him.' Similarly, Sir Alex Jarratt was private secretary to two permanent secretaries in the civil service. From Sir Donald Fergusson, he 'learnt the intellectual rigour he brought to bear in reaching conclusions . . . he would put his reputation on the line at times . . . as a young man watching it, that helped to stiffen my backbone.' Sir Leonard Peach had two mentors: at West Midlands Gas, Vincent Young 'took great pride in ensuring that his protégés made progress,' and at IBM, Parry Rogers.

Other individuals who acted as mentors from a more independent position included the lawyer, Gordon Cowan, who sensed that Graham Day needed a job change and who introduced him to Canadian Pacific. Anne Jones recalled two strong influences in her early teaching career from whom she gained her counselling skills. She went on to comment, 'At various times in my life I've been lucky to have a sort of mentor. I do believe you learn best, not through writing something down, but through talking something through with people. When I was a counsellor I had regular support sessions with a psychiatric social worker. I needed that kind of psychiatric supervision because I was dealing with very explosive situations.'

The final category of 'powerful personality' has to include Steve Shirley's first manager, 'a beast of a boss . . . an example of the sort of manager I didn't want to be' – but a man who 'had high standards. He taught me to be more assertive. It was he who taught me some judo.' In the same vein, Neil Shaw at 25 was assistant to a hardworking, dictatorial chairman, from whom 'I learnt a lot of how not to do it.'

The high ground
Now we reach the culmination of climbing the hill: being selected for the post at the head of an organisation. For a surprisingly large proportion their elevation was unexpected.

> [On being chosen as managing director of Tate & Lyle] I wasn't expecting anything of that kind to happen. (Neil Shaw)

> [On being asked to run Lucas' battery business] . . . they took an
> extraordinary chance and gave this 34-year-old who had never run
> a damn thing in his life quite a big international battery business to
> run . . . They were very brave . . . they really did take a flier. (Sir
> James Blyth)

> [On moving to British Road Services as managing director] The
> uppermost emotion was one of fear! Remember, I had never actually
> run anything. (Sir Peter Thompson)

When she was appointed a deputy head, Anne Jones was 'absolutely
flabbergasted and I went back and said, "Well I wasn't expecting to get
this job . . ."' She then laid down various conditions before accepting and
said, 'Do you want me on these terms? And they said "Yes please".'

A small group reached the top by creating their own organisations. Sir
Richard Attenborough set up his own film production organisation, Steve
Shirley founded her own company, FI, and Tim Waterstone started his
own chain of bookshops.

Many agree that the post at the top is different in vital respects to all
others. Sir Alex Jarratt, speaking of Smiths Industries, said, '. . . we had a
pretty flat organisation – that leap from running a subsidiary to running a
division is quite a big one. The leap from there to running the whole
thing, or being number two, is a hell of a leap.'

> . . . the very largest step of all is from the line of managers
> immediately below the chief executive to the chief executive slot.
> (Tim Melville-Ross)

Among our leaders, there are varying reasons why they were selected for
the top post. In Ann Burdus' case, being chosen as chairman of McCann
seems to have been a combination of three factors: her ability as a
strategist, her international experience and her unique ability to understand what her predecessor had been trying to do! In Brandon Gough's
case, his colleagues at Coopers & Lybrand had a fairly stark choice, they
'could either have a senior partner who was about 55 or one who was 45
or under . . . The partners were very brave when they chose someone who
was under 45, particularly as he had no managerial experience.'

If our sample provides a template for selection for top posts, the template certainly depicts a track record of vigour and impact.

> . . . out of the blue I had a phone call from John Gardiner, chairman of the Laird Group. He asked me if I would like to run a shipyard. He knew about me because I had spent four months in 1970 trying to sort out Cammell Laird's problems . . . with Canadian Pacific I had knocked around a wide range of engineering activities and had bought and sold more ships than Cammell Laird had built in ten years. I knew the blunt end from the sharp end in shipbuilding. (Sir Graham Day)

Sir Peter Imbert moved from superintendent to chief constable in three years. '. . . although the Thames Valley Police Authority put their trust in me, I was very green in the provincial scene . . . I had got to summon all of my energies and political nous and use my personality, such as it is, to get the support of everybody around me.' Clive Thornton was asked by a selection consultant why he wanted the job of chief general manager of Abbey National. 'I said, "So you think it's a great dinosaur of an organisation?" He said, "Yes" and I said, "It won't be." The attraction is to do something about that.'

It is always fascinating to see how a person tackles the 'honeymoon period' immediately on taking up the top post. Within the organisation and outside, all eyes are on the new chief. What style will he or she set? Will it be 'business as usual' or a bloodbath? Sir Peter Thompson assessed his task in BRS, 'I hadn't inherited a disaster scene . . . My first stance to the guys who were running the business was to say, "Look, I've come in from outside. I don't know anything much about BRS . . . I'm going to spend the best part of six months just walking round the patch".' Baroness Blackstone, in taking over as master of Birkbeck College, knew she had a financial crisis to tackle, and decided to bring in management consultants, '. . . the financial problems weren't going to be solved by slashing spending here, there and everywhere. Something else had to be done.' In total contrast, Neil Shaw felt on becoming managing director of Tate & Lyle that the company was 'inundated with consultants . . . They all had to get out within one week! I felt that the issues that needed to be dealt with were simple – the answers weren't, but the issues were.'

In the same vein, Clive Thornton abolished fifty-one committees in his first week.

Decisions about organisation structure and accountability feature strongly in this phase.

> [Commenting on his time at Ironbridge] I also learnt that the organisational structure of a museum must equate with the nature and style of the job it has to do. If it doesn't then don't be afraid to change it and change it again as circumstances change. If the systems don't meet the needs of the day there probably won't be a tomorrow. (Dr Neil Cossons)

> [On becoming chairman of Metal Box] The first thing we did was to take a big head office, with six hundred and thirty people, and disband it. And we said to all the people who were running businesses in the head office, 'Out.' And they said, 'Where shall we go?' And we said, 'We don't care where you go – just give us your telephone number when you get there', and they all went off . . . (Dr Brian Smith)

Sir James Blyth had learnt the same lesson from his time with Mars, 'the value of decentralisation . . . They still run the entire corporation with about twenty-five people at the centre.'

> [On becoming chief executive of the NHS] The Management Board . . . had been created within the DHSS but it had no thick line reporting to anybody – it was just there. But that didn't worry me because all my background concerned indirect authority. (Sir Leonard Peach)

This is an interesting example of the effective leader's ability to discriminate between issues which have to be addressed and others which may look untidy but can be lived with.

Hand in hand with putting in the right structure goes the need for a clear strategy. When Anne Jones became head of Cranford Community School, she consulted not only her staff but also her pupils about the school's objectives. 'We involved the pupils in this same consultative process so that they were also committed to seeing certain changes in the school.' But what if staff and pupils had come up with unrealistic ideas? '. . . I would have known where I stood with them. You have to work from where people are now, not necessarily from where you would like them to be. I believe people learn by doing and they will also learn from their mistakes.'

For Sir Alex Jarratt, becoming managing director of International Publishing Corporation not only meant learning to manage thirty thousand people instead of two hundred and thirty, but, 'Restoring its credibility as a profitable organisation. It had lost its way . . . It was under-managed but it wasn't under-managered. The managers were there but they had not been led properly. Once they realised I was on their side and could see the potential that this enormous company had got – I got a very quick reaction from them, and that helped enormously.'

Sir Graham Day was asked about the four companies (Cammell Laird, British Shipbuilders, Dome Petroleum and BL) where he had transformed their fortunes: was there anything in common to each of those? 'Common to them was a management at the very top which, at best, had lost its way through absence of strategy . . . you always had to start off by saying, "Where should we be going, how do we get there?" . . . I then put in hand two key exercises. One which I called the "operational audit", which is an internal evaluation, and then an "environmental scan", which is an external evaluation . . . You then have two packages of information and assessment from which you can analyse and develop a strategy. You then run like hell . . . I progressively changed out the top managers . . . Then I started to address the financial problems . . . '

Brian Smith had been a main board director of ICI with Sir John Harvey-Jones as chairman, and there he had seen the value of main board directors focusing on strategy as distinct from day-to-day management. So on becoming chairman of Metal Box, he left the managers of the operating businesses to construct their own budgets, but, 'I don't want any excuses about not doing it, because I haven't changed it . . . now you go and do it.' He then asked each business to prepare its strategy, asking them to be ambitious. When the resulting package was 'the dullest, most unambitious thing we have ever seen. It doesn't seem to take the company anywhere . . .' he threatened them with closure. On a second attempt, the results were far better and they were pursuing not only their operating budget but a conscious strategy of change.

Sir Alex Jarratt makes the same point about the role of the operating businesses, 'At the end of the day if it's [the business plan] going to work, people have to *own* it.'

In order to set a clear direction for the organisation, the leader needs a signal ability to concentrate on essentials. Tim Waterstone learnt this from Sir Derrick Holden-Brown, 'It's a process of looking down at a business from above and sorting out the wood from the trees and seeing what matters and what doesn't.' Steve Shirley learnt the same skill during the recession of the 1970s, 'It is the survival instinct that actually brings out the recognition of what is important. There is no future for British industry unless we get the focus right.' Lord Donaldson developed this skill as a barrister, 'A barrister has to have an analytical mind in order to analyse the problem, strip it down to its bare essentials, and then be able to communicate those essentials.'

> . . . if you believe in yourself, and can reduce the basic problems of the business down to three or four well-understood problems, you will then be able either to deal with them directly or turn them over to people who do know how to deal with them directly. By identifying the issues and talking about them, explaining them and obtaining confirmation that these are indeed the issues, you gain a lot of support, because clarity about what needs to be done is the most important management attribute. (Neil Shaw)

The horizon

Having got beyond the 'honeymoon' period, the leader has to maintain the momentum. Some leaders, including Brian Smith and Clive Thornton, believe that a fixed term of about five years is appropriate. Although that is a minority view, most of our sample would agree with Tim Melville-Ross that leaders go on learning, 'No question about it . . . However successful an organisation may look . . . the chief executive himself and the organisation make mistakes along the way.' He instanced his own softness with poor performers, 'I've learnt now that I need to be quicker off the mark and more decisive about dealing with people who are clearly not up to the mark.' Brandon Gough finds that a good way of keeping up momentum is 'targeting one or two big developments each year.' Sir Peter Imbert works to an annual planning cycle which entails consultation with the public, meetings in workshop format with over one hundred senior officers and finally the setting of annual objectives with his top team of seven.

The distinction between the role of chairman and that of chief executive (or equivalent job title) was approached in a variety of ways. Sir Alex Jarratt said, 'The difference between those two roles is what two people make of them.' Clive Thornton sees a dynamic, even ruthless role for the chairman who, 'should bring about change when [directors] have had their day. He should see that the board has constant birth and rebirth.' Sir Richard Attenborough grants 'massive autonomy' as chairman to his chief executives, whether in Capital Radio, Channel 4 or other organisations, 'It seems to me, apart from anything else, to be eminently stupid to engage superb chief executives like Nigel Walmsley or Michael Grade or Wilf Stevenson and not to give them rein, breathing space . . . You've got to be available and if they need you, you've certainly got to be there.' Sir Peter Thompson found that, 'Operating at management level is to me the most satisfying thing that there is. It is about making things happen. Whereas operating at board level is . . . much more about gut and feel and analysis.' 'At the chairman level,' he went on to say somewhat wistfully, 'my world is all about longer-term decisions and unquantifiable things like values.'

Taking decisions which will have a long-term impact on the organisation is inescapable for the person at the very top. Clive Thornton gathered his top team in Abbey National once a fortnight for what he called 'make-your-mind-up time', and when he felt insufficient minds were being made up, he himself announced decisions to the Press. This brinkmanship – 'bouncing them into it', in his phrase – is untypical. Most of the leaders interviewed for this book prefer to obtain agreement within their team. But, as Tim Melville-Ross ruefully realised, '. . . the decisions that come across my desk: they're nearly all difficult. Of course, the reason is that the easy ones have already been taken!'

> Challenge issues that drop right on your desk . . . do we or don't we do it? If you cop out of that the whole place will find out and judge you accordingly. (Dr Brian Smith)

> [From his time as a Chancery judge] I'd got a difficult bail application coming up. I went and asked Lord Parker, the Chief Justice, what his policy was, and he told me. I heard this bail application, and came to the conclusion . . . that his policy didn't fit, and did the exact opposite of what he had advised. When I told the Chief Justice I had departed from his policy, he said, 'But my dear John, that's what you're paid for.' And he was right. (Lord Donaldson)

One of the characteristics of these leaders is their concern for customer service. It takes various forms including an obsessive drive for quality and excellence and an enthusiasm for becoming personally involved.

> [From his time with Mars] regarding the wrapper on the product as being as vital as building a huge manufacturing plant. They drummed that into people. (Sir James Blyth)

> One of the things that I have been very anxious to do has been to demonstrate that we have a clear obligation to deliver to our customers. For some of my staff that has been a novel and in some cases a quite distasteful rhetoric. (Dr Neil Cossons)

Even in the more protocol-bound environment of the courts.

> I'm concerned with the throughput of cases. I'm concerned with delays. I'm concerned with providing a service to the public. (Lord Donaldson)

> On returning to IBM after his secondment to the NHS] The vocabulary now is clearly that of a market-driven company. It's difficult to think how IBM could be more market-driven, but it genuinely believes that it has to have greater contact with its customers. (Sir Leonard Peach)

> One of the things I want [the firm] to carry for generations to come is a reputation for superb stock and staff quality. (Tim Waterstone)

One way in which leaders continually take the temperature of their own organisation is by networking and using their external contacts as sources of fresh ideas. Sir Alex Jarratt is very much in favour of his executive directors having outside directorships.

Perhaps this degree of symbiosis with the external environment contributes to another notable characteristic of these leaders, namely their keenness on face-to-face communication. For sheer scale, it would be hard to match the National Health Service, and when Sir Leonard Peach was its chief executive he decided that getting out and about was a major priority, '. . . you need to carry the message out into the sticks. I must have spent a great deal of time out there talking to people and being talked to by people – I did up to six sessions a week.' Tim Melville-Ross spends 'a lot of time in the field with branches trying to understand how they are feeling, what are the problems that the front-line troops are having to cope with . . .' Sir Peter Imbert insists on visiting at least one outstation a week; Clive Thornton visited four hundred out of Abbey National's seven hundred branches.

When Sir Graham Day was trying to turn round Cammell Laird, 'I talked till hell froze over', and then as a rider the supreme understatement, 'On Merseyside discussions are long, but nevertheless always interesting.' Brian Smith described the battle with Elders for control of Metal Box, 'You had to go out and persuade people; people will understand all the logic but in the end, they are only convinced by passion and the belief you bring. I don't think people work for logic . . . they work because they believe in things.' Even at the most mundane level, this face-to-face contact is seen as vital, as Anne Jones recalled from her time as a head teacher trying to help troublesome students, 'I found that as I went round the building, or did dinner duty, I could often defuse a tricky situation.' Tim Waterstone, who appears the exception in liking written communication – 'I've always enjoyed the process of inter-office memoranda, which other people hate' – balances this with heavy face-to-face involvement through two days a week of branch visiting, 'I'm very careful to talk to every single member of staff, read their file and look them in the eye. You can quickly pick up staff disaffection. It's always the same reason – bad branch management – and I'm very quick to get on to it.'

There is not much flavour of the omniscient dictator among these leaders. Many spoke about teams: creating teams over a period, and leading a close-knit team at the top. Anne Burdus and Sir Richard Attenborough both actively sought the best individuals to comprise their teams.

> I had a wonderful stable of people because I just went out and hired the best. (Ann Burdus)

> . . . I gathered together, by virtue of my experience in the business, the people whom I thought were the absolute tops of their profession – the best cameraman, the best recordist, the best designer, the best continuity girl, etc. . . . I relied on them enormously. I've continued to do that . . . I've used the same crew in movie after movie . . . I have supreme faith in their capabilities. (Sir Richard Attenborough)

The teams which these twenty people are leading are extremely varied, so the tactics used by the leader vary. Sir James Blyth had to impress his personality on a mixed group in the Ministry of Defence.

> You were managing civil servants. How does that differ from managing people in industry and commerce?

> Not a lot really. You do have to thump them on the head and tell them that the first time they actually try to second-guess you on a 'Yes Minister' basis, you are going to get cross about it.

Still in the public sector, Sir Leonard Peach regarded it as realistic to think of the eight hundred and thirty general managers in the National Health Service as a team. Lord Donaldson approaches his position as Master of the Rolls as 'a choirmaster. You conduct but you're conducting twenty-seven Privy Councillors, each of whom is perfectly capable of playing a solo part, and is entitled to do so.' The same approach, allowing individuals sufficient space, is followed by Baroness Blackstone in her academic environment. In a university [compared to a government department] 'the command structure is much looser. You are a bit like a king or queen with a whole lot of barons in a relatively decentralised state, and those barons must be allowed to develop their own areas in the way they think fit, but within a framework that you set, within guidelines about the policy goals of the institution as a whole.'

Designing such a framework will typically be done by the team at the very top (for example, Tim Melville-Ross, Brian Smith, Sir Peter Imbert) but may then entail not simply presenting the outcome to staff at lower levels but obtaining their contribution to it.

> When we complete the strategic review, before the board endorse it we take it back to them . . . have meetings all over the country . . . so that the workforce are now part-owners of the plan. (Sir Peter Thompson)

These leaders are acutely aware of their responsibility to develop people. Steve Shirley reported that her board meetings were dominated by this. There's a continual attack on costs and productivity but the discussion is invariably about people: management, team working, how to select people, picking high fliers, succession planning. It's always about people . . . I know few key people in industry who are not people managers.'

Tim Melville-Ross is 'a great believer in formal training for the staff of an organisation at nearly all levels. I have very substantially increased the training budget and resource within Nationwide Anglia. I've also moved it right up the organisation to as near the top as makes no difference.'

But a whole variety of methods besides formal courses is used. Sir Peter Thompson combined courses for his managers in BRS with individual coaching. Sir Alex Jarratt uses 'springboard jobs', placing people under managers who are particularly good at developing others. Like most leaders, he believes strongly in delegation, 'The point of delegating is to give them an environment in which they can flourish, to encourage them as much as possible . . .' The corollary of delegation is the willingness to allow mistakes – not of the cavalier kind, but mistakes made for genuine reasons. Clive Thornton told his branch managers in Abbey National, 'You are to cultivate the Press, and you must be your own man on the spot. Dont worry that you'll get it wrong.'

This readiness to trust middle managers in very large organisations characterises these leaders. When Sir Leonard Peach was heading the National Health Service, and trying to introduce performance appraisal,

'Some of the personnel group felt that we went too far, too fast. I don't think so. And it was only the top ten thousand anyway – the managers. Below that level I gave personnel free rein down the line and said ". . . It's a very good learning experience".'

In their quite different environments, Anne Jones and Brian Smith concur that leaders are not infallible.

> [As a headteacher] You mustn't think you're over important. There's something wrong if you think you're the absolute linchpin of everything. (Professor Anne Jones)

> I'm a negative macho person. I have a great antipathy to the godlike figure that drives the world or the business – the charisma man . . . it contains the seeds of disaster, no matter how good that person is. (Dr Brian Smith)

We have seen how leaders regard the role at the very top of their organisations as different in key respects even to those immediately below. Perhaps the supreme difference is the leader's responsibility for the long-term health of the organisation: establishing a vision of where the organisation should be heading. As Sir Alex Jarratt pointed out, the timescale will differ from business to business, 'In aerospace and defence there is no way you could operate on an annual basis let alone a weekly basis . . . In publishing, the horizons are much shorter, you don't start fussing about whether women's magazines will still be there in five or ten years' time.'

Brandon Gough looks on his role as 'the creation and encouragement of a vision for the firm, then relying on other people to execute it.' Over eighteen months, Steve Shirley gradually drafted 'what we now call our Charter . . . It doesn't mention anything specific about making a lot of money, but it sets out our value system.' Sir Peter Thompson, disillusioned by British Steel's lack of corporate vision, put his ideas into effect with conspicuous success in the National Freight Corporation, but points out the need for leaders to balance their long-term plans with short-term realism, '. . . put a great strategy with a reluctant workforce and some poor implementation and you are unlikely to succeed.'

In a way, perhaps, that encapsulates the message from these leaders:

that there is an endless challenge in matching vision with reality. Leaders cannot just be stargazers. They have to have the ability to get things done now as a means to an end. The key is to build up a team working with the leader, who are trusted and given scope to manage the day-to-day operations. That our nineteen leaders positively enjoy this endless challenge is beyond doubt.

> I've loved every job that I've done. (Baroness Tessa Blackstone)

> I try hard to make life fun for people. The work ethic beats hard through all of us. (Tim Waterstone)

> A good manager wants to get at his work every day. He never has to cajole others to get their work done. His people are doing the job because they like to work with him. (Neil Shaw)

> I said to somebody, 'For God's sake, treat each day as an adventure and not as a day of drudgery. (Clive Thornton)

Conclusion

In the last few pages we have selected some of the themes that come through consistently in the interviews. As will be clear from a thorough reading of the transcripts, other factors have also contributed at various stages in these leaders' lives: parental guidance at the point of career choice, support from their spouse in their middle years, international experience and so on. There is a rich array from which any reader can choose the factors most relevant to him or herself.

For those looking up 'the hill', above everything else two signposts stand out:

• seeking continual challenges
• using a mentor for guidance.

For those reaching 'the high ground':

• clarifying structure and accountability
• concentrating on a few strategic essentials.

For those contemplating 'the horizon':

- balancing a long-term vision with plenty of face-to-face contact with staff tackling the demands of today's customers
- demonstrating trust in managers by delegating and giving them breathing space.

For organisations, as distinct from individual managers, the main action points will be:

- to note the above messages which their present staff – and potential recruits – will have absorbed, and plan accordingly
- to develop an environment in which opportunities to learn are actively encouraged, and formal training is one element in a much broader repertoire.

Industrial Society Publications

Other titles of interest from The Industrial Society Press include:

The Action Centred Leader John Adair

> The best managers are not bosses but leaders, and leadership is the crux of successful management. In this book, the emphasis is on the simple actions a leader must take to build a team, develop the individual and achieve the task. Given the basic potential and the will to succeed, anyone can be a leader. This book will help turn common sense leadership into common practice.

The Industrial Society Handbook of Management Skills

> This unique handbook, based on The Industrial Society's tried and tested series of practical booklets, contains everything you need to know to become a more effective manager. By turning into action the points made here, you will improve your performance, increase your leadership abilities, and maximise effectiveness. The Industrial Society is at the forefront of practical management skills training, in this single volume, the Society's practical experience of and expertise in management training is condensed into eighteen chapters.

Notes for Managers Series

> The highly successful Notes for Managers series is a tried and tested resource and information 'centre' for busy managers. Concise, clear and practical, the twenty-four titles in the series cover the key management topics and people skills. The latest title is Managing for Total Quality.

Absenteeism
Appraisal and Appraisal
    Interviewing
Decision Taking
Delegation
Effective Discipline
Effective Management in the
    Public Service
Effective Supervision in the
    Factory
Effective Supervision in the
    Office
Guide to Employment Practices
Effective Use of Time
Induction

Industrial Relations
Involving Young People at Work
Job Descriptions
Manager as a Leader
Manager's Responsibility for
    Communication
Managing Change
Managing for Total Quality
Management of Health and Safety
Motivation
Selection Interviewing
Supervisors: Selection, Training
    and Development
Target Setting
Training Your Staff

These are also available in a boxed set.

Communication Skills Guides

A series of eight practical titles on communication.

Effective Meetings
Letter Writing
Dictation Techniques
Interviewing

Effective Speaking
Telephone Techniques
Rapid Reading
Report Writing

For further details, please contact:

The Sales Unit
The Industrial Society
Quadrant Court
49 Calthorpe Road
Birmingham B15 1TH
Tel: 021 454 6769